"Perhaps that's my problem:
My sister says she remembers the sharp bones,
I remember that I felt them."

To my sister, who means the world to me. This book is all because of you (I mean it). Thank you for being my reason to live. I Love you, Love you. Kisses.

BEST BODY
Pretty, Miserable, Perfectness

Jordan's book to sister

(I am so proud of you —? Always want to be here for you. Thank you for giving me the opportunity! Kisses x2)

A MEMOIR BY
JORDAN LEE KNAPE

SPEED HONEY PRESS

To my mother,

~~please don't read chapters 11, 15 or 21.~~

~~Hell, please don't read any of it.~~

~~Also,~~ to my sister.

I love you both with three kisses

up to the sky each.

A NOTE TO THE READER

I tried for a very long time to write this book in order. Chapter 1, Chapter 2, Chapter 3. The aim was chronology and moment leading to moment, everything in order. The truth is I couldn't write that story. With eating disorders, much like life, nothing is in order. Without a storybook beginning, middle, and end, eating disorders, instead, exist up in the clouds, every moment a singular event and everything connected. And when you try to pin all the points down, you can't. The fact that everything seems so disconnected and out of context becomes the truest context. I could not write a simple story from beginning to end to talk about my eating disorder because eating disorders are not simple. Even though we'd like to pretend, with our schedules and our meal plans and our calorie counts, that they can be neat and tidy and easy to mend, eating disorders are messy and confusing and out of place. That's the real story. Also, please note: I am wary in my writing to say "anorexics" or "anorectics" — or spell out my different weights, or the calories eaten, or the calories purged — the list goes on — as I do not want to promote defining people by their disorder. But, at the same time, you have to look your disorder in the face. When you do, you'll see the pieces floating everywhere.

CONTENTS

1   *2 Sharks*

2   *Best Body*

3   *Intake*

4   *Always Hungry*

5   *On Men*

6   *Best is Best*

7   *Intensive Inpatient*

8   *Hospital Bonds*

9   *Rich White Bitch*

10   *Inpatient*

11   *Suicide*

12   *Merry Fucking Christmas*

13   *Family Matters*

14   *Intensive Outpatient*

15   *Talking Bones, Purge Binging*

16   *Sex & the Little Girl, To Body War*

17   *Outpatient*

18   *Diets, Celebrity, & Addiction*

19   *Promise Me Perfect*

20   *Discharge*

21   *Relapse*

FORWARD

Written by Stephanie Setliff, M.D.

Medical Director of the Partial Hospital Program

of the Eating Recovery Center in Dallas

Most psychiatric physicians have a handful of patients who stick in our minds for the long term. Sometimes the patients motivate us, haunt us, sadden us or even bring us delight. It is something about their story that resonates with us and makes a lasting impression. In my practice I have treated hundreds of adolescent psychiatric patients, the majority of whom have suffered from severe eating disorders. While I treat all of my patients with the same level of care and try to help them all individually, a few patients have stuck out in my memory, far past the time of the patient's discharge. These patients are, for various reasons, my most memorable.

In the realm of my memories Jordan is one at the top of the list. While she was still an inpatient under my care, there was something special about Jordan. I spent a lot of time trying to figure out what it was that resonated with me. Some time after her discharge it hit me. It was gritty determination. At times this was a negative, as it was during her eating disorder. But during her recovery Jordan found a path towards healing that was highly personal, distinct, and, of course, determined. The way I thought of it, Jordan just kept on going.

To have suffered from a severe psychiatric illness before your first day of high school is intensely difficult. High school is already traumatic enough. However, no matter how hard the difficulties, Jordan kept on going. She had a commitment to seeing herself through the difficult times in her life. Even when the difficult seemed huge and her idea of a feasible, positive future was microscopic, Jordan kept on going.

In Texas it's common to see people "pick themselves up by their bootstraps," as we call it. We have a real go get 'em attitude and believe in taking risks and picking ourselves up with our own two hands. However, few people in Texas can do so at such a young age, especially when they are trying to recover from an illness that has a higher mortality rate than any other psychiatric disorder.

Looking back at Jordan's struggles and subsequent recovery, I wonder where she thought she was going all along. A few years after her discharge I talked to Jordan about it and she said something like this, "Dr. Setliff, I knew I wasn't able to recover then, not fully, and I knew that if I thought too much about my life at the time I wouldn't have been able to survive. I wanted to get as far away as I could. In the process I've found myself more strong, more able — more adult — to handle everything I was going through at the time." When she told me this I thought two things. One, I thought how unique, and fortunate, Jordan was to have found health through an unconventional and highly personal method. Two, I thought, when will Jordan decide that she is ready to look back?

We have found ourselves at that time. This book is Jordan's looking back. Jordan has waited a long time. Her story is aided now by the strong self-awareness and understanding that Jordan has developed over the years, both for herself and for her experience with anorexia.

So now I know, this is where Jordan kept on going. I can not think of a more unique or understanding person to write about her experience with anorexia nervosa. Jordan's writing is personal, honest, and moving — just as she has always been. Once Jordan found herself fully ready to look, she uncovered a breadth of experience and detail that is often overlooked in personal accounts of eating disorders, because of the pain that comes with remembering things we would much rather forget. Jordan took the time and we are lucky for the wait, just as we are lucky for the bravery she faced in finally speaking up.

Many people who recover from eating disorders try to get as far away from the disorder as possible. You do not owe anyone your experience; you do not need to share what you learned — instead, many former patients who find recovery welcome a new life and a fresh start. It took serious guts for Jordan to look back at the most difficult time in her young life without triggering a relapse of her disorder. That speaks to the nature of how mightily Jordan was able to find her own recovery, and how urgent her story is for others. I believe that Jordan's story won't just be one that resonates with me alone anymore.

Preface, on Leaving

A person with anorexia is a person who leaves. For some reason — maybe they feel powerless, maybe they are afraid, maybe they want to stop their bodies from changing and revert to a body that is less developed, less sexual — something no longer fits, something doesn't feel right, and they leave. They leave everything they know, the people and the places and things they used to love. The "used to" here as in past tense, as in something soon forgotten, as in joy, even of the small and seemingly everyday variety, is a forgotten, fast-decaying, lost monument to the anorexic's former world.

They leave because they are scared, because they are tired of knowing, of constantly being and thinking and living, and they want, if only for a minute, to feel still. They believe that if they leave the world they know, they can also leave themselves. Knowing, to the anorexic, means recognizing the facts of life that make them sick: the need to grow up, mature, partake in a world full of mature grownups acting immature, the sex, the greed, the material wants. Safely cocooned inside the world of their disorder, they can escape from the world around them. They think that the more that they abandon, the more of themselves, the more people and things that they sacrifice to this disease, the more they can find refuge in the disorder. And it's true. It's easier to hide behind anorexia when there is nothing left to distract you. The more you leave your life and escape into anorexia, the more you whittle everything you used to be away until you become someone entirely different, someone entirely inauthentic. You leave until it feels like you aren't yourself at all, until it feels like you are just the disorder, until every part of you has been tightly wrapped and put away.

Finding and hanging on to our compulsion, with no time or concern to spare for other things, that is the goal of anorexia.

When I first found my home in anorexia, I disappeared from my factual present. I quickly left the surroundings that were familiar. The people who knew the old, real me. The disorder first arose, that little voice, in June 2001 and by mid-July, I had left most of my friends. The disease took me captive with surprising force, shocking speed. I stopped seeing my friends because, as much as I didn't want to admit it, I knew that I was different from the person I had been before. I knew that I was changing quickly, and I didn't want them to worry about me, to suspect how I was hurting myself, to gossip about me, or worst of all, to step in my way.

By August, I had given up most of the places I used to enjoy: the country club pool, the library, the movie theaters, malls, and restaurants I used to frequent with my friends and family. These places were a distraction. I needed to count my calories. I needed to exercise to exhaustion. I needed to plan my future meals and recount what I already ate. And in order to do so, I needed to stay in set areas that wouldn't spoil the agenda. I couldn't have fun. There simply wasn't time. I didn't deserve it.

Once school started I left it, too. At first, I dedicated myself to schoolwork more than I ever had before; schoolwork became the perfect excuse to lock myself away in the pursuit of perfection and discipline. But by October, the little voice was no longer whispering, insisting that I count every calorie and run one more mile, but was howling full-volume through every part of me. By November, I had lost all conventional, healthy, human contact with my family. The more they reached out to me, trying to connect with the girl they loved, the more I left them behind.

Even now, ten years after I was first diagnosed with anorexia, I still leave. It's a remnant of the disorder, the leaving. It's a habit, one I struggle to stop. I want to believe that I am truly, authentically happy. That after years of deprivation and sacrifice, I am finally satisfied. When I realize that I am not, I want to escape. I don't try to fix myself, to learn to deal with my complicated feelings of inadequacy or imperfection or sadness. Instead, I run away. If I change where I am physically, I believe I can change where I am emotionally.

With people, it's more complicated. I don't like that I can leave people like I can places — truly, I don't. And yet, I have left everyone I know, everyone I love. With everyone significant in my life, I get close, I let them in, I allow them to love me, to know me, and then I leave. Often it is a physical and very literal departure but always, without question, the physical departure is spurred by a spiritual departure. My true, authentic self, that soul resting within my body, becomes disinterested, or desensitized, and while it might look like I am actually talking to you and engaging, I am not.

I have left all of my best friends. On the surface, it's because we grew out of touch. Peel that layer back, and it's because I grew out of touch. Peel that layer back, and it's because I ask too much of them. Peel that layer back, and it's because they can't give me what I want. Why be with someone unless they can become your moon and your stars? Why be with someone unless they can consistently stand in as your other half, the beam that keeps you standing straight? Why be with someone unless they can prove the test of that last peel, unless they can be your everything?

I have left all of my previous boyfriends. I'd get angry with them for what seemed like no reason. But, in the end, I knew it was my only one: they weren't enough. I want too much; my expectations are too high; I leave. I pretend to be someone I'm not, really. I bend myself backwards and twist my spirit into knots in an effort to appear to be whatever else, whoever else, they want me to be. Then, frustrations explode from inside. They don't understand my anger because they thought they knew me. So I leave.

With my family it feels like I am always boomeranging back and forth. I get too close and need too much, and because they have known me so well for so long, they may actually detect it. Then, because I want to be an independent person, because I want to prove to them that I don't need their help, I flee. To me, being strong means being able to live so independently that I can exist without love, without support, without comfort. Of course this mindset is the reason why that final peel has endured despite its impossibility: My attempt at being strong is so extreme that whenever I feel a movement from the other side, I run to it. I boomerang back and forth from trying to be strong to being exhausted by my failed attempts and needing to recuperate by living through the dictates of another person. I become what they want me to be, for a while, because it is so hard for me to be my kind of strong.

I have left everyone I know, at some point in time, because when I ask them to fill me, they can't. I'm still hungry. I still want more. I leave them because I am unsatisfied.

Nothing, no one, is ever enough to make me not feel so — the word I'm looking for is close to empty, but it's not a hollow, darkened empty, it's an empty implying loss — and when I try to go one way, I always go so far that I have to run back to the other extreme just to keep my balance.

I want to be completely self-sufficient, defiantly independent.

Then, if I am with someone whose presence feels comfortable and I let them help me, let them know and love me, I may get carried away. I forget myself in a way that I don't want to exist anymore without them. I want to exist as me + whomever. I want the little support they give to become all my support. Because, I realize, my life has been so heavy and difficult without them and, now that it is easier with them, I don't think I can go on without them. I don't think I can go on unless they carry the whole load and help me open all of my doors.

My eating disorder did that the best. All doors opened, I was free to say goodbye.

With my eating disorder I left every place, every person, every friend, and family member I cared about.

I left and turned the corner until I had nothing left to call my own — everything remaining so entangled with the disorder. At that point I knew that finally my penchant for leaving had done me in; I'd been replaced entirely by my false person, the girl capable of pretending to the extremes.

I left myself when I left my friends and family.

But that is not what this story is about.

This is about coming home.

I

2 SHARKS

June 1, 1998

When you sink underwater you don't hear the loud sounds of the world outside. You hear your own soft exhales, those little bubbles of air that expand and disappear before they reach the surface. Underwater, there is a division between you and the other people in the pool. Much more than gravity, it separates you from me, the way I feel from the way I want to feel. Peace. Quiet. Calm. Underwater it's like we're ghosts, in our own little coffins, and though you might be smiling for me, I don't have to see.

Each summer morning, I'd wake up early for the Dallas Royal Oaks Country Club swim team, my dad would drive. I'd open the big iron gate, take off my clothes, stretch my arms and legs, shivering in my Speedo. When our coach blew the whistle, I'd be the first to jump in. I always chose the middle lane.

I would pretend that at each end of the pool there were doors that opened to reveal a shark that would bite my toes each time I did a flip turn. I had to swim as fast as I could so the sharks wouldn't rip me apart and bloody the water. The problem was that I could never get away from the sharks — once I splashed my way from one shark at the end of the pool I was already in danger from the other shark at the other end of the pool. My summers were a constant fight to stay in the middle.

The sharks came to my imagination first not out of a desire to swim faster, and not out of a want for entertainment. I had never seen a shark in real life or been told they exist in artificial, mechanical pool doors. Instead, the sharks came to me instinctively. Like they were always there — a dark part of my imagination that it behooves me to ignore. I didn't create the sharks, but they arrived, fully formed in the dark corners of my mind, and I can't not see them.

In fact, this rather masochistic tendency follows me around in other places too: a deep attraction to the dark or hurting, hurtful world that I can't avoid.

Even today I turn on the oven, and I hear the gas blow up in flames like a meth lab. I safely change lanes on the highway, yet I hear the sound of crushing metal and skidding tires. Perhaps as an adult, the severity of these imagined moments has lessened through a peculiar and funny normalization — a multiplication of the variable points of harm makes each one less powerful. But as a kid there was one point of injury. The sharks. I could see them.

Yet I never saw the sharks until I was in the water. I could walk by the pool a hundred times without fear. I could stand at the pool's edge, feeling the hot scratchy-stone under my feet while my big toes curled into the cool water. I could outstretch my arms like Superman, and my torso could bend with my chest meeting my knees, my fingers pointed towards the water, and still I thought nothing of the sharks. But then I would dive in. And I would kickkickkick, and my body would stretch and swim smooth up to the surface, and I would take my first stroke, take my first breath, and the memory would reset: There are two sharks waiting to attack, one at each end of the pool.

As I swam towards the end of the lane, the white tile would become a heavy cast iron door. Once I was three arms' lengths away, the door would start to open, and out would come the shark. First, I would see four razor sharp teeth. Next, the shark's two nostrils would appear. Then I would see its eyes, sentient and round like human eyes, sometimes green and sometimes blue. They always felt cold, always looked sad.

Once the shark was visible an inch past its eyes, I would give one big butterfly kick and roll my body like a caterpillar, spinning until the tip of my head faced the other edge of the pool. My toes would flex, my feet would hit the wall, my body would spread out like superman again, kickkickkicking to reach the surface.

I imagined the shark's bite, what it would feel like to be torn apart. It felt like watching a horror film, being both repelled and attracted to the violence and gore on the screen, unable to turn away no matter how much I wished I could. I tried not to see the shark's bite, but the more I tried, the harder it became to ignore. I would see the sadness in its eyes, a pit of dark that had no end, and I would see the shark open its mouth and envelop my feet, then my legs, then my butt and stomach. I would see the shark bite into my torso until I was torn in two, and I would see it swallow one half like a wild snake while the other half lay limp and dying, floating in crimson water while my friends swam alongside, happily unaware. Don't you know that we are dying soon?

One thousand times I'll say it: Nobody ever told me to imagine the sharks. I invented the fantasy all on my own. I created it and added to it until it was no longer something that I imagined, like a dream, but rather until the sharks were real, something that I couldn't get away from. Even though I knew — I must have known — that sharks weren't really behind the walls of the pool, lying in wait for me.

Two totally different sides, I am purposefully swimming towards each — no this one, no that one — a constant motion, stuck inside this self-induced and yet oh-so-important, if only I could remember why, terror. My swims were like a calling, the most real part of the day.

· · ·

The summer before fourth grade, I met Samantha. Samantha had vanilla ice cream colored skin with not even a single freckle. She laughed like a hyena. We ate soft pretzels and drank raspberry-flavored slush puppies on lawn chairs. We back dove off the highest board and rubbed sunscreen on the parts the other couldn't reach. Samantha understood. We confessed our troubles to each other and they were the same: We both felt like we had to pretend to be people we were not in order, not so much to be accepted, but to be, in general. Neither one of us felt comfortable exposing our true selves, who we really were, and it wasn't because we didn't know who we were. It's because the person I have known to be me has always been contrary to the person I was expected to be.

Swimming at the club offered me a summer world, a world separate from the one I knew at school. Different schedule, different people — it was a separate, secret life. I felt like I could talk with whomever I wanted, something I knew I wasn't allowed to do at school. Because none of my school friends were around, I didn't have to pretend to like the all-boy band Hanson or pretend to enjoy spending all day making up dance routines or liking or disliking certain boys. When Samantha told me she pretended to be a vegetarian in front of her friends because they had all converted to vegetarianism, I told her that when I was with a friend who invited me to sleep over, I would call my mom in front of my friends to ask permission and my mom would ask the secret code — "Say orange if you really want to sleep over" — and I would often say a different color so it wasn't my fault. So I could just go home and be alone.

If only temporarily, summers with Samantha meant no more hypersocialhappy-person with our hypersocialhappypeople friends; no more false delight at going to see PG movies with our many supposed best friends (conveniently all named Jessica); no more joining Jessica #5 and her family at their lush summer house in the back ends of Texas, the palm trees transplanted straight from California; no more pretend, no more fairytales. And so Samantha and I became great summer friends, people who grew close not just out of convenience, taste in bathing suits or our parents' play-date wishes, but because we were the same.

You love her so much you call her a sister. We said that we'd go to the same high school, graduate from the same college, move to the same town, live on the same street, in houses side-by-side, with matching cars and perfect jobs, pretty husbands whom we would marry, at the same wedding, side-by-side.

One day, we'd say, we would become matching grandmas with granny packs in techno-color sweatpants who would march slowly through malls as per our doctor's orders to exercise; or that one day we would be on our deathbeds, at the same place, the same time, the same hour, arguing like lovers ending a phone call: *"You do it first," "No you do it first," "No you."* We were joking, I know. But for me it felt not like a joke but like something faintly hidden. A thing that looked like truth and talked like truth and even though it wasn't truth, well, it was *close enough*, I thought. I thought I wanted for my life to blend with Samantha's and for her to be my constant.

Add to the list Samantha's love of rules.

Like me, Samantha saw the swim team as one big secret code. A code for the beauty, the supremacy of summer, for that time you can never get back. For that time, as we saw it, where we could finally, for no second more than a heartbeat, be ourselves. The problem was we both thought that our true selves could only come out in the summer and, in thinking so, we began to understand our true selves as something that was passing, changing, always in flux and never the same from one season to the next.

· · ·

My dad read Rudyard Kipling's "Just So" stories to me before bed, and my mom rubbed my back, sang me songs. There was a routine routine routine. I could say the word forever. On Sundays, we went to church. On weekdays, we would wake up, get dressed, brush teeth, eat breakfast, carpool to school (It's Montessori, meaning my parents want us to love to learn, love to learn), get stuck in traffic, arrive five minutes late despite all of my whining to Dad to hurry hurry and pick up the other kids fast, walk to the head desk with sister and other carpoolers in tow ("Sorry I'm late. Please let me into school"), go to class, smile at teachers and friends so they don't think I'm a) embarrassed or b) care (I am both a and b), learn, eat lunch, have recess, learn, wait for mom to pick me up from school at 3:30 sharp, though she's never there on time, smile and wave bye like it's no big deal to my friends whose mothers play tennis instead of work, go to 7-Eleven and get a Slurpee, go to ballet (or soccer, or math tutor, or singing teacher, or art class, or swim team practice, or whatever else I'm signed up for that year (why don't I take violin?), get home, eat dinner, play, talk with family, go to sleep, restart, restart, restart!

I was safe when I went to sleep, safe when I woke up. I was loved. And yet, that's such a small part of the truth. I did not feel safe. I never have. To me, safe is that happy that people follow you around with, trying to scoop you in. How are you??? It's normal, expected, convenient, and polite. Safe is a comfort, I think, an ease in one's own skin that isn't learned or taught. And even though I should feel safe, and am, I'm not.

· · ·

I was late the first day of practice the summer before fifth grade. I know this for a fact because my younger sister could not find her swimming goggles, and we had to stop at 7-Eleven, but they only had kid goggles that were green and looked like alligator eyes, and she did not like them. Typically, I'm late because of my sister.

When I open the big heavy painted-black gate to access the swimming pool, all the time waving bye to my father and shoving my sister through, I see Samantha. She is so happy to see me that she is smiling wide. She has lost a lot of weight. Her bones stick out more prominently now, her knees seem to have grown while the rest of her legs have shrunk, her shoulders look sharp, her once rounded face looks more angular; there is a deep cave at her temples and her cheekbones seem to jut out like her nose, screaming. I'm worried but, Samantha, she is a Very Smart Girl. And I think, when you get the flu, you can lose a lot of weight.

My coach is whistling for my sister and me to hurry up and get to the spot by the pool where we do our morning stretches. With his eyes he says that we are late, that we are bad, that it's far past time to jump in. My sister follows my moves as I lift my hands up to the sky then down to the floor, up to the sky then down to the floor. Next she follows as I outstretch my arms so I look like the letter T, or a cross, or a forked road, and we bend with our hips to the left, then to the right, again and again. Then, I raise my arms up to the sky once more and start winding both of my arms forward in circles like the butterfly hand movement, then again, backwards and simultaneously. Finally, I wind one arm forward and one arm backwards at the same time. This movement is my favorite, though it's my sister's least. She says it's too fast, that when her arms spin and spin, they start to feel uncontrollable, like they are going to fall off. I say I like the feeling. I like going fast every which way. While we stretch, my sister and I look at our snot-nosed friends as they hold onto the edge of the pool and listen to our coach's welcome back speech. I don't really listen to the speech, though. I am busy looking at my friends, the people I have not seen since last summer, and trying to act cool by rolling my eyes as I stretch, trying to pretend that I don't care that I'm late to our first practice, even though I do.

In front of everybody our coach turns to look at my sister, "Why did you stop, you have five more minutes of stretching!"

By now I've finished spinning my arms and hopped to the floor, bending and flexing my toes a couple of times and then in one quick motion hurling my chest towards my knees, my fingers outstretched well past my toes. Since I'm bending so and my eyes can only see the dark in between my legs, I didn't notice that my sister hadn't followed me to the floor. Instead, she had stopped, her hands folded over her tummy and her feet stilled on the ground somewhere in between first and second position.

My sister stares back, wide-eyed and blinking with her big chocolate-brown eyes totally confused. I feel like I need to protect her — she's my little sister.

"I'm sorry, it's my fault. I told her not to continue because she is having back troubles."

"Back troubles?"

"Yes," I lie. "She is having back troubles, and so I told her not to keep on stretching."

"Hmm. An eight-year-old with back troubles." My coach looks unamused. He looks like he's on to me, like he knows that my sister's back is just fine. My sister keeps silent, her eyes still blinking wide.

"Fine. Just get into the pool already."

I win.

We jump into the pool. I get in the lane with Samantha, and my sister gets in the lane with her group. The people in my sister's lane look at her funny because she looks like some weird fish in a light blue Speedo tankini with yellow stripes and alligator eyes.

"*Beep,*" says my coach. The first person in the line starts swimming 100 freestyle followed by 50 with the kickboard. "Beep," the second person starts. "Beep," the third person starts except for in our lane, where Samantha and I are not sure who is to go next as we are too busy catching up and not thinking about first person, second person. *"Beep BEEP,"* says my coach, and Samantha starts swimming.

Goshdarnit, Gosh-Gosh-Gosh. Immediately, the sharks are back. I hadn't thought about them at all through the school year, or while I was stretching. But once I start to swim they are back as they had always been, one at each end of the pool.

I near the end, and I see its teeth, its eyes, I see it coming towards me. I swim faster, wanting to get it over with. Faster, I can't stop. I have no other option but to keep on swimming fast, hoping, blindly, that the faster I swim the less time I have to spend with either shark. In reality, swimming faster means that you have to see the sharks faster and again. But I didn't know that then. I thought that, through the cycle of swimming back and forth, I could get out of the cycle. I thought that if I was good enough, I could break free.

I swim underwater, finally breaking up to the water's surface in the middle of the lane, between the two ends and the two sharks. Perfectly stuck in-between.

When you swim laps while imagining that there are two sharks at either end of the pool, you end up swimming a lot of laps. Nobody knows that you are swimming for your life. Instead people think that you are actually a good swimmer, not a person with shark phobia. That's the goal, of course, to swim fast. But there are problems too. The big one is you are always passing by people, even those that are on your side, because you are on a super top-secret mission. For instance: Samantha. I had to pass her that day because I was swimming fast, and she was not, though she began before me.

Luckily, like all the other Good Girls of the World, Samantha is compliant. An extra-happy reproduction. So when I find my fingers suddenly graze the back of Samantha's toes, Samantha sweetly moves from swimming position to standing position. With her toothy pre-braces smile, Samantha allows me to calmly and sweetly pass her. To smile wide, to beat the sharks.

After practice we get out of the pool. We use our arms to pull ourselves up and twist around so that our butts flap against the stone ledge, thereby escaping any embarrassment that a stick-your-butt-out-as-you-get-out-of-the-pool move might cause. Our intention is to order an early after-practice lunch of the delicious, carbohydrate-necessary variety. Since it is the first day back to practice, it is also one of the first days that the club pool is open for the summer. My sister and I told our parents to not pick us up after practice. We want our day at the pool.

We grab our towels and wrap them around our bodies. My sister wears hers like a strapless sundress. I fold mine and wear it like a rolled up skirt. Samantha wears hers like a shawl, then a headdress, then she gets self-conscious and wears it like a shawl again. Samantha says she's cold. "Me too!" I say. "Me three!" says my sister. We bundle up in the towels like Samantha and begin walking towards the food counter wearing oversized towel shawls in one-hundred-degree weather.

Our hair is wet and snake-like, creating tears of water dripping down and forming individual puddles below us as we wait in line.

"Did you have a good time in second grade?" Samantha asks my sister.

"Uh-huh," says my sister.

"Did you learn anything?" Samantha asks, like a parent at

the head of a dinner table.

"Oh yes," says my very smart sister, "We learned subtraction, and I read every single book from <u>The Boxcar Children</u>."

When Samantha asks me what I learned, I say, "Oh, you know, fourth-grade stuff," even though I skipped ahead three grades in English. Me, the master self-deprecator.

Finally, it's our turn. My sister and I, defiantly vegetarian, order one grilled cheese with fries on the side, one pb&j (*"strawberry*, please!") with chips, and a big, American, monster-sized regular soda to share. We discuss whether or not we also want to order an Oreo cookie milkshake and decide that we can get it later as a snack. Next Samantha orders. Here's what she orders: comparatively, and practically, nothing. Can you believe it? *We just finished practice! She is so thin! She neeeeds a sandwich!*

The oh-no, watch-out, feed-her soundtrack repeats, but we don't say anything.

Perhaps it's even worse in memory. We were so young. Can a ten-year-old kid and her little sister really be held accountable — as good friends — to witness a problem, identify the itching ugliness? I remember my sister looking at me in line, the fear and the sympathy in her eyes. But maybe the memory is more fantasy than reality. I know Samantha ordered a chicken salad, the kind with mayonnaise, with a bag of chips — maybe now that wouldn't even be a red flag — of course it wouldn't be, today. Perhaps it was the way she ordered. The way she stared at the menu unblinking, the hesitation and obvious self-doubt in her eyes. I saw, I know I saw, torture. An anguish. A deep well of hurt that I knew I couldn't possibly quench.

Perhaps that's my problem: that even as a ten-year-old kid I was able to spot the hurt in the sea of summer friends. My sister says she remembers the sharp bones; I remember that I felt them.

Years later my sister and I will, again, find ourselves in similar positions. At these times we will both be much wiser but, still, we won't really know what to say. Or, rather, we will know, exactly, point-blank, without a touch of doubt what to say: Treatment. We just won't want to say it. *Once is enough,* I know that she, my sister, rightly thinks. *Once is enough,* a mantra I try so hard to live by. And so we keep quiet, waiting until we can't take it any longer, until we feel like exploding, the imaginary hot lava words bursting every which way. We speak up. And then we *remember,* and we almost wish we hadn't spoken. Because reliving things is almost just as bad as living them.

We take our food and sprawl out on the lawn chairs closest to the diving board. This is the summer before they replaced the old lawn chairs with new, sleek lawn chairs. As usual we complain mildly about the rubbery white strips of the chair that stick to you in the heat, causing those temporary red stripes to tattoo themselves into the back of your thighs. Quickly, we stand and turn our shawls into sheets, plopping back down onto slightly more comfortable, newly padded old lawn chairs.

My sister and I dig into the food. We shake the ketchup bottle so that when we pour it near the fries a sea of ketchup emerges. (When annoying-boy #8 from practice walks by us he smirks, *"You want fries with your ketchup?"* like he had been planning the joke all day.) The food tastes greasy and finger-licking good. But the meal is also very filling, especially in the heat. And so we, smart children with a healthy relationship with food, stop eating once we are full. Later we will go home to a healthy home-cooked family meal filled with family talk and vegetables. And we will eat from all the food groups and we will ask, first, for second helpings of broccoli and then for pink sprinkles with our peppermint ice cream (dessert!) because we were raised to enjoy food, to eat with sanity, to even enjoy the occasional helping(s) of fried food when the parentals aren't looking. It's yummy, and it feels good, eating like this.

But Samantha's meal goes differently. She eyes us as we bite into our sandwiches. A tinge of disgust flares up around her eyes as she sees me dipping a potato chip into ketchup. Humppph. Even though she never actually changes positions, her voice becomes distant, her eyes glaze over and she grows further and further away from us, closer towards a lust for the food and the chomp of the bite. Well, this is no fun.

When we finish eating, my sister and I lie back in our chairs, like full-bellied cats sprawled out with satisfaction. Samantha smiles and asks if we are ready to go swimming. "Sure," we say. Before we can stand Samantha has already piled-high on the tray all the paper plates and remnants of food to trash. For a second my sister and I look at each other, as real sisters do, wondering if perhaps she does not have a Catholic babysitter or a Depression-era grandfather to remind her of all those hungry children when she doesn't finish her food.

We're standing in line at the big diving board. I'm first, then Samantha, then my sister. When it's my turn in line I confidently climb the six steps to the top, walk to the edge fast so as not to make anyone wait any longer than they have to, and turn around. I smile at Samantha and my sister and raise my arms as I bend my knees. When the diving board swooshes down, it whooshes back up, lifting me off to make a perfect backwards dive into the water. "Yay," says Samantha. "Yay," says my sister.

Next comes Samantha. She's always a tad more hesitant,

treating the rails at either side of the board like crutches instead of gymnast bars. Samantha gets to the end, makes an effort not to look down, smiles at me and makes a perfect frontwards dive. "Yay," I say. "Yay," says my sister.

Then, my sister, the enviably mature little girl with an endearing goofiness, walks up, nears the end, and smiles at the lifeguard named Jenny who sometimes watches over us on Fridays when my parents have date night. I don't know what kind of dive my sister was planning on doing but Samantha yells, "Cannonball!" and my sister pinches her nose, springs off the board and makes a small kid cannonball. "Yay," I say. "Yay," says Samantha.

Then we swim under the lane rope dividing the diving section from the swimming section to follow the play routine: next come water handstands. Along the way Samantha's ponytail holder has gone missing somewhere in the pool and as she swims underwater her dark hair floats to the top like a life vest. We stop at the shallow end and count: "one" — we glance around awkwardly to see if anyone is watching, "two" — we take big, shameless gulps of air, "three" — we plunge in, and our feet stand where our heads did moments before.

Like always we quickly find that it is nearly impossible to hold water handstand competitions while everyone plays. Someone, or everyone, eventually ends up having to strain their necks to see who is winning and, unable to see well through the sunscreen-soaked water, someone, or everyone, ends up giving up only to claim above water that it was unfair and we need a rematch. Samantha decides that we will all take turns and that while one of us is underwater, the other two will count together to make sure that neither person is cheat-counting. "Okay," my sister and I agree.

Samantha goes first. Her pale vanilla legs stick perfectly straight up to the sky. However, time, not aesthetics, decides the winner, and she underwater-trips at six Mississippi. "Good job," we say and smile.

Next goes my sister. Her feet barely stick out from under the water because she is so small. Samantha and I count to four Mississippis and my sister underwater-trips. Before she returns from hand standing to plain standing, Samantha and I agree to add two Mississippis to my sister's total count. We're pretty sure she can't hear us underwater, because we can't hear us underwater, and, since Samantha also tripped, we want them to at least be equal.

Next it's my turn. One, two, three. I take a big gulp and my tummy expands to the left and the right as air fills my lungs. Fast, I plunge into the water, my hands touch the stony-white surface of the pool, my fingers spread out to ensure proper balance, elbows slightly bent and locked. I close my eyes and count the Mississippis myself, making sure not to pay attention to the splash of the underwater waves or the bubbly gurgling sounds of kicking feet and toes, or the sharks faintly present at either end of the pool. I remind myself to be cautious of my exhalations and only let air out through my nose in small, measured spurts. Up above Samantha and my sister keep on counting, becoming ever more impatient. "Six-*teen* Mississippi, seven-*teen* Mississippi, eight-*teen* Mississippi."

And this is how it all begins.

PSYCHOLOGICAL EVALUATION

(Confidential)

Name: Jordan Knape

Date of Birth: 1/8/88

Date of Evaluation: 5/14/02

Age: 14 years, 4 months

"She was born following an uncomplicated pregnancy and delivery weighing 7 pounds, 11 ounces. She was an active infant who had some difficulty with colic and establishing regular sleeping patterns. Developmental milestones were within normal limits, if not a bit early. Jordan walked at 8 months. She fell at 14 months and needed facial stitches. Otherwise there have been no serious accidents or illnesses requiring hospitalization. Even at an early age Jordan did not seem to focus very long on one activity. She was 'into everything' and would play with a toy only for a few seconds before moving to something else. In preschool her teacher described her as 'spaced out…' She was initially somewhat resentful that she needed to take more tests. However, rapport was easily established and she was fully cooperative. She did not evidence undue frustration and appeared to put forth good effort... Her understanding of math concepts and how to apply them to practical situations is at the lower end of the average range. This is below expectations given her high IQ... Mr. Knape reports that his daughter is somewhat anxious and shy, and mildly perfectionistic. No attention or hyperactivity problems are reported. Jordan's parents describe her as loving, generous, and creative, with a 'wonderful' personality. Jordan's teacher, who is also the Director of the Middle School for St. Alcuin, filled out a Child Behavior Checklist and Conners' Rating Scale and the behaviors she reports for Jordan can be compared to those of other girls her age in the school setting. Mild problems with withdrawal, anxiety and depression, somatic complaints, and attention are reported. The Conners' Hyperactivity Index is well within the normal range. Jordan is seen as a hardworker who is not as happy in general as her peers. She is creative, 'a great appreciator of literature,' and 'a sincere and earnest young woman...' She performs above grade level in all subjects except math, where she is at grade level... There is a family history of mood disorders."[1]

---

1   Excerpts from a six-page psych evaluation.

2

BEST BODY

March 11, 2011

I can hear all the cliched ways I'm supposed to talk about my illness: My battle with anorexia. "Hello my name is Jordan, and I've been sick for ten-odd years. As in, I was put in the hospital, a danger to myself at thirteen, and ever since I've been pretending not to be..."

I think it is best to just begin.

I started all of this because I wanted to be healthy. I was 13 and got some books on proper diet and started to read fitness magazines. I thought that was what you were supposed to do. I had always been hyper-appreciative of the concept of health — even though I grew up in a physically healthy family, even though its concept, that glowing idea of what it means to be healthy, was always familiar, never foreign. I wanted to be healthy. It was something I was supposed to have and something I could reach. Yet there is a point we can cross where the very good spills into the extreme and becomes very bad. The magazines told me to eat this, not that, and that to lose weight you have to eat a certain number of calories every day. I didn't even want to lose weight. I just wanted health.

That was seventh grade. Where I come from, the end of seventh grade means it's time to start thinking about the high schools you are going to have to apply to, the tests you are going to have to take and the essays you are going to have to write to get in. Just a minute ago you were a little kid, and now, you have to start thinking about high schools, which means you really need to be thinking about college, which means you really need to be thinking about what you want to do when you get out of college. Before your summer has even started, your whole life has been written in bold letters, permanent ink, on stone.

I wasn't ready for my entire future to be decided. I know I was just a kid and my braces weren't even off yet, but that's what it felt like for me to finish seventh grade. It felt like I was one summer away from having everything figured out for me, from having dinner parties instead of sleepovers.

I wasn't ready.

I also wasn't ready for the attention I was starting to get as a maturing young female-thing (don't call me a woman).

In the fifth grade, maybe mid-fourth grade, I started getting attention. Attention from boys who thought I was cute and attention from girls who would have much preferred themselves alone being cute, not me.

There were a couple of boys in particular who started joking about me, because they thought I was attractive.

I was uncomfortable with all the extra attention, and nobody believed me. They thought I was joking. That I really liked being noticed.

But I don't like attention. I know I should, but I don't. To me attention feels like a bright sunbeam shining on me so hard that my insides start to bleed. It takes mere seconds for the blood to reach the surface of my skin, igniting a sudden urge to vomit. I can't accept a compliment without feeling squeamish, like there are worms in my stomach, and I can't smile because if I do, who knows what will happen?

A big, flaming, red-hot spark for my eating disorder boomed on a weeklong school campout in the seventh grade. The boys in my class made a list of the girls in the class and rated them from top to bottom. They itemized them. They picked off their parts and pieces and they said who had the best what and where. Of course the list only involved looks — what else was there to talk about?

Best face, best body, best eyes, best lips, best arms, best butt, best legs, best breasts. On the list there were three spots for each item: a Number 1, a Number 2, and a Number 3. So, out of all the seventh and eighth grade girls from our school, there could only be 3 arms, 3 lips, 3 legs. And one of them was best, and one of them was worst, but still visible, still noticeable as a number 2 or 3. I appeared on the list a lot, and so did one of my best friends, but my other closest friend did not appear on the list at all. So how was I supposed to process that? What was I supposed to say to her, and she to me?

I was voted best body. And a friend was voted best face. If you took us apart, we could create the perfect girl. If I just lent her my body, she could be it.

By late afternoon, someone had counted all the votes and found out that I was the winner. I got the most Number 1 votes, even though my body was better than my face.

I don't know where my teachers were, and I don't know what the boys were thinking. I don't even know if the boys realize now, as grown men, how wrong they were for making the list. I do know that the boys were acting well within our social standards and trying to process and become Real Men. I do know that they meant no harm. Perhaps they even thought I enjoyed being singled out. I'm sure a part of me, somewhere, must have.

(I know I am supposed to enjoy it — to want that attention, to crave it.)

I was ashamed and embarrassed. To this day, the thought of the list hits me in the gut.

And what's funny/sad is I know, I just know, that if you ask any of the other girls in my class about the list, they will be able to tell you about it no problem. They will be able to smile and laugh it off. Life went on, for them.

Just a couple of months after that list I started starving myself. To this day talking about the list makes me want to starve, to tear the flesh off my thighs, to pull the covers over my head and kick everyone I know in the face. I know that that list hurt me.

Of course at the time I didn't have the perspective that I do now. I was humiliated by the list. And scared for my future life. I was confused about how I was going to keep my friendships secure, now that I was no longer Jordan but best body, and my friends were breasts and eyes or nonexistent and competing to become Top Three. But I didn't talk to anyone because I knew that people would laugh at me like they did when I tried to get Alexander to stop writing me love letters. Everybody thought I was "asking for it," even though I never asked, or showed any remote sign of interest, or indulgence, any ability to stay in the same room as him without my eyes watering and my hands cutting off all circulation to whatever body part of mine I decided to squeeze in total tension.

I was ten years old when Alexander wouldn't stop writing me love letters. He talked to his friends and they talked to me about all the different ways he wanted to kiss and touch me, all the reasons why he liked me. I was ten!

I was twelve years old when I was voted best body. Twelve!

I know it. I KNOW IT. I know everyone is laughing at me for talking about the love letters and the list. I had horrible things happen in my life. Terrible, sad things. Things that are Not Supposed to Happen. And yet the first bit I think to tell you about is the list. It is just so important. I know it, I know it, I know it!

At this point you should know that an eating disorder is not about food.

An eating disorder is not even about lists or risk factors. Instead eating disorders are about everything you could possibly imagine all stuffed into a tight container, you, and there's no exit. There's no word you can say to make everything all better and clear. There's no way you can verbalize or act on how you feel because you feel so much, because the whole wide world is on your shoulders and nobody understands you. Because everyone else is just so worried about the day-to-day and here you are worried about the end of the universe — it's coming quick, and nobody believes you or cares. It's being unprepared to cope, a feeling that you have seen too much and become the perpetrator plus the victim. You hold all the cards yet you can't see even one.

Eating disorders are complex and destructive diseases. They are also poetry. Because they ask real, important questions, questions so big their weight can kill you.

I know that I had an eating disorder not because I lost so much weight I almost died, not because I counted calories and carbs and protein obsessively, not because I over exercised, or binged and purged, or binged and didn't purge, or chewed and spit, or abused laxatives, or fantasized about suicide, or loved the company of food more than the company of anyone else, or loved the avoidance of food more than anyone else, or wasted hours upon hours thinking about my weight and how marvelous everything might be if I just shrunk myself down a little more.

No. In the end I know that I had an eating disorder because one day, when I was thirteen years old and eighth grade was looming large and scary in the future, I asked the questions.

Where other people have anchors and foundations and personhoods to rely on, I've got questions, volatile questions, and besides temporary avoidance and denial there are no answers.

Medically speaking, an eating disorder digs deep holes and question marks into your insides until the holes engulf you. These are important questions, huge questions, questions that disprove and ridicule and take the blinds off of everything you previously accepted and maybe even bowed down to and took part in. The questions make you feel like everyone belongs to this animal herd, walking in the one direction that you just won't walk down. But I can't pinpoint the questions. The minute I try to put my finger on them, they run. Perhaps the questions don't even exist. Perhaps they are mere question marks inside, swimming and bumping into one another, with no formed words or sentences to precede them, with no real or verbalized issue.

I think that's why you can't rely on the existence of the holes and the marks when you diagnose someone; since you can't get to the big questions bumping into one another inside, because who can define them, you have to instead go to the externals, to the appearance of things, to diagnose someone.

I know a few things.

I know there is hunger and emptiness, a black hole that you learn to either listen to or ignore.

I know that someone with anorexia thrives on self-deprivation and has such a great degree of, and respect for, control that she or he can become disgusted by those that lack a similar code of discipline.

I know that someone with anorexia becomes the sort of superhero that can exist with the Independence that negates the need for Relationships — both with other people, friends and family, and with themselves.

What I know most is what I have become: a perfect, by the book, check-me-off-the-list definition of someone with an eating disorder. At different points in my life I have been composed of the different checks required for diagnosis of the different eating disorders — anorexia nervosa, bulimia nervosa, binge eating disorder, eating disorder not otherwise specified.

Right now I think I am a mixture of all the different disorders and the scars they left behind and the continuous attempts I make to forget the past and live day by day, disordered thought by "recovered" person thought.

It's all because of the questions — and the list. They took my girlhood from me and replaced it with this bubbling, excruciating, dark-hole, fluctuating, and inconsistent, blank.

3

INTAKE

April 3, 2011

When I was sick, I loved to look in mirrors. My body often felt so detached from my day-to-day existence it felt like a separate being entirely, and so I would look in the mirror. I'd look to make sure that whatever was inside of me was still encased within my skin. That's what I was doing on the day I found myself headed to Children's Medical Center of Dallas' Psychiatric Unit. I was looking in the mirror to make sure that I was still, actually, there.

Specifically, it was between brushing my teeth and reaching for a hair tie when I caught my reflection in the mirror and it didn't look like me. Instead, I looked like the opposite of me. I looked hollowed out, like someone mistook my cheeks for cantaloupes and dug out all the seeds. I looked yellow. My eyes hid like night under the mountains of my brow bones and the bone of my cheeks jutted forth like the skeleton wanted out. There were bags the size of three squished cotton balls under both my eyes. And when I ran my fingers through my hair from root to tip, I saw scalp where there used to be hair.

Later when I start to recover I will stop seeing the badness in my body; I will stop seeing how far from health my body has come. I will gain weight and suddenly feel huge — the body dysmorphia finally kicking in in full force. I will feel bloated like a sea animal, all salt and protruding flesh.

As a thirteen-year-old kid headed to the hospital, anorexia still fresh in my blood, I think my body dysmorphia — that inaccurate perception of look and weight — was the slightest it has ever been.

Then I thought I looked sick and seeing myself scared me. Now I see old pictures of myself, and I see how untouchable I was then, at a weight that my body will never physically reach again, not just because of my own improved mental state but also because my body doesn't trust me anymore. It wouldn't let me if I tried.

In addition to sadness, I also feel envy for my former self. For how young and pure of heart, for how naive I was thinking I could fix all my problems myself, as an inward struggle. For how stupid I am to still think the same.

I remember looking in the mirror that day so clearly, like I am there now.

I placed my right foot on the top rim of the bathtub and lifted myself up, grabbing the curtain rail after the lift to help stabilize my balance. For a minute, everything was black and dizzy, then my vision returned to me with black spots fluttering all around. I used one hand to lift my shirt, the other still holding on to the shower rail above so I wouldn't fall. In the mirror I saw that my stomach curled in and my hipbones jutted out. All at once, I thought I looked normal, and sick, and, oddly, beautiful. But mostly I was unsettled by how I looked.

This was not supposed to happen.

I moved my body ninety degrees and cranked my head around to look at my back. My spine looked like a dinosaur's should. Like a hunched-over old man in need of a cane and two deep breathes of air for every step. I looked breakable. But I also looked sharp, like I could cut someone with my bones. I wondered then how I had gotten to that point and I realized that I already knew. That I always knew. That this was one swift fall that came so easily for me.

December 20, 2001

This morning I woke up at 7 to my buzzing alarm clock. Time to do my stomach exercises and stretches. Time to do my arm exercises with my five-pound weights. Time to go for my morning run.

Like every morning, every day, I am incredibly cold, tired to the point of sandy-eyed grogginess. Yet I have such a definite sort of energy at the same time. When I run, I feel like there is a string attached to my belly button, like an umbilical cord is pulling me forward, pushing me to keep on running.

It feels like the exercises are a personal ground rule, an offshoot of the familiar household tasks like doing the dishes or feeding the dog.

My mother doesn't want me to exercise so much. She says it

is *too much*. She says I should *slow down*. That I need rest.

I know my mother is scared. That's why I try to comfort her by eating all my meals in front of her. I know I'm not eating as much as I used to, or as "normally" as I used to. But I want her to see that I still eat.

This past month I also know I have gotten progressively worse. I have lost a lot more weight and my eyes bug out so that I look like some bug-eyed insect. My mother has taken time off from work. I don't know what she did exactly, but she's here with me all the time. Since she works in advertising, this is hard for her to do, to take time off. But I appreciate it. I feel like I need it to go on. Need her.

Because Christmas is coming up we have spent the last month running Christmas errands and going Christmas shopping and getting ready for the annual big-family-friends-Christmas party that we had at our house this year because we pulled our last name out of the hat at last year's party, which was held at my friend Shannon's house. We have been doing Christmas stuff and that used to be really fun for me. But now it just encompasses a lot of driving around, me being tired, my mom running in quick to get whatever thing we need and coming back fast to me in the passenger's seat, still tired, still waiting, with the seat buckle still locked across my chest. It's not so fun anymore. And what's really not so fun anymore is the clothes shopping part. The part that used to be my favorite.

My mother and I went to too many stores and tried on too many clothes, and the clothes marked for people who are size-less, or are venturing too close to being size-less, did not even fit. I pulled the pants up, and they fell to the floor. I pulled the pants up, and they fell to the floor. I pulled the pants up, and my mom, my poor mom, looked at all my bones jutting out every which way and for a moment you could see disgust and sadness in her eyes before she wiped the feelings away saying, "Okay, we'll go to another store." You could see that she probably felt like a bad mother for raising someone to grow up to look like this. Like some big ski accident with bones pointing out in ways they shouldn't.

Eventually we did find a pair of pants that didn't fall when I pulled them up. Unfortunately, they were the ugliest pair of dark tan, faux-leather pants. The pants whistled and screeched whenever I uncrossed my legs to stand, the fabric getting stuck together when it touched, like bare skin on a hot roller-coaster seat. A cheap copy of Ralph Lauren riding pants, the pants were much too shiny and much too sticky.

After we left the store and started walking to the car I remember being so worn out. My mother said, "Please, Jordan, please see that you need to take better care of yourself. I am so worried about you."

My mom and I are able to have lunch together every day because I am taking time off from school, just as she is from work. Usually we go to a place called Mercury Grill. Inside it is so dark your eyes have to adjust from the light outside to the lack of light inside and it takes a good twenty seconds. The restaurant is always cold. Even for people other than me. They serve fried calamari and steak tartare, endive salads with orange and fennel, big juicy heirloom tomatoes piled high with balsamic and buffalo mozzarella, risotto with mushrooms and chicken. For lunch we always split a hamburger, super-well done, with Cotswold cheese. My mother asks for fries, "extra crispy." I ask for a side salad.

Before I start doing this thing, this lose-weight-and-count-calories-and-exercise thing, I had been a stubborn-child vegetarian. But then a health book I read said that everyone needs complete protein.

We ate at Mercury Grill for lunch today. My mom had half of the hamburger with crispy fries and a big iced tea. I had the other half and a side salad and one diet coke, two diet cokes, three. My mom ate her half like a normal person. I try doing that, but it doesn't work for me. If you do that then the food goes away too quickly. And I don't eat enough food for it to go away too quickly. Instead I eat everything on its own, slowly. First I jab the meat with fork and knife. The meat is soft and beef-like crumbly, and it breaks off into baby bite-sized sections easily. We run out of ketchup and my mom raises her hand, asking the waiter for more. The waiter looks at the meat. Thanks to too much salt and pepper, I have made it look like the streets of New York in February. The waiter looks at me, makes a face, and turtle-scuttles away.

I am used to that at this point, as is my mother.

We keep on eating and I start with the Cotswold cheese I had siphoned off from the meat, nibbling and sucking on tiny pieces from the tip of the fork. We talk about Christmas things and our upcoming birthdays. I move on to the hamburger bun. There is half of a top and half of a bottom, which makes one whole slice. The bun is toasted and buttered, and it is my special treat. It tastes warm and comforting. I miss foods like this so when I eat lunch with my mother I really try to enjoy it. And I want to make my mother feel better, so every time I allow myself the treat of eating the bun in front of her without even being scared.

I know I can't lose any more weight and I think, *maybe this will help.*

I am upstairs looking in the mirror, seeing what happens to my
stomach when I eat half a hamburger, shocked that everything
still looks the same. Downstairs my mother is talking to a doctor
about me. I can't hear the conversation, but I know she is talking
because I heard the phone ring. She never told me she was expecting
a call, but I could see it in her face. All week my mother has been
forgetting names, misplacing keys, accidentally dropping things.
And I know it is because of me. Because she is worried about me
and has *had it up to here* and cannot take it any longer. Like she
is holding back tears. During lunch, my mother keeps looking at
her phone and with each screened call there is disappointment.
My mother is very worried, I think.

I hear her walking up the stairs.

"Jordan, that was Dr. Kay on the phone, the head doctor
at the unit we were talking about. She says you need to come in
immediately."

"Okay."

"So pack your bags."

"Pack my bags?"

"Yes. Try to hurry. We need to leave in fifteen minutes."

I am confused about why I need to pack my bags. I know
that my mother is about to drive me to the hospital, that I will
go to that unit and be taken care of, that I will have to spend
the night there. But I don't really understand. Nothing clicks. I
have never even been to summer camp before. My only experience
living away from home is with sleepovers, Monday to Thursday
school campouts, YMCA Indian Princess retreats with my dad.

I pull the pink ballet duffel bag out from under my bed. I
quit ballet a few months ago because I was tired of having to go

there every afternoon after school. Now I store all of my stuffed
animals inside the bag. I have a large collection, though I never
particularly liked stuffed animals and always thought I was too
grown up for things like teddy bears and blankies. I take the
stuffed monkeys and rabbits and put them on the bed.

Next I go to my closet and stare. How are you supposed to
dress for these sorts of things? Probably you should wear lots of
black and try to look cool and tough. Probably you should try to
look like those people in *Girl, Interrupted,* my favorite film along
with *The Virgin Suicides.* (Please don't tell my mom. She doesn't
know I've watched these films.)

I pack the ugly faux pants. I pack a black sweater, the only
black-colored thing I own because I used to like to wear colors,
not black. I throw in some shirts, pink ones, green ones, blue ones.
All of the shirts are of the same cut and style. My mom and I
found them at Gap two weeks ago. The T-shirts are the only ones
we could find that don't totally drown me in their fabric so my
mom insisted that we buy several in every color, wanting to take
care of me as best as she could. If I were still me, I would have
been annoyed with my mom for doing this. I like clothes, and I
wouldn't have wanted to have so many shirts that look the same.
But not anymore; now I don't particularly care. I pack two pairs
of workout shorts, a sports bra, and my running shoes.

Downstairs my mother is waiting by the front door. She is
pale and looks lost, like she's the one being sent off to the hospital,
not me. I smile. She quizzes me to make sure that I packed
everything I need. She tells me that my father and sister are still
out running errands and that we better go ahead and leave now.
I offer to carry the shopping bag by her feet but she says she can
take it. The bag has a pillow in it so I figure she might sleep in

the chair next to me like family members do in hospitals, and this makes me happy.

I don't remember the drive.

When we get to the hospital we don't know where to park and drive around for what seems like days, and by now I wish we could just keep on driving, that I didn't have to go away. I feel fine. I worked out this morning, ate lunch with my mom, I am fine. My mom finds a parking spot. We walk to the entrance, find the elevator, and go up to the fourth floor. From here we take a quick right, another right, another right, and then we go through a long pathway with offices on either side until we finally wind up in a waiting area with a desk surrounded in Plexiglas. It takes a long time to enter the building and get to this place. I think maybe the architecture is a protective measure to ward off escapes. At least it is for me. I want to run fast away but the route we took is all a maze, and I don't know which way to turn.

My mother bends down to talk to a nurse through a hole in the Plexiglas. She says that she just talked to a doctor at the hospital and was told that I had to come Right Now. The nurse smiles, presses a button, and in seconds a woman in business clothes appears. The woman asks if I'm a new patient; I nod and she smiles. My mother is given a stack of papers to fill out, and a nurse asks me to follow her.

The nurse leads me to a small room filled with medical equipment. First she measures my height. Then my weight. Then she listens to my heartbeat at different points mapped on my chest and listens to me breathe from my front and my back. Next she asks me to lie down and takes my blood pressure lying down, then sitting up, then standing up. She tells me to sit back down. I am dizzy because of all the quick movement. She takes my temperature by sticking a thermometer in my ear, and when she sees the reading she asks me if I'm cold. "Always," I say. The nurse looks into my eyes and hits my kneecaps with a small brown rubber hammer. My legs barely move, and she is obviously disappointed in me, though I barely know her. I tell myself that next time I will remember to force my legs to move when the little rubber hammer hits.

The nurse says that she is done checking things and that I will need a wheelchair. I don't ask her why but she tells me, "Your vitals are dangerously low, and you need to exert as little energy as possible." Someone knocks on the door and a man appears with an empty blue steel wheelchair. It's for me. Suddenly, I feel like resting my head on my thighs and falling asleep. They tell me to get in the wheelchair slowly, and the nurse grabs me by the left underarm while the man grabs me by the right. They slide me into the chair.

Tomorrow my underarms will be bruised from the process of moving from sitting-normal to sitting-wheelchair, but I don't know that yet.

We're in an office filled with medical texts, lots of files, and children's toys that I might have liked if I were eight and not thirteen. A business lady introduces herself as Dr. Kay and says that she is the head of Children's Medical Center's Psychiatric Ward. When she says the word "psychiatric" I feel like vomiting. I know what that word means.

Dr. Kay says she wants our family history.

My mom speaks up, "Well... Jordan was a normal, healthy child until around this past June when she became interested in healthy eating and exercise. I was worried about this because I had an eating disorder around her same age, but her primary doctor told us that there was nothing to worry about. She said I should be happy that my daughter was concerned about her health."

This is not our family history. Family history implies moms, dads, sisters, and grandparents, not just me.

"But then she kept on doing what seemed like extreme dieting and exercise, and she lost a lot of weight. So I took her back to her primary doctor who suggested that Jordan might have an autoimmune disorder — because why else would she be losing so much weight. This was around late August and, from afar, Jordan still appeared healthy. She lost too much weight, which wasn't good because she didn't need to, but she appeared to be functioning well... I had my concerns but listened to her physician."

Dr. Kay keeps looking at me while my mom talks, as if to check my response, to see if I agree or disagree. I still don't get why my mom isn't giving the family history. That's what the doctor asked for!

"And to be totally honest, I was hopeful that there was some physical thing going on with Jordan. If there was something physical, we could diagnose it, give her a pill and treatment and maybe that would have been simpler."

Dr. Kay looks at me for my response, and I don't give her one. Instead I look at my mother. Her skin is pale and her eyes look sad, but there is less tension in her face than there was this morning. She keeps smiling as she speaks and using her hands a lot, the way one does when they want to look agreeable.

"So we had all these tests done and found out that Jordan has hypothyroidism in September. But by this time, right after

9/11, Jordan had really gone downhill."

Suddenly I want to scream. I want to scream at my mother.

"She stopped seeing her friends and stopped going to school, altogether. She just refused! She said she felt too tired and sick, but then she would run out the door to exercise. I was worried, but tried to give her space, because of the hypothyroidism."

I finally get that *this* is the family history. This is it. *My story.* It's becoming the family history. Hot tears well up in my eyes and I don't know why so I try to focus and tell myself, *"Don't cry, don't cry."*

"But my intuition was telling me that it wasn't just her thyroid, that there was a bigger problem, and so I set up a meeting with someone here, Dr. Berman, and we both met with him on November 15. By this time, I really knew that she had an eating disorder. But Dr. Berman said that we needed to fix Jordan's hypothyroidism first to see if her symptoms went away once her body got used to the new thyroid medication."

I cry. My mom keeps looking in her red Filofax as she talks. Her Filofax is sitting on her lap and looking at it is too much for me to handle. Her organizer is meant for business and schedules, not for me. I am supposed to be her daughter, not a page in the book. I am supposed to be normal. I am not supposed to be the family history, a page nestled in between the work to-do's and the addresses of friends.

"So we went home, and on my own I hired a nutritionist to come to the house twice a week to set up a meal plan that Jordan could stick to in order to gain back the weight she lost. This woman was experienced with eating disorders and she talked to Jordan and seemed to get to her. The nutritionist told Jordan that she needed to start eating a set amount of calories every day to stabilize her weight and asked Jordan to keep track of her calories, which made sense to me as Jordan was already very obviously counting calories."

Dr. Kay's face looks like it is listening. But it also looks like it has heard it all before. Her eyebrows stay flat and they never jump or perk to the side or anything.

"The nutritionist asked Jordan to stop exercising so often and just to work out for a little bit five times a week, and then they could taper off from there. Jordan seemed to want to follow the nutritionist's advice, but she wasn't able to stick with the meal plan, and she kept over-exercising and losing weight."

This is embarrassing. I don't want to be here anymore, I want to run away. My eyes are so hot it feels like they will fall out of their sockets if I keep on crying. My eyes will just fall right out with the tears. I want to scream. I want to jump up and kick, to hammer the walls with my feet and hands. I am dying inside, I can feel it. Yet I don't move one bit. I'm hunched over, my eyes dropping hot tears onto my kneecaps and I can feel the tears, they seep through my jeans, wet my skin. But, besides the wetted knees, besides the need to kick and scream, I can't feel anything.

"Then the day after Thanksgiving I took Jordan to the ER. I didn't know what else to do. We had eaten dinner, our family, and afterwards Jordan sat on a chair in our living room and didn't move. For thirty minutes she was completely still and quiet and she looked really, really pale."

I don't remember this.

"I'm always used to Jordan... the Jordan before... running around, laughing and making noise with everyone and seeing her like this scared me to death. Because she looked like she was dead. Her dad was asking her questions. He was worried that she had had a concussion or something. So we put her in the car, and I took her to the ER. Her dad had to stay home to take care of her sister."

I want a turtle's shell. That is exactly what I want. It has never been more clear: a turtle's shell! I simply cannot be here anymore. This hurts. I hurt. *Let me out!* I scream inside my own head, silent to the outside world.

"At the ER, they immediately put Jordan in a wheelchair and she sort of haphazardly rested her head on the side of the chair, like she passed out. She didn't appear to be upset at all about being in the chair at the ER. It looked like she had been there a thousand times but, of course, I knew differently. Jordan was a healthy girl, the only medical thing she had ever dealt with was stitches!"

I hear the word "wheelchair" and look down at the one I'm sitting in. I look back up at my mom. I look back down. *I am in a wheelchair.* I went running this morning and now I am in a wheelchair. *I need to get out of this thing.* I need to get out of this thing while my mom isn't looking. She can't see me in this. This is ridiculous. This is crazy. *This is not where I am supposed to be.*

"I really thought, 'This is it.' I scratched her back like I used to when she was little, when I was putting her to bed at night. And I thought, 'This is the last time.'"

Dr. Kay looks at me, her eyes questioning. Her eyes ask me if I get what my mom is hinting at. "I'M NOT STUPID!" I want to scream. "I KNOW SHE IS TALKING ABOUT ME DEAD."

I'm crying more than ever, and my eyes will surely fall out. When I feel myself wanting to scream those words, I don't actually mean it. I feel the words but I don't feel the meaning, I don't recognize it. I do not like thinking of me, my mom, and death in the same minute, in the same hour, in the same day. I do not want my mom to scratch my back one last time. I do not want to be put to rest like a dog. I need to get out of here. I need to kick the wall, and I need to get out of this wheelchair.

"We waited *eight hours* to be seen. Finally, they said that Jordan was very dehydrated. Also everything was too low: her blood pressure, her temperature, the time it took for her to respond to questions, move her body, and adjust her eyes. They drew some blood and gave her an IV for a couple of hours, and then we went home. They said that we should call her physician and come back the next day if Jordan still wasn't doing well. The next morning when I woke up, Jordan had just gotten back from a run."

Dr. Kay looks angry now. She says that I should have had more treatment that night, better care. She says that she is mad at the hospital people, but I know that she is mad at me. I know that she sees what a total failure I am, that I am stupid and not right.

Maybe I should be here right now. Maybe I need to be here.

So many tears are falling from my eyes there is a traffic jam of tears piling up between my pupils and the lower lash lines — they need to take care of th at.

My mom agrees with Dr. Kay. She says that that night one of the nurses at the ER suggested, offhand, that we visit Dr. Berman again. She says that that is why we are here. Because when we met with him again, he said it's not the thyroid, it's me.

"It's good you're here." Dr. Kay smiles at me and my mom. I feel bad because I realize that Dr. Kay is a lot like my mom's friends, she has the same posture and jewelry and is both fun and professional. Dr. Kay and my mom could be friends. I need to get out of this wheelchair.

Dr. Kay looks at my mom. "Jordan has a serious health condition. Her body cannot last much longer the way she has been treating it."

My mom looks at me, I look at my mom, our eyes meet. I see that she is also crying hot tears.

"Which is why you have to be admitted today."

Dr. Kay looks at me. I can't take the feeling of four staring eyes at the same time. I don't know where to look. I look at my kneecaps where my tears have sunken through from cloth to skin and this doesn't feel sufficient. This doesn't feel like enough.

"I am sorry that you have to be admitted right before Christmas, but your body cannot wait."

I look at my mom. I want her to take me away. Her face is so pale it blends in with the hospital white walls. I feel that I can't get out of this — this is the real deal. No more hypothyroid business, no more pushover nutritionists, I am here to stay. My eyes cry uncontrollably but my eyeballs stay in place. *I can't do this.* I have to think of something. I have to think of something quick.

Dr. Kay asks my mom about our family and any history of mental illness. No, no, no. A little depression, yes. A little eating disordered, yes.

Dr. Kay asks my mom if she thinks that I am suicidal. No. Does she think I have been binging? Purging? Taking laxatives or diuretics or diet pills? No. Anything else? No. Just under-eating and over-exercising? Yes.

They keep on talking but I stop listening. I can't take it. I wrap my hands around my chest to center and anchor me down, but it does nothing, I feel out of control. I am shaking, rocking in this wheelchair and everything suddenly feels very surreal, like it's not happening. Like I'm an angel up above flying around and watching this horrible thing happen to some other person, not myself, down below.

Dr. Kay asks me my side of the story. All I can say is, "I'm sorry," as I rock back and forth, drooling salt tears. As I keep telling you, the tears have become so hot and heavy, so traffic jammed, that I am having difficulty seeing clearly. With my vision hazy, I feel like we are all underwater. Or like everything in the room is drowning in Saran Wrap, making the image of my mom appear splintered and multiplied with shattered body parts stretching out every which way from her glowing center. Like a picture of the Virgin Mary seen through a kaleidoscope.

Dr. Kay says that it's time for me to be admitted and my mom must say goodbye.

I stop crying.

Dr. Kay says my mom can visit me tomorrow from 5 to 6, and my father and sister can come along, too.

I wipe the snot and tears from my face with the sleeve of my shirt. Something inside me remembers that I am about to go inside the ward and so I must clean up and look cool, no matter how much I want to kick and scream, to run away with my mother.

My mom stands up and seems to not know what to do next. She leaves her purse on the floor and fumbles to the back of me and my chair. Dr. Kay says that a nurse can wheel me. My mom says okay.

Someone knocks on the door, and Dr. Kay says, "Come in." Another nurse appears. She grabs the reins to the back of my chair and wheels me out of the room. I want to look back to make sure that my mom is following, but I am so incredibly tired and cold. I spent all the energy I had left crying. I had saved it for so long and now it's gone, I have no more. All I have left are hot tears becoming colder and colder against the skin of my kneecaps, making me wish I had one hundred gazillion dryer-warmed blankets just this moment to keep warm.

The nurse comes to a halt right next to a big door with a square glass peephole that lets you see inside. The peephole is not made for people in wheelchairs, though, so I can't see anything.

I hear my mother say, "uh-huh, uh-huh," and then I see her. She is standing almost right in front of me and looking at Dr. Kay, worried. Dr. Kay opens the big door with the peephole, pops her head in. In a minute a younger-looking woman, maybe late twenties, comes out. She has big brown eyes like my sister and lots of brown hair piled into a loose and falling-down bun. She looks nice. Dr. Kay says that she will be my nurse for the day.

Dr. Kay shakes my mother's hand but not mine. She tells me that she will see me again tomorrow, smiles, and goes away with the nurse who first wheeled me.

The new woman, my "nurse for the day," introduces herself as Andrea. She shakes my mom's hand. She doesn't shake mine. She says that it is time for me to say goodbye to my mom.

My mother kneels down to hug goodbye. The worry that spotted her face has completely vanished; now she looks supportive-happy. I am upset that she is treating me like a sick person, giving me that *"you'll be fine, don't worry"* fake-smile that translates into *"I have no idea what's going to happen, and I'm scared for you, too."* Then I smell that wonderful mix of gardenia perfume and baby powder that is my mother, and I feel so sad, so homesick, because as I smell the perfume and powder I know that in just seconds I won't be able to smell her anymore.

My mother squeezes me tight for a minute and then loosens the hold. She grips onto the sides of my arms and pulls me towards her and with our foreheads touching she whispers, "I love you." I want to tell my mom that I love her too, but I am so tired my voice has gone mute. I nod my head to let her know that I agree, I love her too.

She keeps her hands gripped onto the sides of my arms as she inches her body away. "I don't want to have to leave, sweetie. I love you so much. But I know that this is the right thing to do. Okay?"

Tears well up in my eyes again and I tell myself, *"Don't cry; don't cry."*

"You have to get better, okay?"

"Okay," I tell my mom. Her hazel eyes look so sad and tired they look blue to me, like different eyes altogether. I can see shiny wet lines running down her cheeks from the bottom of her eyes. The lines are ruins marking the tears she shed today. She tried to wipe them off but they can't go away completely.

Next my mother says my absolute least favorite word: goodbye. I am expected to say it back to her but I can't, I have gone mute again. She gives one last squeeze to the sides of my arms and then she lets go. She stands up. She looks at me, new tears welling up in her eyes.

My mother turns around and walks away. I watch her as long as I can, hoping that she will turn her head around and wave one last goodbye but she never does. Instead my mother turns the corner and disappears.

Immediately I feel a sharp sense of panic. For the first time in my life I feel truly alone.

I woke up this morning in my own bed at my own house and now I am here, thirteen years old and away from everything I know, five days before Christmas.

I have been abandoned.

A few tears roll down my face, remembering their path, and then they stop falling. I sit stick-straight in my wheelchair and take in one big gasp of air, wide-eyed. I realize that all of the teary, Saran-wrapped haziness, and the fluttering, black-spotted dizziness, and the hovering, angel-views from up above have gone away. Everything appears harshly in focus. Like rapid movement, captured and made quiet.

This is it, an important moment, the memory of which will spook me for many years. This is the part where the whizzing stops too fast and crashes into the wall, and I can't walk anywhere because the picture frame fell on the floor, and there is glass everywhere. It's the sad still frame from the happy feature length film that tells a different and a more true story: the story of *me* leaving, not knowing if I was ever going to come back.

. . .

How did this happen?

My eating disorder was a fight to stay in the middle, a fight to stay away from the extremes. A fight between those two sharks. I had my "real" self on one side and my "sick" self on the other. I had my old self on one side and my new self on the other. My dead self and my alive self. My clean self — my first bout of anorexia — and my dirty self — my future bouts with bulimia and EDNOS.[2]

---

2   EDNOS = Eating Disorder Not Otherwise Specified. It's an eating disorder that doesn't fit the set criteria of anorexia, bulimia, or binge eating disorder (criteria that is rather difficult to reach) but it still present, harmful, and needing of treatment, in some way.

My good self and my bad self. My scared self and my fearless self. My tipsy-topsy curving self and my disciplined and structured self.

Always, the two extremes were positioned on either side of me, and I was pinned in the middle, unable to make a choice. I am very bad at making choices. I am because you can't have one part without the other. Extremes depend on each other in order to exist.

And so you keep swimming back and forth between the two extremes. You can't get out because you see you have no other options. You keep on going and it feels like someone is dragging you. It feels like it's the question of who you are, who your real self is, that is always up in the air. No wonder you find it necessary to count those calories and track that weight. Counting anchors you to something solid and unquestionably true; something with a quantifiable answer that could define you as one whole thing, one whole calorie in versus calories out, one whole center with no extraneous business flanking you on either side.

With an eating disorder there is a left and there is a right but there is never a center, there is never a real you.

Eating disordered people can't have real, normal, balanced selves, selves capable of choosing not to swim. But I think I used to. Way back before the eating disorder, I can feel her memory, this most perfect self. This unadulterated, spotless, ideal version, the first edition we can never get back. She slipped from my hands before the summer. Before I turned thirteen, I could feel her increasing absence. Perhaps that's why I clung to the disorder: because I could feel myself disappearing and had nowhere else to go.

In my childhood pictures I think I look authentic. I look

happy. I smile and it's genuine. I look excited, full of energy. My pictures don't look like that anymore. Ever since the disorder, you can see the dark shadows of a ghost hidden behind my image. You might say I look happy or pretty, or whatever, but I say look harder. You can see the hurt. You can see the Disappearing Girl.

It's no coincidence that I started disappearing when boys started to take notice, when hormones started shaking, bodies maturing faster than some might like, faster than the mind. Around fifth grade I stopped being happy. I felt like something wasn't right, and that feeling lasted, steady and true, for some time. As I disappeared, I searched for something to hold on to, to ground me. I could have tried all kinds of things, there are so many ways that young people rebel or self-destruct just to prove that they still exist, that they still feel something. It took me just a few years to find the behavior — really the inevitable behavior — that clicked for me.

There is lots for you to know. Like, my father is insufficient compared to my mother. I know it's a common story. The father is absentee while the mother provides love and care and stability. And as girls mature, the fathers of America become more and more distant as the mother/daughter bond grows. But for me, the difference between my parents and the feelings I have for each are even more distinct. I love my mother. I am confused by my father. And sometimes when people ask about my father, since I never mention him, I immediately say, "Oh, I don't have one." It's become a protective measure, an instinct to shield me from the pain of saying I have a father but we don't keep in touch; I have a father but after I turned fourteen I have never had a meaningful father/daughter talk; I have a father but I'm not sure if he cares — and I don't want to care anymore.

When I was thirteen I still loved my dad and he loved me and my parents were together and everything was supposedly happy. Only it wasn't. And I knew it wasn't. Not because anybody told me but because I felt it instinctually. I just knew that my mother and my father did not get along, that something was uneven, that everything wasn't so normal and that it couldn't possibly stay normal much longer.

Years later, my mom will tell me that my eating disorder was the warning call she needed to confront my father and eventually divorce him. My father, off and on, will blame me for breaking the family apart. If it's not me that's the problem, it's my mother. To him we are one and the same.

It's painful and I do not want to talk about it. And, even if I had a fantastic father I know that I would still have gotten sick. Because I do not, did not, like myself.

It doesn't have to do with how I look but it has to do with something similar. A feeling I have about myself, often brought on as a reminder when I see myself in the flesh, brought on to remember that I have a body and therefore exist. I have a body and am therefore repulsive.

It is not the body that is to blame. It is just the fact that the body belongs to me.

Studies say that kids as young as five demonstrate preoccupation with weight and body image, and that dieting is a pretty sure-fire response to bad body feelings.

I think that on some level, even before I started disappearing and before I disappeared completely, I have always been disgusted with myself. The idea that *I am repulsive* was always there. It just came out bigger and badder when I left myself and the disorder came in to fill the void. So it was easy to justify my "healthy" monitoring of food: I need to watch out for myself, punish myself, change myself before people start to notice me. Again, it had nothing to do with how I looked. It had to do with how I felt.

What am I supposed to say now, to those who love me who I have hurt so much with my disorder? *I'm sorry?*

I am sorry for the things I didn't get to do because of the disorder. I am sorry for the things I did do because of the disorder — things you shouldn't do. But I just can't see any other way around it. Who would I have been, if I didn't get Sick? I'm not totally sure that a me minus disorder could even exist at all.

I got sick and stayed sick for a very long time. And somewhere in those years while I was fighting in the deep dark of my disease, I walked away from my own father — for the health of myself and my family. Now that I'm doing much better, he's not here to cheer me on at the finish line.

I miss him.

· · ·

Though I wasn't fully aware of it, in the seventh grade I was terrified of growing up, of having to become that sex-symbol woman that I knew I was expected, and didn't want, to become. I was scared of the family fights I could feel bubbling near the happy, nuclear surface. I was scared of having to go to high school soon, of my friends who were becoming meaner and crueler as the days went by, of the boys that looked longer and longer at my parts. I felt like this life that I was growing into wasn't even mine to begin with. That I never said it was okay.

That's why the disorder felt safe: because I said, without

really knowing how or why or what, that *it was okay*, that I could be sick, that I could start to disappear and that I could do it all to myself. I could, in essence, pull the covers over my head and for a while nobody would even have to know. Everyone would think I was still fine and functioning as I burrowed myself deeper underground.

But an eating disorder is an addiction. The food, or the lack of food, becomes a drug. There is the high of a binge, the deep lows of the purge, the hurried, itching denials of self-starvation and also the walking on clouds, best high you've ever had that comes from the brain fog of malnutrition — or purging, or overeating. Each has a different cloud, but they all feel better than the everyday.

Still, before it kills you, anorexia feels like the most rewarding of the eating disorders. While bulimia and binge eating make you feel — outside of the high-cloud — sick, weak, and metaphorically bloated, anorexia often makes you feel pure, sublimely clean, and protected, as if you are impenetrable, untouchable, and wonderfully ice-cold, frosted over, one-track-minded. Like a strong sheet of glass is protecting you from the outside world, softening the sounds. You become unbreakable. I suppose it makes you feel like cocaine is supposed to make you feel, or crystal meth, or whatever those drugs are that make you feel super-human and then break you down to nothing.

Plenty of people with eating disorders struggle with drug abuse and a fistful of other addictions, too. I think the reason why I'm not a pill head is because my anorexia happened so fast; one month I was a healthy, normal teenager and six months later I was dying on the floor. Typically, it's a slower progression — easier for the friends and family to ignore, easier for the health complications to glimmer and grow as everyone plays dumb. For me, anorexia quickly became impossible to ignore. It had devoured me whole. Thus, I don't do drugs. Sure, I've smoked a cigarette, I've drunk too much, I've taken painkillers when I had no real physical pain. But those things don't last long for me. I'd rather eat a cookie. Or purge a cookie. Or avoid a cookie altogether.

My anorexia taught me that I need less than an ounce to turn my whole world upside down. It also taught me that it, along with bulimia and overeating, is the only drug I need.

Dear Reader,

The next two chapters are problem chapters.
They are academic and boring and slow in pace.

They are also necessary.

4

ALWAYS HUNGRY

April 22, 2011

When I was seven, I went roller skating with my sister around our block and, unable to tell her that I needed to eat — because I already knew hunger was not something to admit — I thought I was going to die of starvation like the Ethiopian children with big bellies that my neighbor told me about. Hunger was my near-death experience.

When I was eight, my sister and I spent the week at one of my friend's houses while my parents went on a business trip. Her family ate a lot of things I didn't like, such as beef and fish and spinach dip with rye crackers. And while my sister was able to ask for something else, I was not. Hunger was my inability to ask.

When I was eight, I also learned to equate food consumed with bodily size and began to compare what I ate to what my friends ate and felt guilty, as a black-and-white thinker, if I happened to eat more.

When I was nine, I went on a weeklong school camping trip and came home weighing a few pounds less. Hunger was my mother's attention.

When I was ten, a friend started pulling up her shirt and looking at her stomach in the mirror; if her stomach looked big she would do thirty sit-ups; then, when she ate, she promised herself she could eat the last bites she wanted but did not need if she made up for it in pushups. Hunger was my friend's problem.

When I was eleven, my looks became the whole big wide world and even though I didn't like it, I knew I couldn't stop it. Hunger was my real self, quieted.

When I was twelve, I stopped eating lunch at school because none of my friends ate theirs. Hunger was my competition.

When I was thirteen, I fell fast into anorexia's companionship and organized my life into calories in versus calories out. Hunger was my suicide pact. When I was hospitalized for anorexia and told I might die, told I might not survive the night, hunger was the only thing grounding me, connecting me to this body, this life.

When I was fourteen I was let back out into the real world equipped with extra pounds, meds, and meal plans. Hunger was my downfall. A few months later, I refused to eat certain foods unless there was a toilet nearby that I could throw up in, and I watched as messy, uncontrollable bulimia replaced my perfect, ascetic anorexia. Hunger was my button pressed.

When I was fifteen, I became tired of binging and purging, so I stopped purging and the depression worsened as my weight shot up well above my comfort level. Hunger was this private, lonesome pain.

When I was sixteen, I started dieting like "normal" people do, and you'd swear I was recovered. Hunger was my past complaint.

When I was seventeen, I had a cold and lost three pounds and remembered the benefits of self-starvation. Hunger was this exhilaration, remembered.

When I was eighteen, certain events made me feel that pain so great one can't actually feel it, the mind instead resorting to numbness, and I started binging without purging. Hunger was a numb shell to fill.

When I was nineteen, I tried to get my life back together, which included trying to lose the supposedly "extra" weight. Hunger was my attempt at getting healthy. The healthy diet and exercise quickly turned into binging and purging, chewing and spitting, laxatives. Hunger was uncontrollable.

When I was twenty, my bulimic self met my anorexic self and I became an anorexic bulimic. Hunger was my pattern.

Now I'm twenty-three and my hunger is a lot of things: My hunger is the thing that is tucked inside that I, so tired, don't like to acknowledge; my hunger is my reminder, like a panic button, that I still feel and want and need; my hunger is the thing I hate; the thing I trust; the thing that defines me as, often, someone I do not care to be.

Sometimes my hunger is all I need. Sometimes, I feel as if it is the truest, most dependable thing in my life. At my lowest points, this dependability feels like safety; it masquerades as a protector. But most often it's too real, a deep ache that I need to superficially fill with more, and more (or, with less, and less). And if anything I now know, after over a decade in bed with Ana,[3] that my hunger, though multiplied and contorting, can always be explained in either one of two ways: first, my hunger is exhausting (and so I am often Healthy by defeat — defeat, as in, I can't go on pushing) and, second, I am always, irretrievably and uncontrollably, hungry.

Yes, my mother did everything she could. She fulfilled all the obvious requisites of body-positive parenting for her daughters: raising me to think that one's beauty comes from the inside so I should not put much attention towards diet or looks. But she also did much more: She wanted me to be independent (thus my first name, a boy's name) and told me that my intellect was most important, that it was okay to cry, okay to laugh, okay to talk about uncomfortable things. My mother never bought me a Barbie doll and, because I never had one, I never really wanted one. My mother taught me how to eat healthily and that sometimes eating healthily includes peppermint ice cream before bedtime. She taught me to play outdoors and love my body for what it could *do*, for the trees it helped me climb. My mother made sure that our family ate dinner together every night, talking about our day, and she never told me Cinderella stories.

Once I got older and started taking note of fashion magazines, my mother, who is both beautiful and fashionable, pointed out the air brushing and told me, "Darling, please understand, being fake — so tightened and stretched — never looks good." As I grew older, my mother never even encouraged me to get straight A's,

---

3   Otherwise known as Anorexia – many websites, both "Pro-Ana" and against, refer to her in this slang. It's probably distorted to refer to anorexia as a friendly human name. Well, I'm distorted, as are the people of the internet.

though I always did.

Most of all, my mother never, ever, taught me to give a crap about weight. My whole life, she has never owned a scale. My whole life, she has never talked about weight or fat or the look of her thighs — not to me, not in front of me, not to anyone, I presume. She did these good things in part because she used to be sick like me — as I would later discover sometime before my intake. When I found out, it's like I already knew. It wasn't surprising. Not because she still demonstrated eating disorder behaviors but because my eating disorder felt so familiar, it only made sense that she knew it once too.

Hunger is about disappointment. It's about wanting more and not knowing where to find it. It's about feeling empty and aching to be filled. It's about being, about becoming, a woman. It's about hurt.

It's the hunger my mother felt. It's the hunger I feel. Every day, it won't stop.

More than once I've been anorexic. More than once I've been bulimic. More than once I've been a compulsive exerciser. More than once I've been a binge eater. More than once I've taken laxatives religiously. More than once I've chewed and spit. Only once have I been Healthy: that was before I turned ten. And I attribute all this mess to hunger, to that pain in the upper regions of my stomach, so close to the heart I mistake it for an emotion.

I am always hungry. And I know that everyone has been at some point in time. But I am convinced that my hunger is different, more extreme and life-threatening, more visceral. My hunger is my womanhood and my incapabilities and my insecurities. My hunger is what I am. And more than anything I wish, pathetically, that I weren't hungry. I wish that I weren't, in essence, me.

My eating disorder has left me with two physical scars, one per hand; two constant reminders of the life I've had and the experiences I've lost, one horrible way to touch and feel and live in the world, always remembering and, therefore, always living in the past.

On my left hand I have a scar from anorexia. I was beyond malnourished and when I bumped into a brick wall, my hand was cut and it never fully healed. For almost an entire year, the small cut was a scab. Then it became red. Now it is a pale white, almost undetectable, but it's there. On my right hand, at the same point as the one on my left, where the second tallest finger curves inward down to the thumb, I have a scar from bulimia. I put my fingers down my throat, suffocating and wanting to vomit, so many times that a scar developed. Now the scar has turned pink. One day it will turn pale white and some people might not even notice it, but I will always know it's there.

And that's what an eating disorder does: You know it once and you know it always. You live it once and you can never get away. It leaves a scar that you can't get away from, a scar much bigger than the spots on my two hands, a scar that is always radiating hurt, and loss, and thoughts of who you could have been. If only you hadn't gotten Sick.

· · ·

A person with an eating disorder can use the word "hunger" as a metaphor for just about anything. They think the word is fantastically huge and meaningful and can sum up all of their sadness and neuroses, memories and feelings into one word: hunger. And they think it is a universal thing, the way they feel about hunger. They think that people will instantly understand all of their trials when they use the word. But mention hunger to a normal person and they don't think loneliness, fear, wants, and needs — a normal person thinks the physical need for food, a temporary if not potentially serious phenomenon. That's it. Normal people think hunger is the need to eat. Seriously! And here I am, thinking that hunger means my insatiable need to be more, more perfect and more true, and my insatiable need to exist and feel alive and to hide and feel numb, and the crying child I feel somewhere deep inside, crying for warmth and never satisfied, never safe. If I could pick one word to define me that would be it: Hungry. If I could pick two it would be: Hungry, Always.

It's true. For me hunger means being a woman, ultimately. Hungry means having to do with being female, with my relationship to my mother, and with my thoughts on having to grow up and become the one thing that I absolutely do not want to have to become: a woman.[4] It's like hunger is my womanhood and my eating disorder is the thing I sought to rid me of the feminine entirely.

My hunger tells me that I am not enough. I want more, so much more, but I do not deserve more and I cannot ask for more. My hunger tells me that I am out of control, impatient, and wild; that I need something, anorexia perhaps, to reel me in, to put its hand down and scold me, telling me that I don't need as much as I say. My hunger is embarrassing. *Why can't I just be happy with what I have?*

For people with eating disorders, hunger is a mess of a thing that is often tied up with family relationships, the push towards

---

4   The use of the word woman here refers to the traditional, nuclear sense of man versus woman; a woman in a world where trans doesn't exist, where homosexuality doesn't exist, where the end goal of a woman is always to serve — even in the smallest sense, even when it's not so obvious — a man. It's a woman that's stuck as subservient in a world without choices.

perfectionism, sex and emptiness and love, the confusion between what we need and what we want. It's the fear in asking for the things we need, as if to need is to want and to want is wrong. In essence, my struggle with hunger is immovable from my struggle with anorexia. They are the same thing.

Here's a game. Simply replace the word hunger in everything I say above with the word "anorexia." Everything still makes sense. Try it with the hunger metaphors below. The big ones are: *Hunger is my mother. Hunger is not my father. Hunger is a little girl. Hunger is fear of sex. Hunger is hurt. Hunger is loveless.*

And, just like my hunger, my anorexia cannot be cured by food alone.

+*1*

Hunger is My Mother

The one thing my mother never taught me that she should have is where my hunger comes from. She didn't tell me because she doesn't know. But I do. The hunger comes from my mother.

Even though my mother tried so hard, the anorexic person sees the things that aren't spoken aloud and thinks they are more important. So even when my mother taught me all those good things and even though we had dinner as a family every single night (a simple event that has been said to help prevent a long list of adolescent troubles including eating disorders), I still heard what she didn't say out loud: *oh no, watch out, be careful, it's getting closer.* Because of my mother, my eating disorder was inevitable, unavoidable, and it wasn't even entirely because of her as a person with DNA but because of her as a figure, too. My mother is my *mother*, my caretaker, the person that is supposed to love me a thousand times as much as the whole wide world. She is the one who is supposed to pass down the family stories from generation to generation. And guess what my family story is? Hunger. Wanting more.

To those that are wondering now, yes, my little sister struggled too. At the same age as me, even. Only hers didn't last so long. It wasn't imprinted in her person as much as mine was. Partly because anorexia was already mine, a sort of taken hobby, but primarily because, by that time, family circumstances would not have allowed for any more serious, serious illness. If she had gotten too sick, we would have fallen apart, fallen to the point of being unmendable. My sister, I think, did not want that. Instead she wanted us to get normal again. (This is said not to minimize the difficulty — or, for me, the impossibility of recovery — but to recognize that there are things that we can tell ourselves, particularly at certain fortuitous times, that help.)

In regard to my mother as an actual living person: My mother works. She always has. And while her career never took away from her capacity to love me and showed me the wonderful ways that a woman must contribute and benefit from her work, her work also taught me, though she never said it out loud, that being a woman in business sucks. Don't try to tell me differently.

I know that the fact that I am female will keep me from boardrooms, from old boys' club networks, let alone from walking down any street, just name a street, without people looking at me too long.

When I was little my mother and father owned their own ad agency and often held their very own take-their-daughters-to-work day. While I was playing in the office, I saw how my dad stayed my dad while my mom had to juggle so many different characters and be extra-girly nice or extra meany-tough, always conniving — not in a manipulative way but in a survival way — to satisfy the needs of a lot of different people — and that understanding sunk deep inside of me. The expectations of who I was supposed to be stuck. And when I finally got to that age of becoming that woman, I said No. No, it's not enough.

It's not enough to be my mother. It's not enough to have to pretend to be a thousand different people in a day, to be liquid and move from one character to the next with a fake smile always shining. I want more authenticity, more comfort in my own presence, more food, more security, more stuff, more happiness, more contentment when I can't be happy. And that, in essence, is my metaphorical mother and what she as a living person passed down to me: the feminine need for more and the feminine fear of asking for more and the feminine disgust, aimed at oneself, because it's not nice to be mean and it's not nice to want more. We women made all the big and little people of the world and yet, we women are afraid to have more. It's our job to do, not to have. To give, not be.

Anorexia, for me and for thousands of others, is a direct response to the bad draw of having to be a woman. We want all those things the boys got to play with, and we want to play like girls with dignity and respect. We want more than we could ever imagine — who even knows where to begin. *We want so much that we want nothing. We want so much it hurts.* And with the pain we ask for even more.

So here's what you decide to do: Shut it up. Stop wanting so much. Stop thinking so much. Figure yourself a Spartan, sleeping on wood floors. Figure yourself as nothing. You can't have anything, just the gift of anorexia. That sweeping nothingness, the void left from all you can't have.

+2

Hunger is Not My Father

My hunger is not my father because my hunger is my mother, and my mother as a figure is the opposite of my father as a figure. The mother nurtures. The father pays. He is the provider, and she is the caretaker, and in a society where we have so much stuff sold as replacements for love, which do you think is more important? Love, the actual thing, or money, the sorry yet necessary substitute?

Absolutely, this mom and pop idea is dated. I grew up in a mom-funded, *mom's hard work* family wherein my dad did not and perhaps even could not contribute in the same way as my mom. I understand that the roles are changing. That in even more traditional, nuclear family households, women, or well-to-do, supremely educated women, are reaching up higher and that sometimes the man stays home and takes care of the kids. What I can say, from my background with such a household, is that the mother, or at least my mother, still had to foot the bill as prime nurturing caretaker no matter her long hours at work. It wasn't a role reversal so much as it was a role acquittal — my mom took on a two-for-one while my dad's contribution subsided into Neverland. And, absolutely, trust me I know, for many families, money is not something to scoff at, it is a primary concern thanks to its deficit. The same can be said, for other families, of love.

A girl's relationship with her father is supremely important and it has been shown that girls with strong, supportive relationships with their fathers have a lower rate of mental illness including eating disorders. Conversely, for so many women suffering from anorexia, bulimia, or binge eating disorder, it is the lack of this foundational relationship that exacerbates the disease. For many anorexics, the father may seem to have nothing to do with her eating disorder, but that's because he doesn't exist. As in, she has learned to adjust to a life spent pretending not to notice his absence.

It's okay to lose that important figurehead of safety because the anorexic doesn't ask for safety so much as she asks for death. *Women need men in order to exist.* So the anorexic pretends she has no father. She pretends she has no opposite. No protector. And just like that, the anorexic doesn't exist in the conventional world at all.

+3

Hunger is a Little Girl

When I was little I used to joke with wide arms. Someone would ask me how much I wanted to do something or how much I liked someone and I would stretch my arms out as wide as I could and say this much times 84,372,043 thousand, trillion, million, gazillion. This number made a lot of sense to me, much more sense than the algebra equations and the x over y minus z's I learned in middle school. It made sense that I could outstretch my arms and say I love you as much as my arms times a hungrazbilliontwenty. I love you immeasurably and ginormously and more than anything you and I could ever imagine. I love you so much, I love you *this much*. I love you like I love eating grilled cheese sandwiches by the swing set. That's the kind of number that I know best. The kind you can only measure with wide arms and an imagination.

These numbers work when you are a kid and the whole wide world is ahead of you. But something changes to the formula when you get older. You realize that the world is huge, yes, but you see that you are just this little microscopic speck. That you don't mean much at all, that you can't ask or receive the things you thought you could. And with the chase for adulthood comes the realization that limits and choices will have to be made. Because you can't possibly have it all, you have to downsize a bit, decide what you really want, make choices.

My hunger was the ever-expanding span of my arms but I felt, as one growing towards adulthood, that I needed something more solid, something more of the specific, calculator-necessary variety. In comes my eating disorder. It squished the fun and the random and the numbers that stretched out to magical infinity; it wasn't enjoyable but it felt necessary.

My eating disorder became the sixty-two calories in a small apple. The eighty calories in a slice of whole wheat bread. The me minus the mother, the father, the happiness when you wake and when you sleep, the joy in not having to know everything, in being satisfied with my two outstretched arms.

+4
Hunger is Fear of Sex

Eating is sexual. It's consumption. It's biting into something juicy and discarding the core, licking your lips, digging in. Eating can feel greedy, selfish, and incredibly, sinfully fun. And when you eat, your body matures. And as you mature from a little girl into a teenage girl, people want to have sex with you (before you reach the tipping point and become yesterday's news).

An anorexic wants to stop the process of maturing into a disposable, sexual plaything.

Because she doesn't want to be abused or taken advantage of either physically, mentally or emotionally; she wants to have respect for her mind, for her body, for her being. For the anorexic, avoiding sex — what so often seems, to a child, like the manifestation of adulthood — is a way to not only avoid the chance of being raped, we'd hope, but also the world where rape exists.

So there is a comfort in childhood. It is a place to stay static where one is hopefully protected — where engagement with the adult world is not compulsory.

The happier, normal, no-harm, and supposedly beneficial sides of human sexuality are scary too, coming so quickly to the forefront of the adolescent experience once your age reaches double digit status, from nine to ten. The dating. The first kiss. The soon-to-be mandatory short hemlines on Friday nights... pretending she's still a child, she can avoid what she wants to.

When an anorexic enforces real and meaningful dietary

restrictions on her own body, she does it so that she will not grow up, so that she will not have to be catcalled, so that she does not have to take part in a world that hears no yet demands yes.

+5

Hunger is Hurt

Eating can be sedative. Just as many unwind with a glass of wine, there is something peaceful and almost anesthetizing by the act of eating. You turn the switch and exist in the clouds as you chew. You chew and you don't have to think.

When you are in the privacy of your own home, food can feel like freedom. You can slurp loudly and drink the sugary cereal milk straight from the bowl; you can eat and let the crumbs fall to the floor, you can flip the channel and pig out — nobody cares as nobody sees. It's a less visibly destructive way of acting out, eating. You can rebel from that real or imagined push to please. You can disobey your parents or whoever told you to act a certain way and behave. That's part of the high for over-eaters: Eating too much is addictive both in the fog and also in treating yourself to misbehavior. And that's also what the anorexic fears. She has somehow felt, has empathized, with the reliance on eating for rebellion or emotional appeasement that the over-eater has and this makes her disgusted with herself. She becomes afraid to eat because she doesn't think she knows how to stop; she will consume too much, she will mask all her hurt with food.

The anorexic knows that with the good feelings that eating supplies also come addiction and the scary need for more that makes her feel slovenly, impure. The anorexic is hurt, she is hungry, and food and eating is something that can help stop the pain. However, the anorexic fears that she will rely on the good feelings too much; she fears that she will become an addict and consume too much to mask the hurt, so she consumes too little, so that she has the control, so that she does not become a slob.

To the anorexic, the person with impulse control in spades, the person who knows discipline too well, the threat of over-eating supersedes the need to eat. And with the growing pang of hunger comes the knowledge that, once we eat, not being able to stop is a very real possibility.

Here she is, left hungry and hurt. Left with the bad feelings that the overeater masks with food. Too afraid to eat because, more than anything, she fears herself. She fears what will happen, what she will make happen, if the too-tight hold is lifted and she can act out. The anorexic fears that she has no discipline, no will power, that the safest thing to do is to bear the pain. It feels simple, pure, basic. Like a personal suicide pact that is the key to her survival.

+6

Hunger is Loveless

Food is supposed to be nurturing. In lots of cultures, food is synonymous with love. We eat to celebrate; to gather as family and friends, we eat as questionable self-care to survive the four o'clock slump and the 10 p.m. bore. When we don't eat, that means something is wrong. Our bodies send off warning signs and if it gets bad enough, then every single body limb starts to quiver, shaking for calories and a proper fat to carb ratio. We have to eat. It's only natural.

Sometimes, food feels like it is the only real pleasure in life. As if eating is the only thing worth being thankful for: the consistency with which the sugar will always taste sweet, the way that time seems to stop when you chew and the way things like warm vegetable soup steam up your face when you lean in close.

No Thanksgiving would be complete without an apple, a pecan, and a pumpkin pie, thanks to my grandmother Mimi and my desire to recreate her presence every year.

There are things we are told to do in order to survive that do not feel so innately full of love. Drinking water. Maintaining decent hygiene. Aerobic exercise, paying the electric bill. Consuming food is not just warming, or reminiscent of happier moments, or nurturing as a bond between family and friends. Instead, consumption connects us to something much deeper than our daily life touches upon; something that we can't get away from or avoid, something that is real today, tomorrow, for everyone.

I may not understand your life, the sorrows you yourself have experienced. I may not know your circumstances. But if you tell me you are hungry, I can understand that in some way. Maybe my hunger is only a ten-minute thing; a sugar crash that I can quickly remedy thanks to access and monetary means... but I know where you are coming from, to some degree. I have felt your hunger too. And if I know, for a fact, how miserable it is to be hungry for ten minutes, or to diet for weight loss, or to suffer hunger pangs from an eating disorder, then I too know a particle of your own hunger. You who are from a different world than I.

Without access to food, a core in our person goes missing. We become unhinged. We can no longer concentrate on matters of business or politics or day-to-day concerns, our sole focus becomes limited to the pressing need to eat. Once this vital need to eat is met, we can better focus on other things. It's a first step. A starting point. A blessing. Something that feels so incredibly good, when realized, that you know this has got to be necessary.

Much more than love, eating is a gateway that allows the full spectrum of emotions to be experienced.

Eating is a memory of a better time that we can't possibly go without. Eating is a promise of possibilities. Eating is the first thing an anorexic tries to go without. Devoted to sacrifice, the more meaningful the things the anorexic gives up, the more meaningful the anorexic feels she becomes. Anorexics do not give up easy things, we give up the things that are impossible. Love, nurture, community, fond memories, the ability to open one's life up to the possibility of accomplishment, a core person from which to start. You lose your family when you stop eating with your family. You lose the history of what your family was, of who your ancestors were, of your connection to the past. And with the denial of your current existence within a family — as a person responsible for your own health, and as a person capable of recognizing the gift of existence of the people around you — you lose the possibility of a future family, too.

· · ·

I could continue with this nonstop as most things have a part in anorexia, really. We "overthink" everything and incorporate our findings into a logic to starve.[5]

---

5   Stage Notes: Please put an emphasis on the word "starve" in relation to starving her mind, not starving her body, when spoken aloud.

The Troubles of a Too-Smart Girl in a Too-False World. Prior to reality television and ticker news, anorexia was a disease that spoke of the troubles of a too-sensitive girl in a war-torn world. A high-expectations girl in a gentleman's world. A self-doubting girl in a puritanical world. Worlds wherein the girl's sets of beliefs were in vast opposition — or were instead too close for comfort, too close to budge an inch from being that idealized perfect she feels she has no place in being.

Sometimes it feels like the Too Anorexic Girl is the only sort who has stopped for a second to think of who she is and done something, anything, to cope with her findings. The anorexic has justifications for everything she does and even the fact that she thinks theoretically is part of the problem, I know. I know because there are far too many bad things going on in this world to be aware and live a happy/healthy life, too.

At least that's what the hungry anorexic thinks.

Also, on second thought: I lied. *My hunger is my father.*

5

ON MEN

Men develop eating disorders, same as women.

Men are capable of starving themselves obsessively, binging and purging, over-exercising. The disorder can affect every age, every race, every gender, and every sex. The first person I knew who was killed by anorexia was, in fact, a boy. He was eleven years old and passed away from anorexia during the first week that I entered the psych ward for my own treatment. The next day, all the twelve- and thirteen-year-old girls cried for the boy because he died, despite the fact that he actually wanted to Get Better and was "responding well" to his first week of inpatient treatment. But he had been sick for much too long before anybody recognized it as a disease. While it took a little over half a year for me to develop anorexia, be diagnosed, and put in an inpatient treatment facility, it took this dead boy three years before his family even took him to the doctor.

I know there is a stereotype that says homosexual men are more likely to develop eating disorders, that a straight man could never be that concerned with his body size or caloric consumption. I think that's bullshit. In fact, it makes much more sense to me that an uber-macho man — a man who excessively identifies himself with a dated, heteronormative masculine identity — is more at risk. That's because, if you listen hard, an eating disorder is something that the dated, heteronormative, uber-masculine and feminine norm of society approves participation in. Gay men aren't yet part of the norm — straight men are. And look who is sick: out of the (documented) cases of anorexia and bulimia, men generally account for up to 15 percent while the prevalence of eating disorders in gay versus straight men is comparable to the prevalence of eating disorders in gay versus straight women — as in, not anything to phone home about.

However, this is a controversial stat. In fact, it could be quite wrong. Most psych doctors say homosexual men run a higher risk than straight men of developing eating disorders. The social pressures of being a gay man and living in a heteronormative world are debilitating, the eating disorder born in part out of an anxiety of being less than, Other or different. Yet the same trickiness that subverts my own beliefs about eating disorders in women exists with gay men too. Meaning: the very obvious push by women to lose weight, be thin, and fit into the impossibly small sizes the fashion world dictates compel most women to diet, some women to over-diet and even others to walk the line between compulsive, disordered dieting and eating disorders. Dieting and eating disorders are entirely different in terms of one's response to the strict beauty worlds — one being "let me in" and the other "let me out." Like women, some gay men want into the world of looking beautiful, some gay men want out — and sometimes it's hard to tell which is which as the physical signs can look the same and our reliance on using the stories and phrases we've been taught — "I just wanted to be beautiful" — are easy catchalls to fall back on — for both the extreme, obsessive dieter and the eating disorder-afflicted, too.

Straight guys get sick. Gay guys get sick. Straight girls get sick. Gay girls get sick. Grown women and men, it happens to them too. The question remains as to whether being a homosexual male is as Other as it is being female? Is it more inferior? Is that important, a competition between oppression? *Who has it the worst?* Some people say women are starting to take over the world. But, really? Which women?

I wonder if we are all becoming inferior to sales and marketing.

When I was in the fifth grade and boys started talking about me in terms of how I looked, in terms of me as an attractive female to their dominantly attracted male, I was inundated with the ways that I was supposed to respond. I was supposed to like the attraction. I was supposed to respond to the attraction. I was supposed to continue what I was doing — because I must have been doing something, using tricks and potions explicit to my desperate DNA dating back to caveman times — to attract. I was supposed to grow older and have my first lovers-holding-hands moment, my first kiss, my first boyfriend, the line of sexual and relational progression extending until I was married with kids. It's a fine life to grow into and to choose on your own. But for many people, or at least for me, it wasn't a choice so much as a giving in.

Of course I don't like the stereotyped woman that I'm supposed to live up to but, at the same time, I also can't help but think that the tightly wound world of the ideal man is much more restrictive.

Isn't this true: *when you are in adherence with the female or male construct, you must be straight?* And when you are straight you must appeal to the opposite sex in order to fulfill your needs for identity acceptance. And when you try to appeal to the opposite sex, you almost always have to live up to the stereotypes and women, especially, have to be fragile and pretty in pink while men have to display power and can get away with forever avoiding an understanding of sincerity or empathy, an understanding for how it feels to be the person catcalled instead of the one calling. If you try to go any other way, particularly in places outside of certain Other-accepting zip codes, if you reveal that you are a strong-er woman or a sensitive-er man, you run the risk of being rejected, laughed at, or ostracized as a circle in a sea of squares. And some people won't even recognize you because they don't understand you.

Never forget: the world we live in puts sexual appeal at the top of the ladder, the goal we are all striving for. It's what we should all try to exude and whether through power or beauty, wealth, intellect or love, everything comes down to sex appeal — too much, too little, just enough.

Yet people with eating disorders have a complicated relationship with sex and being sexy. People with eating disorders flat-out don't like being treated as sex objects, and they flat-out don't like the race towards the *Ridiculous Celebrity Magazine's* 100 Most Beautifuls and yet still people with eating disorders flat-out want to be protected, safe, valued, and loved. These dichotomous wants create grave and emotional conflicts in heads and hearts, no matter the gender.

I'd like to tell you two things now, and I don't know which is more important, or which I want to tell you the most.

The first is that my story is about being a woman, about needing to scream.

The second is that I, as a woman, will use and respond to the term "you guys," or "guys," or "hey guys," knowing full well that "guys" as a word has come to include myself, a heteronormative woman who wears lipstick colors named frosted pink, dusty rose, and bubblegum. I will also respond to the word "man," as in "hey, man," or "what's up, man?" or "I don't know, man," as my developed sense of identity is strong enough to dismiss type bound by sex organs in rather careless day-to-day conversation. Friends that call me by, "hey, man," or "guy," understand that I am a straight woman who wears pink lipstick; they also understand that women, as far as carefree day-to-day conversations go, answer to the label of men.

As a social experiment I recently spent a few days saying, "hey, woman" to all of my male friends and using "hey, girls" to refer to groups of both males and females. Each time, I had to explain myself.

6

BEST IS BEST

February 3, 2002

There is a hierarchy of psychiatric disorders in the psych ward, and it's required that you know it well.

1. At the top of the list are the cool anorexics, the ones that are lifetime patients and prone to fuck-you's and hate-this's and frequent red-flag escapes and major punishments. These girls are too thin and too in control, yet they are not reclusive. A bulimic's outgoing personality with the anorexic's discipline; cool anorexics are at the top. These girls look like death and they die, a lot. Drop dead goes one, drop dead goes another.

2. Next to the cool anorexics are the borderline personality disorders and the schizophrenics. These people have proven that they are not of the outside world; they are of the inpatient world and so they hold the switch. You can't turn them on or off; they are not to control. They control you (borderline), and they are explosively crazy (schizophrenic — when they can communicate with words).

3. Next up are the depressives and the suicidals. They are cool because they are also not of the outside world and because they are dark, mysterious. They have proven their merit, so to speak. Cutters would fall here if not currently practicing. (If they are, throw them to the pit!)

Next comes a line. It separates those on top from those at the bottom.

---

4. At the top of the bottom heap are the drug addicts. One might think they are cool but they aren't; they are desperate and their hair is not just messy, it's filthy. Their fingernails are black with dirt. The female drug addicts have nail polish on, and it's always chipped. They have eye makeup, and it's always Kohl black. Sometimes they shake, most often they exaggerate. They are desperate to please; they are of the outside world.

5. Next comes the bulimics, the drug user's BFF. Peas in a pod. The bulimic is out of control and so often wishes that she had the saintly discipline and controlled reactions of the cool anorexic.

She is unhappy with herself, she wants to be someone else, to have something else, and she is not cool.

6. Next come the bipolars. If they were able to control their anger better they could perhaps be at the top of the low-level list but their anger management issues make them seem infantile.

7. Then at the bottom comes the most reclusive depressives or the people that claim, for much too long, that they "don't need to be here." Also on this list come the people that cry "trauma" for far too long and claim they are sick for one solid reason, never backing down.

I'd imagine over-eaters would fall somewhere between the bipolars and the depressives, but I've never met one in treatment so I can't say for sure. If they are very loud and funny, they might think they were near the top, but we'd know better. They'd be our playthings.

Here behind the asterisk (*) lies the not-cool anorexic, or maybe even the male anorexic. Typically, they choose to not take part in the hierarchies. For this they would be at the top — if they were in the game.

It's a club.

Notice you are not on the list. And so, no matter what, you mean less to us than do the reclusive and the denial-prone at the bottom of the hierarchy. If push were to come to shove, we would protect them, be their family. But you? We will not protect you. You put us in here, you hurt us, we do not trust you.

There are two circles, one is inside and one is outside. Pick a side. You can't have mine.

Now, please. Tear out this chapter. Crumple it up. Throw it in the bathroom trash when Head Nurse June looks away. I cannot get in trouble. I need my stars for the day before the Treatment Team meeting on Friday. I have to get out of here.

7

INTENSIVE INPATIENT

December 21, 2001

On the morning of my first day in treatment, a nurse probing at the veins in my right arm wakes me at 8 a.m. sharp. I feel like a sacrifice, probed and open against my will — she doesn't even ask me my name or how I am. She takes my blood and inserts a mystery tube at the same pierced point. She puts a blood pressure monitor tight around my arm and takes my pressure both lying down and sitting down. She tells me to stand.

I stand. And then I fall to the ground.

The whole room is black and spinning, and I can faintly hear the nurse, echoing and repeating some stupid cliche like: *just hold still, just rest.* I hear footsteps coming towards me, and as my vision starts coming back with black spots floating everywhere, I see two other nurses, one man and one woman, in front of all the black crows flying by my eyes. The nurses pick me up and float me to the bed. They tell me that my blood pressure is too low, I am Very Sick, I need to Be Healthy, I need to Take Care, I might experience a lot more dizziness as my body is fed, and that I should not worry, I should love myself. To me, they sound idiotic, annoying, and perhaps a little simple and too naive. Don't they know that there are problems in this world? Don't they know there are things more important than health and love, things even more pressing?

Don't they know that I don't want to eat?

The blood-sucking nurse leaves, so does the male nurse, and I am left with a pretty nurse with shiny, dark hair named Sarah. Sarah tells me about the mystery tube — it's an intravenous therapy-thing that I need because I got Too Thin and I Need to Feed My Body with fluids and electrolytes immediately. Sarah tells me that it is Friday, December 21st, and I am in the Psychiatric Unit of Children's Medical Center. Sarah asks me if I remember meeting Andrea last night after intake or if I remember the things Andrea told me. I don't remember and Sarah says, "No problemo, I'll give you the 101 after morning meeting. Andrea said you were so very out of it last night."

"Okay."

This woman, the way she speaks, it's like she invented a new language entirely. The high pitch of her voice is the only reminder that she is from some place not so far from where I come from.

"I'm here to help you do the things you need to do. Okay? Now, let's get started!" Sarah smiles as if life is one big party and she's *just so happy I could come.* She asks me if I can stand long enough to be put into the wheelchair and I say, "Sure."

Here is a secret: I don't like Sarah anymore, and I don't think she's pretty. Her hair is still shiny but instead of glossy sheen, her hair is grease and oil. She disgusts me. Here's why: She has completely ruined my day. She has taken the twenty-four hours and sliced them up and compartmentalized them into bits and portions — just like I try to do with my food, just like she won't let me do with my food — and I hate it. Normally, I love routine. I love control. I love knowing what is what, and I especially love even numbers over odds. So of course, one would think, I would love Sarah! But no. Sarah has taken one of my favorite things, neat little calculations, the schedules and meal plans and the to-do's, and spoiled it. She's here to fill my day with things I don't like or want to do. First, she takes my weight and doesn't tell me what it is. Then, she assists me in deciding what I am to wear as if I am a child and need help. And now, she basically tells me what to eat! She tells me what to do, acting as if I need her help, and I don't.

It started with Sarah forcing me to change from my pajamas into a patient's smock — the kind that's so flimsy it feels like it's made of butterfly wings. The smock is cold, and I'm afraid she can see my backside in it. Then Sarah makes me go outside of my room, in the smock. Turns out there is a whole long line of girls in butterfly-cold smocks with their butts almost showing. These girls look exactly like me. Sure a lot of them are rail-thin, like their bones are needles and their skin is fabric and the needle is trying to pinch through. Their bodies are like diagrams of black and white opposites. You have the stick-outs: the eyes, the temples, the shoulder blades, the elbows, the hip bones, the knees. Everything else is a sunken spot, a deep well of shadows: hollowed cheeks and concave stomachs, deep-set eyes and recesses under collarbones. Their skin looks yellowed, tired, faded. But even more, all the girls look forgotten. And that is exactly how I think I look: Lost. Abandoned. Deserted. *Without.*

Sarah tells me that we must all wait to be weighed. I realize that I should have known this was coming, a trip to the scale. Suddenly all the girls strike me as incredibly scared and if I just close my eyes, I can breathe in their fear. The girls sneak glances at one another that say: *"I know, this is rough, this is bad, I am sorry for us."* None of the girls look at me. Even though I have never had a particularly complicated history with the scale, I follow their lead and stare at the red exit sign and gulp and fidget. I had been striving to be healthy, to be fit, and though this meant I exercised more than I should have and ate less than I should have, I never connected what I did to my weight. They weren't related as weight loss wasn't the end goal. My mother doesn't believe in scales. Our family doesn't even own a scale. The only time I ever hear about my weight is at the doctor's office, where, recently, the declining number has made me more fearful and embarrassed than anything. Now my thoughts on weight are: follow the leader, beware of the scale.

At the front of the line is a girl with strawberry blonde hair. She is not rail-thin. She looks healthy. And sweet. The girl is biting at her cuticles and staring at the red exit sign, and when it is her time to be weighed, her personal nurse for the day has to encourage her to take her first step, to walk towards the sign, to exit the room and disappear.

When my time comes, Sarah makes me do the same. I feel like an animal, prodded to my holding pen. The room itself is cold and sterile and it feels like the end of the world.

If I wasn't sure before the weigh in, I am sure now. I hate
Sarah.

The next thing Sarah does is pick out what I am to wear today.
She decides that I am supposed to wear my brown Gap corduroy
pants, my brown Gap turtleneck, and my black ballet flats with
brown Gap socks that I don't like much. She has made me a
walking ad for brown, brown, brown. I try to tell her that before
I got sick, I had different clothes in many colors and I apologize
for the Gap options, hoping that she will take a hint and chose
something else for me to wear. Sarah says she likes the Gap. God
I hate Sarah.

Since I'm in a wheelchair and not accustomed to a life where
I cannot walk where I choose, Sarah has to help me change. This
I hate the most. This is a violation of privacy, decency, everything
— how would she like to have the tables turned? How would she
like to be dressed like a doll in brown Gap clothes with socks +
ballet flats to top it all off? I try to chalk it up to the fact that
Sarah has no fashion sense. But I really think it's because Sarah
is rude, and she obviously doesn't like me.

After I'm weighed and changed, (waited and chained), Sarah
wheels me to the main room again. It's like the living room or the
homeroom or whatever room you call the home base. To one side,
there is a wall with a long blue couch and tables and chairs; to
another side, there is a smaller blue couch, more fit for an actual
home than a hospital home, with a coffee table and chairs made
for children. To another side there is a check-in desk manned by a
tall and round woman looking over lots and lots of papers. Sarah
asks me if I brought a calculator. Sarah says I need a calculator
and asks the nurse at the desk to borrow one. When she comes

back, she says that I must get ready to calculate my food, that I will have three minutes. Of course I don't understand what she's talking about. Sarah shows me a sheet of paper with my name on it and the words "breakfast," "snack," "lunch," "snack," "dinner," "snack" structuring the otherwise blank space and lines.

We wait near the smaller blue couch, and the scared waiting girls from this morning's weigh-in are still scared and waiting. Three minutes pass and five other waiting girls from this morning walk out of the kitchen and stand near the small blue couch. Next the girls sitting around me stand, hesitantly, and enter the kitchen with their individual nurses. Sarah follows the girls and wheels me in. In the kitchen there are three circular tables all of similar size — even though they aren't the same size — and about five ice-blue and flimsy looking chairs per table. Along the back wall there are many white cabinets and a steel-silver sink, and on the right wall there is a refrigerator standing coolly, almost ominously, by itself in the straight center of the right-hand wall. The fridge is a tan color that looks old and out-of-date while the rest of the kitchen, with the cabinets and the lone sink and no cooking utensils or oven or knife and cutting boards, looks like a pint-sized model kitchen that you would find in a house magazine. It's not a real kitchen, just a fake one with a fridge that we have infiltrated.

On the tables are many tan hospital food trays and on the trays are plates covered by plastic food covers. There is a clear plastic packet with white plastic utensils inside like we are going camping or getting take-out. On some trays there are cartons of milk, on others there are saltine crackers or applesauce, and on others still there are pieces of fruit. Sarah lifts the plastic cover, and suddenly the space around me is overwhelmed with a smell that is both familiar and revolting. On the plate, there is a half-cup of scrambled eggs and a slice of whole wheat bread with butter on it. Sarah says that I need to calculate how much food is on the plate so that I can meet my breakfast calorie requirements and that I have three minutes. I tell her I don't need a calculator and can do the math myself, "it's a habit." Sarah calculates the food on the plate anyways to check my math, "Just in case." The three minutes bing, and Sarah puts the plastic thing back on and wheels me out with the other girls.

We wait en masse by the blue couch, and Sarah explains that I will have food requirements every day and I will need to eat a certain amount of calories divided over three meals and three snacks. She says that right now, since I am new, my daily calorie requirement is low so as not to shock my body by feeding it so much more than it is used to. She says that gradually the amount of calories will be increased so that I gain the weight I need to survive. As she talks, the girls in our group don't say anything out loud but I can feel their internal sighs of disgust. They don't believe her, don't trust her, know better, know they are just feeding us, feeding us to grow oversized and out of size and out of place — *that's* what the girls tell me, inside. Some girls smile squeamishly at me as if to say it's okay, such is life, and others look at me with fire in their eyes, as if the nurses are militants suppressing the girls' truest selves and they will fight to the end to get out, go home, override the powerful to free themselves. I feel like the girls are asking me to choose sides, to be either sweet or harsh, and I don't like having to make choices. To choose inevitably leaves one side lonely while the other side gets used. I smile back at the sad-smiling girls and roll my eyes with the angry girls, trying to fit in.

When I ask Sarah how many days before they increase my calories, she says I have until tomorrow, and then the day after tomorrow, et cetera, that every day they will increase my calories until we get to a steady amount that allows my body to re-feed itself, to gain weight, best. I close my eyes and try to block out all of the words and people around me. *I don't like it here.*

If I closed my eyes and tried not to think at all, sealed my lips, shut it off, I could still tell you what happens next. What happens next is I am wheeled, wheeled without my consent, back into the kitchen and made to sit, to sit in the wheelchair that we can now learn to know as mine, next to all of these crazy people and their clocked-in and certified personal nurses for the day. I am back in the fake kitchen, and the heat trapper has been lifted and a mushy pile of food stinks, like unbelievably stinks, and everything looks so beige yet clinical and cold. Under the stench of the food I can smell Windex and ammonia. I want to scream, to tear out my hair, rip open my flesh. But I know that I will do nothing. I just sit here, unmoving, staring at the food. *Typical.*

In my file it says that on this very day, on this first morning meal, I met all of my calorie requirements. I couldn't tell you that for sure because after the beige and the Windex, I blacked out. Lost my thoughts. I forgot. Or at least on autopilot — they call it survival mode — then, I have forgotten now.

I know I met a boy with clear, translucent white skin, the kind with blue veins peeking out, and black crow-colored hair. He says that we met the night before — *"Don't you remember?"* — and he complains about the food — not a nice thing to do in front of people like me, particularly when I am being force-fed. The boy (really a man, tall and wide-shouldered enough, a high schooler) finally gets what he wants: a peanut butter and jelly sandwich, the only thing he will eat in the hospital. But we, the anorexics, can't substitute anything besides what is on our plate, the milk or the crackers, pepper or no pepper — if we have the pepper privilege, which I don't. It is not fair. He is not like us. He says, "Tomorrow

I am leaving for Aspen. My family is taking me out of here today."
I will learn that he is bipolar, that his family does take him out
the next day, that he does go to Aspen. I don't know what happens
next for him.

I also know I met a young boy named Jessie with shiny
brown hair and blue eyes. And I know I like this Jessie of the
hospital. Jessie has an energy unlike anything I've ever known
before, like a manifestation of the way I privately think to myself,
the skidding every which way. And so, I know, the first time I
meet Jessie I must have liked him, and I must have remembered
it, must have said to myself, *"This is a special moment, one that
I will remember."*

I don't remember, but that doesn't mean it didn't happen.

When your body is starved so too are your muscles and your organs.
Your brain too. My brain lost pieces and important moments, and
I forgot things, things I shouldn't have, and even to this day I won't
remember my first day in treatment clearly through and through.
I won't remember my first three days especially and the rest of the
week, I remember like a dream, like I know it happened because
I was told so many times that it stuck, and it's real, even though
it's not the real version. Like my first childhood memories, they
are not actually mine. They were handed down to me. I believe in
them though I can't recall them.

The first thing starving turns off is your heart.

First, mine was tugged: My mother admitted me and she
left. *Goodbye momma, please don't leave.*

Then, mine was squeezed and tortured, suffocated. Here

is what you like to do, here is what you can't (the same!). Can't count, can't restrict, can't take small bites or hide. *Face your fears. Recover. Get Better.* They're trying to get at my heart and beat it down, to kill who I think I am.

Now, I am subjected to a hall of mirrors, a circus of is this who I am? *Is this?*

You guessed it. It's morning meeting time! Time for us to join together, to grab a chair, to get in the circle, share our Fears, our Goals, our morning thoughts with the crowd! Dr. Kay has come out to play. She sits opposite me in the circle, hands folded. She is the father of the circle. I am the new child, the lowest. The patients sit haphazardly around the circle that has become more rectangle, less circle — it's not uniform as crazy people have no sense of space. The nurses for the day sit slightly behind and to the side of their patients, their representatives and torturers, too. Dr. Kay starts the morning meeting.

"Good morning! How is everyone today? It's just three days away from Christmas Eve so I want to remind everyone of our plans. Since school is postponed until after New Year's, we have more free time and Art Therapy scheduled in. Head Nurse June will also lead some introspection exercises. After morning meeting today we will have an hour of free time, then a snack and then some outdoor time at the park downstairs for everyone who has the privilege. *Okay?* Now, we have a new patient and I'll have her introduce herself to the group in a minute, but before that are there any questions? No? *Okay;* well remember, the holidays are a hard time for many patients, and if you ever need any help, talk with your nurse, journal, express your feelings. This is a good time to learn to communicate more clearly with your loved ones and speak up for yourself. *Okay?* Also, if you ever feel uncomfortable for any moment while your family is visiting over the next couple of days, or if your family is coming to join you at the holiday meal and you get upset, just speak up, use your words. *Okay?* You don't have to do anything you don't want to do, so let's just take it slow. *Okay?* How about we go around the circle, everyone can introduce themselves to Jordan and then, when we come to you, Jordan, how about you introduce yourself to the group and read us what you wrote on your paper? *Okay?*"

The paper is a sheet that asks some questions that I am supposed to answer.

The questions:

What is your name? Jordan Knape

Do you prefer a different name? Danny[6]

Why are you here?

The last question, *Why are you here?*, is the hardest to answer, or so they say. They say it is the First Step. The part where you have to look into yourself, to admit why you are here, what you did that was so Destructive, why you want to Get Better. Just as alcoholics must admit that they have a drinking problem, until I answer *Why are you here?*, I am not a new patient and have not started the program. I have no privileges. Sarah says it might take some time for me to answer, it is a very hard question; some patients take days to answer the question because it is so hard. You have to be honest, to admit how you have hurt yourself and why you want to get better, even though it is hard.

But the sheet isn't that hard for me. One, two, three. I'm done!

---

6   Nickname circa 2001.

See here:

I have anorexia nervosa and I over-exercise and count my calories and eat too many grams of protein. My thoughts are always around food and exercise, I think. I am sad. I want to get better for my family and friends because I am hurting them. I am also hurting myself but I don't care so much about that, I care more about other people and how they are hurting. I know that I want to get better because I am so tired and cold and lonely, SAD, and I don't want to be. I used to be happy and I would like to be again. And I don't want to ruin Christmas for everybody; I feel bad for making everyone worry. They say I am anorexic and I guess I am but I know for sure that I am depressed. I think that is the most important issue, more important than what I eat.

I write it quickly before morning meeting and hand it to Sarah; she reads and smiles and hands the paper back, telling me to hold onto it so I can read it aloud to the group.

Inside I am laughing. Ha! I fooled her! I told her what she wanted to hear, not the truth. I have got this down. If anything, I know how to fool people, how to tell them what they want to hear. And it works!

Inside I am also scared, a tad bit shaken. I do actually want to get better. For my family, for my friends. I want to get better for me, too, but I can't feel that yet. Most of all, I feel a conflict. Opposing truths punching inside of me so fast my body has become numb to the touch, my emotions floating to the top of the room to escape my hurting brain. In fact, the opposite of numb, I feel too much. Intense emotions so great, the stimulation too high.

In my file they record how I feel every day, every hour. The first week, every hour, I say: ambivalent. I thought it meant numb, without feeling, but it doesn't mean that at all. In retrospect, I felt much more than a person possibly could at one time, and that frightened me. It was too much. I was ambivalent: two thoughts so opposed swimming all around.[7]

At the end of the day I am wheeled to my room. I have a single. I see the bag my mom packed up. I thought it was for her but that was before I knew what Psychiatric Unit means, that people only visit after dinner during visiting hours from 7 p.m. to 8:30 p.m. In the bag, there is a fluffy pillow and a shiny new journal in silver patent leather with a matching pen filled with shiny blue ink that writes like liquid pearls. I actually don't remember it this way as the pillow was already on my bed, slept on once by me the night before, and the journal and pen already on my dresser. But I wanted to tell you my memory before it was too late, even though it didn't happen like this in real life as it had already happened when I couldn't remember. Here is the false memory: I see the bag my mom packed and am delighted, I go to open the bag, the one tangible reminder of my mother I have left, and in the bag are presents: a soft pillow, my mother's own, and a shiny new journal and pen. I am delighted to open the gifts, they stand as proof that my mother cares so much for me, I, her first-born and very sick yet well-loved child.

The only things I remember from the first week are sadness. I know they are real, first person, actual happenings because the pain is so great. It carved its name inside of me and I know because I have to know, it's part of me, the real deal.

I once had a boyfriend, five years after being let out of the hospital, when I was nineteen, who thought of me as damaged goods. He

---

7   Yes, Susanna Kaysen does the same thing in Girl, Interrupted — confusing the meaning of ambivalence to accidentally reveal more than she feels comfortable exposing or understanding. As much as us people of the psych ward want to be original, to think things in ways that no one else has, we often fall into line.

said he cared about me and he said, "I wish you didn't have so much baggage. It's hard for me to take care of you when you are so F'd up." But everyone has, or should have, baggage.

I wish that when I was nineteen I had been strong enough and loved myself — my real self, not myself as mirrored by other people or myself with other people or myself for other people, but my real self, alone in the night — enough to tell him to fuck off.

Don't be ashamed, let it out. Overcome.

Don't date bad men. Don't talk to bad boys.

Don't let him think you are more sick than you are.

When you're thirteen you're supposed to know much less about life than when you're nineteen. But for me I think I knew more then. Even though I was killing myself, I understood what it meant to respect yourself, to care for yourself — even though I was doing what looked like the opposite. I think that is what I meant by ambivalent, too, by saying a word to stand in for numb that actually stood in for so much more. I think that when I was thirteen I knew everything I know now and more, just intuitively, and it was so much to take in, and so depressing, that I had to make it stop. The proper thing would have been just not to start at all, I still agree. Life is cleaner before you become an adolescent. The clouds are prettier, the atmosphere bright instead of out to get you. At least that's how it was for me. When I turned ten, the whole wide world started to inch in and claim what I took as fact, turn it upside down, turn future boyfriends into torturers, nurture into greed.

At the end of the night I realize I'm in a patient's bed in a patient's room with a patient's wheelchair and a patient's sink and a patient's mirror that reflects me, the patient. I close my eyes and I try to escape. Soon enough the fear will bottle up, and I will break. But not yet. Right now I just watch as the emergency helicopters lift off and come down, saving the dying children, and not thinking much at all. Often I close my eyes and try to stop taking in so much of the world around me. I try to listen inside and I know I feel safe now. I know I feel like I am being watched and looked after and held and everything is much slower here, and I know that feels good. But at the same time I want to be held more, loved more, taken care of even more. I want to feel warmth, to know something other than the fear of being overwhelmed, other than the thought of being alone and still needing to hide.

I write in my new diary with my shiny new pen: "I want to get better. I will get better, for my family, my friends and for ME."

It's my first entry, and it is also my last.

8

HOSPITAL BONDS

August 14, 2011

I want to go back to the hospital. It was a safe place. It felt more like home than any place I have ever been and, if you've noticed, a home is what I'm after. I know it was clinical there. I know that the red lights of the exit sign singed your skin, that people screamed late into the night. I know that I was denied even the simple liberty of being able to wear shoes with laces. But that doesn't take away the fact that now, I want to go back.

For many years now, the hospital is the place I have wanted most, on some surface deep inside, to return to. The longing is lessening more as I grow older, but it's still there: the longing to return to the place that healed me *(or didn't, or couldn't)*, that understood me *(or tried)*, that allowed me to kick and scream in the quiet room without anyone making faces at me or calling me crazy. I was already deemed sick upon arrival and there is a comfort in knowing that, in being that. There is a comfort in being understood as a certain person and being able to live out that identity to the fullest with other people who are just the same as you. For me, the comfort comes from being known as crazy.

The Group Therapy, the Rec Therapy, the Art Therapy, the people looking at you and treating you as if you are their job, because taking care of you really is their job. I miss the camaraderie of the other patients, the laughs of pure abandon. I miss being able to look into the eyes of another girl and understand her wholeheartedly. Of not having to speak to understand, of not needing to ask questions or do anything, of just being there, being present, feeling and sharing in the pain. Even though the pain was of the individual variety, it was also mutual. A shared family trait or tradition that we could gather around for, the steam fogging our glasses, the perspiration simultaneously coalescing above our lips — it was a physical pain, an emotional pain, a pain in our history and a pain in the realization of our future, of who we could not continue to be. The colors, we knew, would turn to muted tones and the noises would lose their vibrancy. We'd be boring, simple, packaged goods. Much less than fragments of our former selves, we'd be re-envisioned altogether, as these simple little beings, the types that walked and talked and functioned well on the other side of the exit door.

And for some of us, what we knew came true.

Number 2647 has been activated.

I have never known anyone as well as I did those girls in that hospital. We opened ourselves up to each other in ways that don't happen outside. We shared with each other and in sharing we became each other, one single unit, one victim of the universe.

I miss those friends, my closest allies. To me they are the most beautiful people I have ever met, and it has nothing, absolutely nothing, to do with aesthetics. It has to do with the beauty of being able to know a person truly, of being able to see their vulnerabilities in the light of day, of being there, with them, and expecting nothing. We were so low that simple comforts were saviors, easy smiles filled with blessings.

I want to go back to the hospital. Not just because I felt safe there, like I was taken care of. Not just because I had friends there, real friends, friends you didn't have to give anything to or say anything to in order to reap their love. I want to go back to the hospital because it was like our special club. There was a password (I can't tell you). There was a mission, and the mission was to just survive the day. It seems so easy now: just survive the day. There are no other expectations. Just learn to take care of yourself, to love and appreciate and accept yourself, day by day, night by night, one step at a time. The lessons I learned there were so simple, so infantile, sometimes even so incredibly unhelpful in their translation to the outside, fully operating world.

But that could be the problem with number 2647. Perchance she has not fully given in to the simple, functional world. Perchance she is making her life on the outside more complicated than she needs to. Perchance everyone else seems so smiley and happy because they really are going day-by-day.

The hospital was easy.

The hospital was hell.

Having to see yourself for who you are. Having to talk about the things you don't want to talk about; remembering the things you don't want to remember; eating more food, more food, more in order to survive. Some say it's the hardest thing they ever had to do, treatment. Of course it was. We were masters of the dark and somber and put into a bright, bright light. We, the think-for-ourselvers, were given instructions on the basics and told to learn by rote.

But on the days when you didn't much feel like recovering, or even worse, on the days when you decided to swallow the key and sink as far down as you possibly could, on those days we were free.

When you are so far gone that you can't turn around, veering towards death is an exciting way to spend your last supper. When you are so tightly wound up inside, when you are so shackled, you can admit all of your faults, every last detail, and you can let those screaming voices inside come out coolly with your exhales...

It's fun while it lasts because nothing matters.

But then you wake up the next day and you wish, *can't I take it back?*

The lucky ones can, for a time; but every bad has its limit. One day you might wake up and realize this is all the life you've got.

9

RICH WHITE BITCH

You don't get anorexia because you are white and privileged. Studies show that anorexia affects less economically blessed and/ or non-white woman in equal measure; that countries such as India, Nigeria, South Africa, and Mexico report cases of eating disorders; and that even within an all-female kibbutz in northern Israel 85 percent of girls were dissatisfied with their bodies and 60 percent reported fears of "losing control over their weight."

The actual act of starvation can also lead to eating disorder behavior. It's a normal adaptive response to starvation called a semi-starvation hyperactivity response. Like clockwork, the body starves and the mind takes over to help protect the body — perhaps, even, to help minimize the pain of hunger. You starve, thanks to famine, and the mind helps the body to conserve energy by telling it to eat only small bites of food at certain intervals. You starve and you obsess over food, think about food constantly, as a way to feed your brain with the illusory idea of sugars and calories.

Diet for just one day and report back how it feels. The changes in blood sugar alter your mood, cause depression and bouts of euphoria. Starve for many days and maybe, just maybe, your mind will take over. Maybe you too will obsess over food, not knowing what to do when it is actually in front of you. The psych disorder no longer psychological but, rather, what we physically do, how we are supposed to respond, the way we are built to survive starving.

In hospitals they tell you: *eat more, eat more.*

Obsessing about food, hiding food away, eating in tiny, disordered bites. Compulsive over-exercising. Disordered thinking — both circular and completely haphazard.

Because everyone can starve, because everyone can want control, can need control, can feel that mix of hopelessness and determination, that self-destructive spirit that feels like it's the right way to be, can everyone "get" anorexia? Is anorexia something to be had? Because everyone can starve — even though it's not about the starve — anorexia is neither subject to wealth nor race nor gender nor education as things like diabetes or colon cancer are. The experts will agree: everyone can *get it*, as long as it's in your genes or personality traits or as long as you're in a lab and tested or as long as food is in too short of a supply or what have you. But me?

My anorexia wasn't something that could be had. It wasn't something I caught.

When you get sick with a cough, you must determine whether it was caused by bacteria or a virus, as one can be treated with antibiotics and the other cannot.

When you get sick with anorexia you have to remind people that it wasn't something that you asked for.

"It's not fun."

"Being sick is not fun."

"I would do anything to not be sick anymore."

Why is my anorexia so hard, so twisted and contorting that I feel I have to relate everything to an entertainment value when I communicate my experience of the disorder?

Why do I go towards words like "communicate" instead of "talk," "experience" instead of "feel," "value" instead of "need"?

I am not my disorder.

When I was twenty-one and on the surface doing much, much better, one of my mother's friends told me, "I always wished I had just a smidgen of anorexia, just for a month, so I could get really thin."

Anorexia is not something I asked for, but do other people?

If I could I would take my arm and stretch it out as far away from me as possible. We'd fly across cities with skyscrapers and small towns with rivers, people dancing, people sleeping, and my arm would be so far away from me. I would say: *"I am not my disorder. This is how far away she is from me."*

If I could, I'd cut her off.

Would you?

Things I'm good at: keeping secrets, making systems, pretending, restricting, punishing myself for things I don't know, crying, fake smiling, clogging my insides up with food I don't need, lying, withholding emotions, pushing people away, disappointment, panic attacks, wanting more.

Things I'm bad at: letting go, eating, sleeping, keeping promises, not looking in mirrors, staying calm, Health & Recovery, being satisfied, growing up, remembering to breathe, being a woman, not becoming my mother, consistency, trust and anger, wearing clothes that show my skin, accepting me.

I know that when I eat healthfully you try to derail my healthy efforts.

I know that when you exercise you don't tell me because you don't want me to take up exercising, too.

I know that when I was almost dead from anorexia you were mad at me. Not because I was killing myself but because I was thinner than you and so that meant I had more discipline, was more attractive.

I know that you are hurt but is that my problem? It's easy to see it in your eyes, to see the new red marks on your hand as you sit back down at the table after your trip to the restroom. I know you hurried in alone.

There is anorexia, there is bulimia, there is binge eating disorder and there is the way they teach anorexics to think about food when they get out of the hospital: *eat all foods, don't restrict, eat your Fear Foods to be Healthy.*

I want to be healthy but I don't agree. Corn syrup is

never healthy, neither are artificial sweeteners, white flour, and processed, processed former-foods.

The food we eat is also connected to the way we think, our dinner table a metaphor. Anorexics understand interconnection and even though I want to be healthy now, I don't want the hospital's definition of health.

There has to be a middle ground, some point we can reach to draw it out in the sand: We are healthy now. This has been enough.

Rich white bitch. The truth is, I know that I didn't ask for my eating disorder. I know that I didn't catch my eating disorder like a winter cold, that it wasn't my background or my culture so much as my gene pool, I know all of this, I do, but I also know something more. When I was the most sick I had come to a point where all of the confusion about growing up as a white girl in an upper middle class neighborhood, where all the comfort I enjoyed seemed a total denial or avoidance of the suffering of others. I did not understand why I had so much and others little, and instead of thankfulness I felt regret. Perhaps it is a remorse close to survivor's guilt, a survivor's guilt without the industry or motivation to go forward. I had Lucky Rich White Bitch Guilt, and I didn't know what to do with it. I thought a little about the problems, I talked a lot more, and finally the guilt that we try to deny by discounting its legitimacy — *we are equal, that doesn't matter anymore* — gave way.

There are only so many times you can say you're not blessed before you have to fess up to the lucky fate of the draw.

I had a problem not wanting to grow up and being scared. I was scared of becoming a teenager, made to participate in our glitter-loving culture, scared of being looked at as an object, scared of not meeting the high expectations placed on me, of always having to smile. Really, those are lucky problems.

10

INPATIENT

December 23, 2001

Three is an important number in many religions. That's because on the third day the stone rolled and Jesus was swept up into the sky. And that's why there is a God the Father, God the Son, and the Holy Spirit. Jesus, Mary, and Joseph. Three golden gifts from the wise men to the little baby boy.

Because of God the importance of three is everywhere. Like a triangle, we have mind, body, and spirit. We have past, present, and future. We have birth, life, and death. Perhaps historically one is the most important — the Father, the future, the spirit, escape from finite death — but no matter what, the threes complete each other. A perfect nuclear package of the non-familial familial variety. Three is our creation and it's how we tell time. We have years, months, and days. We have hours, minutes, and seconds. We have you, we have me, and we have how we could be.

For a person with anorexia the importance of numbers is never lost, never forgotten. Even though three is the first odd number and even though we prefer even numbers to odds (the more precise, the easier to divide), the number three is right in between the numbers two and four, two very good numbers, and so is also very good.

There are three meals that you must eat each day and sometimes there are three courses. As a kid you hide to *one, two, three-here I come!* and there's three strikes and you're out. If you're slow, you get a first start, one-*Mississippi*, two-*Mississippi*, three. If you're fast, you live in numbers of three. First I want, second I'll settle, third at least my name appears.

I know the numbers one, two, three in many languages.

There are three little pigs, three bears, three blind mice, three wishes, and the third time is the charm. Try and try again.

In seventh grade I learned that atoms are composed of protons, neutrons, and electrons. My dad taught me earlier, in our kitchen when I was in the fifth grade, by using oranges to demonstrate how a nuclear explosion begins. I didn't understand. That was before we moved out of my childhood home, the place where I grew up. In seventh grade, we started a whole new life in a modern home with sleek lines, glass, and limestone, the kind of home that made our things look curated in a museum and impossibly fashionable.

I could make up an eerie childhood song about the family that moves from one house, a very old home with browns, gilded French furniture and smells of gardenia, to another home, a museum-home with white walls, white space, white air, and the song would be fitting. Our lives crumbled when we moved. It was unavoidable in the new home. Everything exposed, nowhere to hide.

There are three acts to every story. I have my first half, I am living through my second, trying to get to my third. *Come on over, there is a way.* Light at the end of the tunnel as they say.

Humans perceive white light as the mixture of three additive primary hues: red, green, and blue. When I was taught that I didn't understand, I raised my hand, asked questions. No matter the explanations, it wasn't enough. I needed more answers. Not just some words or a diagram, a picture in a book, new words. I needed an explanation of the white light made of reds and blues that completed everything I already knew, existed within who I was as a person, who you are, and made everything succinct. I needed an answer, I needed *the answer.* My classmates went along with the curriculum as I was stuck in vertigo — where am I, who am I, what is this light and why? Important questions weren't answered.

In learning about the world, you are supposed to be able to get a red string that connects everything. All the theories, practices, ways of being and knowing should connect with the string to one big center, the foundation that makes everything like a triangle: connected but hierarchal, independent only as much as one single domino is far from the next. But I didn't get that from my education. I got "answers," plain and simple. Behind the answers there was nothing.

To the Teachers of America: if you are going to teach a kid about white bright light, you better know *how, why,* and you better be able to explain it. Light is the thing that connects us all back, after all. To our Gods, to our prayers, to our hopes in the tunnel.

And while I don't believe in luck, I know they say that bad luck comes in three's. I have had more than enough bad luck, I think. I think it's time. *It's time!*

That's right. I have been here for three days. A good number for the good patient-girl.

Head Nurse June told my family that on the third day my anger and resentment is supposed to reveal itself and that that will be a good sign. It's day three and in my charts there is no anger, there is no resentment. All I have is sadness. In fact, my anger and resentment does not reveal itself until day eight, according to the charts. But this is not day eight. This is day three. One sad day.

Why? I don't remember. Really I have no clue.

Here is what I do:

At the Children's Medical Center of Dallas I have many assessments, many of them Physical, most of them Psychiatric. Each one says similar things. I am sick. I am not well. Looking at the charts today, me a grown-up girl who is no longer practicing her eating disorder, makes me feel frozen in place. Far past overwhelmed, I've reached that point of maximum feeling where the mind starts to turn off. A self-protective freeze. To give me breath, I have to focus on the good. *I am alive now. I am not dead.* Looking at the charts also brings me a soft relief. No matter where I am or how I am doing, no matter how well or not well I am, I know that I am no longer thirteen, that I am no longer a patient admitted to a psychiatric unit five days before Christmas, that my parents will not be told, tonight, that I might not survive the night. That has passed, the ship has sailed. *I have survived.*

I look at the paper now and I try to remember the woman (the nurses and doctors are always women in my memory, though in real life, around seventy percent of the health care workers I saw were female) who was quizzing me, taking my pulse, writing things down with pity in her eyes. I know that one day, not today but when I was thirteen and dying, I was sitting in a wheelchair and another person, fully capable, was sitting too and she was quizzing me, trying to find me, who I was. I know the papers were next to me when I was almost dead and now that I am so far removed from that time, the papers are the thing that bring me back. Lots of lines, doctor's handwriting, medical terms that I don't know. *I was there.*

Here is what I want to remember:

Early swim team practices in the summer, family trips to the few white sand beaches in Florida, my dog, a collie named Kelly when she was still young and playful. I want to remember when my sister was so young that her cat Maryanne was still mine. I want to remember playing in the backyard, coming inside for dinner and the dimmed lights and jazz, the calm summer moods. I want to remember Friday nights with my sister at our grandparents' house. Our grandmother Mimi would play with us, Go Fish, and make buttered popcorn and we'd play fashion show with her many colored scarves, the purples, pinks, and yellows bright.

Here is what my chart remembers:

Rn note Pt. upset & apprehensive Sat C pt. Pt compliant c staff, but struggled c meal plan. Fam TX Note Summary miscalculations yesterday. CRI Note. Teen group patient said she is going to be herself now.

My chart remembers now like I was living in the moment, then. My chart is cold, it is past tense, it is far removed even though it is all knowing and present, on the verge of a cliff with the power to make or destroy me.

I don't know why I existed then in the hospital as if it were a memory, something that I could choose to recall and be present or not present in according to my will. After all, you can't recall something when it is actually happening, there is no *remember* until it becomes part of the past, close to forgotten, until you age out of the moment and walk away to the next. The first week I lived in flashback even though I was there, in the moment, I lived it through recall — so tricky, so magical, I was two places at once! Past and present, whizzing back and forth so fast I was a person fit only for the clouds.

Forgotten.

In the hospital, I am present but on the fringe, watching these particularly pressing moments of my life pass by as if they are entertainment. Sometimes I am interested, most often I am not. To watch the entertainment I was given a pair of fuddy, unfocused glasses and through this enhancement of vision everything became both so so very far away and also so very near. Perhaps it's because I was tired. Or starving. Or rapidly regressing towards death instead of growing up healthy and more mature as a thirteen-year-old should.

I've always known that it's easier to be outside of the moment, even when you're in it.

Here are the things I remember, through the glasses, for my entertainment:

There is a new girl and her name is Al. She is actually not new, no newer than me. She came the morning of my first day.

Usually when a new patient comes in, you have to stare them up and down, inspect them, find out who they are, assess how they are different from you, the same, better or worse. I didn't with her. I didn't notice. But you're supposed to, and I'll learn that fast, it's fun — it's what I want to do in real life. *Stare.* The new girl is named Al, short for Ali, which is short for Allison. Her skin is yellowed (anorexia) + tanned (sun exposure) and if it weren't for the sag, her skin would look like leather. The sag is from her weight loss; she was overweight and her doctor told her to lose weight *(Lose, lose! Lose here, lose now!)* and so she did. She couldn't stop. I like that she was overweight before she was underweight. Cut goes the competition, she is out of the game. Undeniably flawed. When she raises her hands way up above her head you can see her stomach and the skin, it drops.

I am happy that I am not her.

Al lifts her hands way up above her head because she is exercising, which is strictly forbidden. One night while I was brushing my teeth to go to bed in my patient room I started exercising too, I couldn't help it — that little voice inside kept saying *exercise, exercise.* I did three quick plies. In rushed Head Nurse June, in rushed Sarah, I am a very bad patient — *I must stop, must stop, must!*

But Al doesn't hear any of that because she is tricky. She is organizing the bookcase in the public school classroom, saying she wants to help. The books are leftovers from old patients. J.D. Salinger, *Franny and Zooey*, more J.D. Salinger. Al says she wants to help as she lifts her hands up over her head, stretches and repeats. The nurses for the day smile, they write in the charts, Al is a very good patient girl. Al continues, burning calories and exercising her OCD — Z's go here, R's go here, la di da.

Al is a bitch. She gets away with things that none of us could because she used to be bigger, and that makes her different.[8] The other girls and I hide our scowls with smiles. We don't like her but we can't let it show. And though we are "jealous," Al may never Get Well. She tricks too much, she is sick.

I tell my nurse for the day Andrea that my will to exercise is so strong, louder than all else, and I can't avoid it any longer. Andrea congratulates me for not listening, says it will get easier. No. I am exercising now. What? I am exercising now. Andrea asks how. I tell her I am squeezing my legs together tight, *forty seconds, fifty seconds, sixty.*

For the next five days I can't sit in my wheelchair with my legs touching, they have to be apart.

I don't like sitting with my legs not touching, it feels dirty.

I cannot be trusted, that I know I remember.

The day before Christmas, I remember that we made holiday cards with colored construction paper. Scissors are dangerous, they must be locked up at all times and even then they must be child-safe, the kind that doesn't really cut. But on special occasions, like Art Therapy on Christmas Eve, the decent scissors are let out, closely monitored. We decorate with sprinkles and with glitter, writing and drawing for the holidays. I started making a card for each of my family members — my mom, my dad, my baby sister, and

---

8   Really horrible thing to say. I apologize for my preteen self. Many young patients with eating disorders come from a background of being overweight before they developed anorexia and or bulimia. It is very easy to understand why — losing weight, once you learn the secrets, feels so awesome, and it can be hard to set a limit and stop once you start feeling the high. Unfortunately, those who experience anorexia and or bulimia after having been overweight have a much more difficult time being diagnosed and treated; much like the bias that comes from being male, having a history of being overweight sets individuals up for blinding their loved ones and physicians to their sinking reality. Another fact to keep in mind: you can be anorexic or bulimic and be obese or overweight. Regardless of what the DSM-IV says, the two are not mutually exclusive.

also one for me that matched. I take a big sun-faded yellow paper and cut out four large squares and fold them all in half. I decorate the folded squares with glitter, dramatic shapes, forms that look spectacular, like a celebration. I start to think about what I am to write. Now is the time.

As soon as I start to write, Art Therapy is over. Time for Group Therapy, we must wrap up.

On Christmas Eve this is what you are supposed to do:

Be with your family, eat Christmas Eve dinner with your family, listen to Christmas music, go to church, sing Christmas music loudly in the car with your sister, sneak peeks at your mom finishing up the gift wrapping, eat Christmas cookies with your mom and sister, snuggle up next to your dad in the living room next to the fireplace, call your family members in different cities and wish them a *Merry Christmas!!!*, leave milk and cookies out for Santa, talk about the reindeers, get tucked into bed, just as your sister, cross your fingers for the stockings, get excited, get happy, be loved and at home.

Here is what I'm doing this Christmas Eve:

Finishing what I started.

Making the Christmas cards feels necessary, like a calling. I need to apologize. I need to say I'm sorry. I need to say *thank you. You are loved. I love you.* As soon as I start writing, I start to cry. I'm embarrassed, maybe even tortured. Both physical and psychological, I'm in serious pain, and if my mind could just stop flying all around, hovering over me the dying patient, then maybe I could explain it better. I'm cold, understand that.

Dear Mom,

We have come so far and I love you. I love you for recognizing me before this and for loving me since the millisecond I was born. Thank you for watching over me and singing songs and driving me in cars to fall asleep when I was a baby. Every blink of the eye you have spent with me has been loved and cherished. I love you. Thank you. You took great care in looking over me while I was growing and you even noticed when I started struggling. And you took action. You've been more than a mom for me, more than loving, you've saved me in more ways than I will ever fully understand or be capable of thanking you for. Now I feel like I can talk to you and make promises to you that I never would have been able to earlier, even though you were always available to me. I am grateful at least for this struggling because from this struggle I feel closer than I have ever felt to you and I love you. Thank you for being so dependable, smart and loving. Thank you for teaching me. Thank you for feeding me. But even more, thank you for being my mom. I love having you. Thank you and please never stop. I love you. Thanks for the songs, the back rubs, the talking and the listening, thanks forever and to eternity.

I love you impossibly.

Jordan

Dear Sister,

Hey my sister! Merry Christmas. As terrible as this Christmas must be for you – I am sorry — you have no idea how good I feel here and how good I feel knowing you are still here with me. Even if this time it means giving up our traditional Christmas. But some day, there will be a day, I will make it up to you. I love you more than anything and I feel your love for me more than anything. Thank you for that. You are a very special girl. And I thank you for hanging in there and being there for me. Thank you for always being there for me. I'm always here for you as well. Whenever you need any advice, any help, or just a set of ears to talk to – I'm ready and waiting. I don't know everything, maybe even nothing, but I do know one thing (okay so I do know something) and that is that I love you. I love you forever and I love you no matter what, each part of you and your beautiful insides I love. I love you because I was made to love you. I love you because I'm your sister. Sometimes I'm the older sister, sometimes I'm the younger one, but I'm always your sister.

Don't ever stop being you.

Jordan

I also wrote a card to my dad and a *"you can do this"* card to myself, though I have since lost both my dad's and my own. I still have the cards for my mom and my sister, because they kept them safe.

Together the cards say: I'm sorry. Thank you. I love you. Please love me.

My sentiments have never changed.

When I make the cards I start to cry, to let it all out, and for the first time since I've been in the hospital I feel truly alone. I don't mean an emotional alone because ever since I have been Sick, at least and perhaps much longer, I have felt emotional-alone. But this time in the hospital I am also physically alone. I got to go in the Art Therapy room all by myself while everyone else played a game in the main room; they let me in because I said I needed to and they believed me. Since the walls are mainly composed of windows, they can see me cry.

This is how I cry:

First my head falls down like a paperweight connected to a tissue. I have no core to hold me up. I start to cry but exteriorly it looks more like a seizure, a shaking instead of a release, like more problems are being caused instead of expunged. Eventually the head to table isn't enough and my head must fall to my bended knees, my absent core so totally empty that it needs to fall in entirely. My chest meets my knees. My head tries to curl inside. I convulse until I become stilled from exhaustion, and from this recognition of sad I am quieted. Whatever tears had fallen become stuck on my cheeks and they don't seem to move — *this is my permanent expression*, I think. This girl with tears frozen to water marks on her cheeks, my quiet becomes poetry. I misplace the anger and for a time I find understanding. *How hard it must be for this girl to do so many things.* How hard it must be with all that pressure and no core to help her stand up straight, all she wants to do is shake and fall so her chest meets her knees. All she wants to do is frame the tears on her cheeks in gold, to let everyone know this is who I am, the incredible crying girl, so unfit for the hard, hard world.

When I cry I try my best to let everything out. To wipe myself clean, to experience the fullness of the cry as I know I don't cry as much as I should. I allow myself to explode in hurt because it feels good and far away from my normal composure of plastered, immovable smiles and nodding yeses.

My patient chart says I have difficulty expressing emotion. By this they mean I have difficulty expressing honest emotion. I am fine with expressing artificial things — I am fine at acting and pretending to be someone else. Since crying is so obviously my normal state of existence, what I so obviously find unique pleasure in doing, since crying to the fullest capacity feels true, unlike anything else, since it feels so good... it makes sense that I have to make my way through life by smiling. You can't cry when you meet new people or talk to your friends — even though I'd often like to.

My friends have never seen me cry. Their parents think I am strong of will because even during unhappy movies, petty fights, tumbles in my roller skates, I never let a tear fall out. What they don't know is that it isn't composure but a stiff fear holding back tears that I want so desperately to fall.

I want to experience things. I want to cry. I want to be allowed to be sad. I don't want to be happy all the time. I don't want a happy life. I don't want a perfect life. I don't want what I'm supposed to want.

I want to show my suffering.

Everyone, everyone should see my tears. So you know who I am, see my cry.

The people of the psych ward are proud of me. *Do not disturb. Let the patient confront her grief.*

What the nurses don't tell you is that tear marks become

permanent on paper. Far from washing away history, tears create swamps and puddles that stay forever in memory.

They say: I cannot be happy because I cried so much for so long, how can I ever forget it?

In the psych ward while you sleep you can hear the other patients screaming for extra showers and access to razor blades, petitioning for sleeping pills, getting down in the trenches of anger in the quiet room, or opening up in the sanctuary of midnight exhaustion to say the things they would never say in the light of day — their fears of never recovering, their fears of being stuck inside the walls of a hospital or psych ward forever. You can hear the nurses change shifts. You can see the little red dot on the overhead cameras that means you are being watched and inspected. You never have your space. Even in the quiet room there is so much padding on the walls and such an invite for fits of rage that you are not alone. I guess you could say I don't know what to do when I am alone, emotionally or physically. Who am I supposed to be? If I am honest I will fall apart, I hurt so much. But how can I pretend? When I am by myself I can't fool me, I know better. I quiver, I shake, my chest meets my knees. I succumb.

Outside of the hospital, while I was sick, my only alone time came in the form of my long daily walks and jogs. Obviously I didn't use that time well, either. There is a limit, they say, a point at which healthy behavior becomes an obsession. You can kill yourself by exercising too much. Did you know that?

I am sorry. I don't remember. When will I become something other than a broken record? *I am sorry. I apologize. I don't know. Thank you. No thank you.*

I am so polite, it hurts.

As I cry in the fake classroom making Christmas cards on Christmas Eve for my family that is not here and is very well disappointed in me, scared for me, heartbroken, and as I feel guilty, so guilty, and disappointed in me too, Jessie walks into the room. He puts his hand on my shoulder and he says it will get better. Jessie sits beside me as I shake and for a moment I think it must get better, too. Schizophrenics deserve moments of calm, a release from hurt and happiness void of fear, I think. Anorexics deserve that too.

. . .

If there is one thing I want you to know about anorexia, it is the inability to sleep, the floating. It's not that you can't sleep it is that it is impossible, you forgot how. You put your head on your pillow, you tuck yourself in, you pray and you wish more than anything else that you could fall asleep. It doesn't have to be a fast sleep or a restful sleep, a sleep without the 3 a.m. wake ups or the tosses and turns, all you want is *a sleep*, any kind will do. The problem is your head is too loud. It's like what happens when you have a major moment the next day, a moment that could make or break something for you, and you just can't sleep because you can't stop thinking about it, there is too much nervous energy in the air. That's what it's like to have anorexia, only the anxiety never ceases as there is no clear end.

While you are awake during the day, everything feels like a dream. You are in this cloud, in a haze of a bubble that distorts the things you see and makes everyone talk so funny and a little too loud. Then at night, when all you want is a release from the noise and the things that look and feel so much like insanity, when you want to touch the proverbial switch and turn it off, you can't. You wish you could. Sleep, to you, seems like the most perfect death. It's not permanent, you can wake from it, but you can also escape.

Instead you think of: calories, fat, protein, carbs, exercise, yesterday's meals, today's meals, and especially, especially, tomorrow's meals. What you plan or don't plan on eating tomorrow is so important, so important that you must stay up counting the calories, making sure they work. While I was sick at thirteen, the now popular computer calorie counters didn't exist, there were no apps to add the numbers up for you — and since I was so young and lived at home I wouldn't have used them even if they had existed in the same way they do now. To write the calories down is to provide proof, to gather all the reasons why and hand them over, spoon-fed evidence. Not smart.

To count the calories up in your head is a hobby, the most addictive one there is. Nobody knows when you're doing it and you can do it always.

$$\begin{array}{r} 35 \\ \times\ 2 \\ \hline 70 + 60 + 140 = 270 \end{array}$$

Adding and subtracting, multiplying, figuring it all out and reworking, redoing, it's a way to live that supersedes everything else and makes it all obscure. With calories you have solace. You have an escape. It's nice until you try to sleep and you can't get away.

When I try to stop thinking, this is what happens:

Black clouds of vertigo, roller coaster rides over tempestuous waters. You float on the bed as if you were a ghost, going round and round, up and over. You get seasick but you must keep going, you can't help it; after all it's not you that's doing the floating, it's your body, and those are two very distinct things.

Even before my eating disorder, I would count. I remember counting numbers nonstop while coming back from a school campout in a bus filled with screaming kids, my friends, people who thought I was happy and pretty and never cried. We drove past a building with its telephone number listed, and I memorized the full number and then counted to see what all the numbers added up to. It wasn't about reaching the final number but about the ritual of counting. About how, by counting, I could escape. Each time I got to the final sum I would start over, adding and rechecking, stopping at each additional number to make sure that it was right. I remember walking out of the school bus, all of the screaming kids laughing and smiling at me and expecting me to play along, and feeling the numbers still counting on my fingers. I didn't want to stop counting, and I didn't think I could.

Numbers have always been most important.

II

SUICIDE

Shut up. I can't take you, take this. I need quiet, peace, and I need it so badly I need it forever. Sometimes I get so tired I don't think I can go on anymore. Sentences run on continually and I think, truly, I need it to stop. I can't go on. Freeze-frame. Blank space, dark. I have always been fascinated by suicide. There it is! I said the word. I admitted it to you, to me. I have always been fascinated by suicide. To be able to stop everything, to say the word and go away for good. To have peace and a blank spot and whatever comes next. Sometimes everything just gets so big I don't think I can take it any longer. And I literally think: How easy it would be. Suicide! That's the answer. Quick and simple and over. No more pain. No more suffering or pretending. Just one quick burst. I wonder, why don't more people commit suicide? Doesn't anyone see how easy it is? It is easy. Really it is. We all have the capacity to live, to die, and to kill. We hold it in our hands like moths, yet we faintly remember it. We act as if it weren't true. We go about our lives and then people die, people commit suicide, people kill and we gasp and act like it's impossible. I have thought about it several times. Specifically when I was a little girl, the world as big as I was scared. The idea felt soothing. I don't think I fully understood its pull. I still don't. I hope I don't sound insensitive. But that is the appeal to me: a place to go home, to find quiet, where people don't get to me like they do when I'm awake. I just want quiet and sometimes quiet seems so impossible that the only option is a quick suicide. When you carry so much weight on your shoulders it's hard to think clearly. And who is to say that people who commit suicide aren't thinking clearly? Couldn't they, in fact, be thinking the most clearly? They don't have to deal with what comes next. They can wash it all away, sleep peacefully. To understand the position of the world and to give up, to throw in the towel, to do the little you can to steer your own life. That's all we can hope for, isn't it? To steer ourselves to safety? To stop the sentences in their tracks. I fantasized about suicide when I was a little girl because the world held too many things, too many things that I couldn't understand and it was overwhelming. The days would go on, nonstop, and if I could I'd stop for a second and I'd think, *wait, where has the time gone?* Have I not slept for a second? Have I not had any rest? Even as a little girl I understood that we people don't really sleep when we are alive. We never get to rest until we are dead. Because even when we sleep the time keeps passing and as our lives are directly correlated to the tick of the clock, so too are we active in our sleep. Sleep is just a decision to spend our lives a certain way. It is active. It is not really restful, not really a stop. Perhaps if the time machines in science fiction stories were invented, then things might be much better for the suicidal clock in me? Perhaps the idea to commit suicide would have never come to me because I could stop time whenever I wanted and still have the option to wake up again, once things were better and more clear? I know when you really contemplate suicide, you don't think it will ever get better. I know when you really contemplate suicide you are certain, in your foggy and clogged-up mind, that death is the only certain thing, the only true thing, and you are certain you want to be true. Am I making any sense? I did, for the record, say the word suicide out loud.

II.5

SUICIDE
PART II

September 16, 2011

Quite simply, my eating disorder was an attempt to leave myself, to die. I didn't like who I was, I always wanted to be better, far and away better, and I was afraid of the person that I was expected to grow into. I wanted it — my life — to stop, indefinitely. To be done with it already. I can act cute and innocent and say, "Why no, I never wanted it to happen." I can tell you that I totally loved myself before the disorder, that I was totally happy. I can feign shock when you mention suicide, I can act like I never considered it. Yet I know that the eating disorder I experienced was an outright flirt with death. It was my suicide pact.

I was thirteen years old and, for my age, I was incredibly innocent and naive. Yet, at the same time, I was also hyper aware of the hardships that life could offer, and the great struggles, and the energies that one must exert in order to get what they want out of life. It's like I skipped six decades: I had the maturity of a ten-year-old and the tired pessimism of a seventy-year-old. I was an old soul with a pink lunch box and ribbons in my hair. And so, when my friends talked about sex and boys I would giggle hysterically and refrain from speaking until they changed the subject — I still do. But when I was in school, and the teacher asked us to describe the meaning of a sad sentence in a sad poem, I was always the only one that could comprehend and articulate the sentiment. Not because I was particularly smart or mature, but because I was abnormally weathered. I had seen it all, somehow, already, deep within my imagination and understanding of life as is. I was totally unable and unready to connect with my friends when they talked about more "age appropriate" things. I would look off to the side and fidget until they changed the topic. But when my parents, for instance, talked about some horrible thing that happened on the other side of the world, I would get it. I could feel and be connected and in the moment. I was comfortable being a little girl and I was comfortable being what I considered a grown up to be — a person who deals with "important" things — but I was unwilling to be what I was supposed to be: a maturing adolescent girl, someone that specialized in talking about school crushes, all boy bands, flavors of ChapStick, and lip gloss.

What this age-split led to, I think, was an absent perspective on my future. I rarely thought of it. I knew I wanted, or rather needed, to become a hard-working career woman who achieves like my mother, but I never imagined lovers, babies, white picket fences. I never thought about my dream wedding or my future husband's ideal qualities because I was afraid of these things, these aspects of growing up in a box.

Still believing in cooties, I no doubt stunted my growth. I pushed myself to go from sixth-grader to sexless career exec, an impossibly overwhelming task grounded in denial. I denied the development of a whole part of myself, because I was too scared, and in doing so, I denied my ability to really envision myself in any sort of foreseeable future. I would try to think of what I would be like, who I wanted to be when I grew up, but I couldn't get there. I couldn't fathom ever growing up.

Even today I have difficulty motivating myself to do the small things that will help the future me, like crafting a better resume or boosting my credit, because I am not totally sure that I am going to exist tomorrow. More than my friends, I struggle with pushing myself forward into the future. And I feel that this is related to my childhood age-split, to my fear of growing, not older, but into a teenager. I denied myself a proper age incline, I refused to budge from number thirteen to number fourteen, and so, now, I never really now who I am or if I will even be around tomorrow.

I was so anxious, as a thirteen-year-old, about doing what is expected of a teenager, like going on dates and having your first kiss, that I trained myself to think that I didn't have to, that I could skip over everything that went along with my supposed-to-be widening hips. I trained myself to deny that that part of me existed, so much so that I wasn't sure if I was anything at all. I began to believe that my life had no value or foreseeable, or wanted, future.

I thought, *"Since I don't have a future, why not end it now?"* For me the suicide-by-eating-disorder path was the obvious choice. I was too naive to know about guns or ropes and didn't have what I considered the brand of courage that would allow me to fully commit. Being anorexic seemed like the easy way out. It felt wishy-washy, slower, and less painful. No one could trace my steps.

The doctors told my parents that my heart could stop beating. They said that when you starve, your muscles, including your heart, shrink. They said my heart was weak, all my organs functioning slow; they said they would work with me, *as long as I first survived the night.*

The body eats the heart.

This wasn't exactly what I expected to happen, this specific unfolding of events.

Sure, I wanted to die. I stayed up late in the night, unable to sleep, fantasizing about getting some horrible disease that would make me sick, help me die quick. But I wanted it to happen thanks to external forces. Which is what an eating disorder can feel like. It takes some time to realize that it is very much internal. That your brain, so close to the heart, is doing all the work.

To that thirteen-year-old girl, dying didn't mean death. It meant escape. I wanted so badly to get away from what I knew, if only temporarily. I wanted to get away from the private high school applications, from my gossiping and vicious yet sweet-looking friends, the boys that were showing me I was attractive in the crudest and the not-so-crudest ways possible, my fighting parents — you couldn't hear them fight, you felt it. I wanted to get away from my dark feelings, my self-pity, and my self-hatred. I wanted to get away from everything around me and most things inside me and I didn't think I had any options aside from death. So it was very practical. A simple equation. I wanted to get away. Dying was the only way that I could. Therefore, I needed to die.

I know my need to escape was also the reason why I welcomed the experience that anorexia elicits of being out of body. It can make you feel, thanks to the intense distortions that malnourishment impose, as if you are a hovering ghost witnessing those final seconds of your death. You see the moment when your spirit seeps out from your flesh and you get to watch the scene from up above. You get to say goodbye to the self you knew, you get an existential passing. Like saying goodbye to a close friend that, despite your love, you never knew entirely. Watching as an outsider before your spirit gets rebirthed or wholly consumed by the heavens.

Your mind is split from your body and here you are left to watch your body, even though you don't care what happens to it — that's how it feels. But it's not the truth. In reality, it's the other way around. In the depths of anorexia, your body is all that is left of you, your mind totally taken by the disorder. But I welcomed the feeling. It felt safe. It allowed me to say, *"I feel sad,"* instead of *"I'm angry,"* and think that there was a great big gap between the two.

I noticed my own feelings as if I was detached from them, as if I were noticing that the plants needed watering, and I didn't think much about my feelings because I wasn't being affected by them. I was up in the clouds watching as this body moved around, talked, and descended lower and lower. I was able to escape from both the life that I had been given, the perfect cookie-cuter extracurriculars and the school dances, as well as from the extreme emotions that were too hurtful to experience directly. I was disassociating and I welcomed the relief. I welcomed the barrier that I was creating inside of myself, that one thing that helped me to get further and further away from who I was.

And that is suicide: denying who you are, denying your ability to exist as yourself, creating barriers, posting stop signs, doing whatever you feel it takes to smash the mirror and break that reflection.

It doesn't feel good, thinking about suicide. But when you are really down in the trenches like I was, suicide, the real prospect of death, can feel like the easiest, most reasonable, and viable option and in that it can feel like the best option, the golden opportunity. The sole thing you have to do to get you what you want: silence, nothingness, the end of the struggles that surround you and make it so hard to breathe. And it can feel logical, too, because you didn't really think you would exist tomorrow anyway.

12

MERRY FUCKING CHRISTMAS

December 25, 2001

In movies, psych patients look like a lot of crazy people running around, screaming. It's just like in the movies.

Particularly on days when the memory of necessary happiness collides with current torture. See: Christmas Day in the psych ward. It was amazing to watch as an out-of-body experience, though when my spirit touched my body to momentarily rejoin as one, it was undiluted pain. As a body and a brain, I remember that I was supposed to be different, that I couldn't compete with the happy life that was expected of me. As I disconnected being, I enjoyed the chaos. It felt amazing to watch. I saw the first members-only club that I loved and appreciated and wanted to be a part of, full stop.

I don't need to tell you by now that when you starve yourself, you forget yourself. So long go your memories, your time, the joy in who you used to be. And it gets worse at the breaking point. Everyone who struggles with addiction has one, as you know. Eventually the addict will come to a point where something has to break.

My break happened my first week of treatment. Passive and hovering overhead on Christmas Day, I saw that I had hit rock bottom and I reached my point, my spot where I had to decide: Will I do the impossible and climb up, or will I surrender to what seems the most inevitable? Will I give up and let whatever shitty thing that happens next, happen?

When you reach your breaking point, it seems like you are most literally choosing between life and death — in the case of anorexia, you are — and one seems possible, the other unreal. And in that sense, to survive means to believe in fairy tales.

While survival is a fantasy, death is a tossing of the rules, living your life in twisted celebration, a temporary and excruciating fun that lasts only so long as your slowing heartbeat. *You might not survive the night.*

Christmas morning I am awoken by the nurse who comes early every morning to draw my blood from my right arm as I sleep. Only this isn't the nurse I see every morning. Since I don't recognize this nurse and since I am terrified, and by terrified I mean *terrified*, of getting my blood drawn (each time more worse than the first), I decide to do what Head Nurse June is helping me to do: speak up. If I am unhappy with something or if I don't trust a situation, I have to speak up, she says. It's like our secret password: just speak up. So I do. I ask the nurse who she is, how many times she has drawn blood, if she could please not squeeze the rubber band around my upper arm so tight and, finally, if she could please just stop so the old nurse could come back as I preferred the old one anyway. The bad nurse stops when I ask her to but not because of me, she stops because she's finished. She puts a cotton ball over my pierced skin and asks me to press, I do, and when she comes at me with the stupid Scooby Doo Band-Aid I snatch it from her and say, *"I'll do it myself."*

For me this is important. It's the first time I learn that the things they teach us inside the hospital don't necessarily work outside of the hospital. In fact, sometimes they can be quite the opposite — and I was still *in* the hospital.

When the bad nurse leaves I try to go back to sleep even though I can't sleep and wasn't even asleep to begin with. I keep trying. I hold the pierced spot with the stupid Scooby Doo Band-Aid. The nurse actually was as bad as I say she was, it wasn't just my imagination. A bluish purple bruise will make itself at home right there on my inside elbow soon and stay for two whole weeks. I'll show it to all of my nurses, Head Nurse June, Dr. Kay. *Look. See? See!* Every time I see the bruise I am reminded: Stupid me, couldn't speak up well enough. Nobody listens. I look at the bruise often — how could I not?

The day before I was complaining with the other patients about the holidays and the fact that we were all imprisoned during them. One of the girls told me, then, that I was lucky. *At least you didn't get here eight days ago.*

Eight days ago the old ladies who run the Art Therapy sessions came in to run a holiday-special Art Therapy. For some reason — who knows why? — they thought it would be a good idea to have a holiday Christmas cookie decorating "Art Therapy" session and brought in loads of pre-made sugar cookies from the grocery story. Another girl told me exactly how many calories were in the cookies: 220 per serving. The 220 calories per serving, the other girl said, meant a half cookie portion which meant the whole cookie was 440 calories with no protein, no fiber and lots of saturated fats and simple, simple sugars. The old ladies also brought in sprinkles and glitter dots made of sugar, green and red and yellow, and canisters filled with cake icing. The icing came in four colors: green, red, pink, and blue.

But what about Head Nurse June? Didn't she see?

Maybe Head Nurse June saw and thought it was a good learning experience for us to Express Ourselves or Face our Fear Foods, Control our Urges to binge or exercise or walk away, stiffen up, count the numbers. The girl says they were all just sitting around the tables perfectly calm when the old ladies started to unwrap the cookies. One box of cookies, two boxes of cookies, three — the girls sink back a little in their seats. Then the old ladies take out the icing and glitter dots, and the girls start looking at one another, asking for help, looking to see if they can't see Head Nurse June in the hall and tell her to *Get Here Quick! Code Red!* The old ladies put the icing and decorations on the table and pass out individual cookies on paper plates to each of the girls along with a holiday-themed paper napkin for clean up. *"More napkins are available here at our table if you need any."*

I imagine the way each girl must have responded to seeing her individual cookie appear. Frightened? Disgusted? Tempted? Or were they ambivalent? Were two emotions running so deep inside of them, did they not know how to respond? I know if I had a 440 calorie sugar cookie put in front of me to decorate I would be scared, disgusted. I would think back to the way I used to put oatmeal raisin cookies in milk as a kid and how I'd use a spoon to find the sunken cookie parts at the bottom of the glass; the way we left cookies out for Santa, baby carrots and apples for his reindeer. I would promise myself that I wouldn't eat any of the cookies, and I wouldn't. I'm an anorexic. I have discipline. I would count the calories I had eaten already that day and the calories I planned to eat. I would get scared and think back to the calories I ate yesterday. *Am I sure it was just 1,400?*[9] *Am I sure?*

The girls start engaging in all of their negative coping behaviors instead of confronting their fears. One girl does jumping jacks in the room and jogs in place, "I'm sorry, I have to." Another eats her cookie and its icing and asks if she can go to the restroom for just a minute. "No, you cannot go to the restroom until 30 minutes after eating, you know that."

"But this is not on my meal plan! It's not on my meal plan!"

Some girls enjoy it, as a way to exist next to high-calorie, delicious food without taking part. They lick their lips, smell the cookies, enjoy the swirl of colored sugars in total anticipation, giddy with delusional excitement for the phantom person who might soon be fed. The rest of the girls start doing what I would have done: dutifully decorating, ignoring the chaos all around while sinking further and further into the chaos and counting numbers inside.

Eventually, the girls explode, they did, I did, and a lone tear starts to fall. It feels so good another goes and another until they

---

9   Had to get this in here, though I didn't want to tell you for risk of being a bad influence. I do not want to give you numbers to hold onto or spark an obsession or competition. I do not want you to compare me to you. But those stories of anorexics subsisting on nothing but a single apple a day for weeks — those are lies. We are human too. 1,400 was my number at 13. That's at least 18 apples per day. And word to the lifelong dieters: 1,400 is not a sustainable number of calories, you need more to better meet all of your nutritional needs.

have become sinking ships, sole proprietors of One Sad Feeling. I know in their heads it must have felt like the room was shaking, like the lights were buzzing on and off, like the end of the world was unquestionable, had so obviously arrived.

Just eleven girls with eating disorders and some sugar cookies, that's all it takes.

An hour after the blood-sucking nurse comes on Christmas morning, another nurse, the one who is always here and specific to our ward comes to my room. I prefer this nurse the most, second to Head Nurse June who is supposedly a nurse but doesn't do any nurse things like draw blood or give out medicine. That's what this nurse does — she gives us our medicine each morning and night in a little clear plastic cup along with a little paper cup filled with two ounces of water to match. Since this nurse is specific to our psych ward, I don't feel embarrassed when I see her. When the old nurse or the bad nurse comes, for instance, I think: What must they think of me? Of this ward? They must see kids dying of cancer, kids with severe diabetes, kids who can't sleep with sticker plugs and monitors to find out why.[10] The sick kids they must see didn't ask for what they have. But me? Did I ask for this?

The nurse who is always here to dole out our medicine takes my blood pressure lying down and sitting up and standing up. Since I have been in the hospital, these times are one of the few moments where I am allowed to stand up on my own two feet. I can stand for a moment when they must know my blood pressure while standing and I can stand to be weighed, for a split second, standing backwards on the scale so as not to see the secret number. When I shower I must use a special seat, the kind old

10   The kids-that-can't sleep ward was right next to the kids-with-psychiatric-illnesses ward.

people use, and my nurse must sit nearby to make sure I am okay — *no broken bones or concussions, no dead Jordans here.* When I change clothes, my nurse helps me pick them out and first I change waist up, then waist down — the nurse looks away and says, *"Ask if you need help."* You might think this means I am extra safe, but I say the opposite: By not being allowed to stand on my own two feet I am growing to appreciate the life of the coddled person, the sick one, the child. I am growing to love being taken care of to an extent that someone who is my age and healthy should not and cannot be.

I am growing to love being the sick and dying patient, the one who needs all the special care and love, the assistance to do such simple things like walk, shower, stand for the two seconds required for the blood pressure monitor to snake around me tight and suck me in, hurting my upper arm with its too tight grasp.

I hate the feeling of being held too tight, I suffocate. And yet I need to be held. This, I think, is due to the wheelchair and the snake. Thank you very much.

As I pretend to sleep, I can hear the nurses moving about, preparing to wake us up. Quickly, Jessie rushes into my room, it's his new thing: *wake up Jordan, say hi to Jordan before the mean nurses wake us up.* I like Jessie. He is my friend. I want to protect him, and I think that I can, I think that he needs it. I also think Jessie thinks the same of me. Two sick patients, trying to take care of the other when we can't even take care of ourselves. It's easier that way — I have never had a problem taking care of other people; the problem is with me.

Jessie rushes into my room screaming, *"Merry Christmas!"* He hands me a green piece of construction paper. On the front it says my name, inside is a drawing of a red gift box with a blue-striped ribbon, at the back it says The End.

"Thank you Jessie... what is it?"

"It's a Christmas gift, from me to you." We hear footsteps coming towards my door and Jessie whizzes away, straight past Sarah, into his room. Jessie is stuck directly on the other side of me, the hallway separates his room from mine.

Sarah walks in and says she is my nurse for the day. Yes, it seems like every day Sarah is my nurse for the day. She says it's just chance but I think it's because they want to keep us comfortable. I have never had a lot of the nurses. I've never had Jessie's, never had Al's, never had Abbey's. That means I know their nurses one way, as sort-of friends. We laugh together and try to make light of the situation together. Sometimes they see my hurt, but it's never as much as my nurses, Sarah and Andrea, do. Sarah and Andrea feel it. The other nurses just see it.

Sarah helps me change from warm pajamas into cold patient's smock. If I had a whole 400 pages to tell you how it feels to be anorexic, how cold it feels, that wouldn't be enough. Anorexia feels so cold it's no longer human. The cold is past your muscles, past your bones, you solidify, become this metal sheet, this too-cold substance open and naked to all the harsh elements. I bet you don't know how cold the things of this world are. Stethoscopes? Ultra sounds? Heart monitors? IV fluids? It's a cold world.

I remember going to swim practice one day, two months before treatment. I hadn't gone for a long time. I felt ostracized — my favorite SAT word at the time — by one of my best friends who I used to go to practice with; even though she was thin, you could tell, she was jealous that I had gotten thinner. My friend chose a side, and it was me against her, our old friends, our whole world with her, and me, by myself, with the cold. As I walked into practice, I remember my mom followed me in, as if to catch my fall. My mom used to just drop me off, pick me up, but now it's different. I know. She stopped her life to take care of me, way before I was in treatment. I know she saw the eating disorder — how could she not? — but when she took me to doctors they said *hypothyroid, Addison's disease, it's not her, it's a disease!*

My mother asked me what was wrong. I said, *"Nothing."* Why would she not trust me?

Why would she not trust the doctors?

I walked into practice and my mom followed me in. My coach stared at me as practice had already started. Everyone was staring at me, actually, except my friend. It was my used-to-be friend's thing: look away, pretend you don't notice her, notice me.

I can see that everyone is looking through me. They see that I am not good — *oh no, too thin*. If there were a phrase to the slight "o" of their mouths, the dropped jaws, and their big gaping eyes it would be: *"Eat a sandwich, put some meat on those bones!"* Everyone says that. It might sound like something your grandfather would say — mine certainly does — but in matters like these, I have found, the new borrow from the old. They fall into the status quo, into what has been done before, into the protocol.

I take off my jacket and sweatpants and try to brush off the stares. This has always been the hardest part, jumping into the cold water. I used to do it with the full knowledge that I would soon kick my feet off the sides of the pool and swim away, moving fast to warm my body. If it was too cold before, I would jump up and down at the side of the pool and scream out: "It's too cold coach! Coach, it's f-f-freezing!" By joking I would warm up. By playing and laughing and all of these things that I can no longer do, not fully, not with my whole heart anymore, I would loosen up, relax. I inch into the pool. Into the water goes the tops of my toes, my ankles, the points of my knees where the doctors tap with their little doctor hammers. I breathe in and out and my heart, it feels like stopping. *Quit me, leave me. Let me out of here!* I sink into the pool with careful calculation, careful not to let my head and hair go completely underwater.

I try to swim. I can't. My coach stares. My mom stares. All the little people, my age, in the pool, stare. My friend keeps swimming. She succeeds in looking away.

I tell my coach this secret that has become ever so clear: "I can't do this."

Why? Because the cold is unbearable. It's like the whole world has frozen over and I'm just this small pocket of air impossibly stuck in the snow. Each breath in and out is an admission of guilt and I have to swallow the ice, swallow the ice, more. It's freezing and excruciating, the cold is impossible. The ice has turned you into a glass that can snap to pieces at any moment. Your legs can snap, the foot and hands, your elbows can part in two. If you've felt it, you know; if you haven't — trust me — you've never been cold.

It might look like cold and it might be cold to the touch, a light blue with specks of ice coating the top, it might make you shiver, make goose bumps on your skin, the cold so deep that you know even a warm bath, a warm blanket, not even the gas turned on high will do. You might have felt all of these things but even still, I promise, you have never felt cold. Your cold is something you can, as they say, *get over it all already*.

I can't get over mine. The cold equates to numbness, an inability to move.

We get weighed. It's interesting to see who works on the holidays and who does not. Everyone working today looks fired-up, awake and ready for the big bad things to happen. As we stand in line to be weighed the nurses eye us all left to right, walking by us like drill sergeants, totally on-call. The girls and I whisper to one another: *Merry Christmas, Merry Christmas.* Al breaks the whisper code and speaks to my nurse. "Merry Christmas, Sarah."

At the scale I try to sneak a peek at my number, but the nurse working the scale is not a pushover.

We eat breakfast. I don't want to talk about it.

We have morning meeting. And then it starts, Christmas. *My Christmas in the psych ward.* Dr. Kay takes out a handful of papers and hands them to Abbey, asks her to pass them around. Abbey is two years older than me, the one with the pretty and still healthy-looking strawberry blonde hair. She is bulimic and a cutter. She says she wishes she were an anorexic, that she envies "the discipline." Once in therapy, I tried to lift Abbey up with the heart. I said cutters must have lots of discipline, too. After all, I have thought of cutting myself, fantasized about what seems like a real manifestation of how I feel, the carving, the open wounds, and yet I haven't been able to muster the strength to find a sharp blade, to open my arm straight. I say I envy "the courage" because, to me, Abbey is strong. As much as I, for one, have thought of cutting, of suicide, of a real and fast response to how I feel — to how I really feel, what I think I really want — I can't find the will to do it. I think of my sister, my mom, my dad. I think of my friends. I think of my future life that I have, by living, promised to those who love me.

I promised, by living, that I would grow up, get a job and get married, and to do what I want, to stop, would be a breach of contract. I am also afraid of open wounds.

It's not like Abbey doesn't feel the same as me. She is just better at listening to herself and hearing what she really wants to do instead.

I say this to Abbey and the therapist Changes the Topic. Even though the therapist wants us all to confide in one another, it has to be under her terms, not ours.

It starts. The papers are passed around and on them are holiday songs. Dashing Through the Snow. Oh, Hanukkah! Oh, Hanukkah! Rudolph the Red Nosed, Feliz Navidad. And on the last page, Silent Night. Dr. Kay has us sing Jingle Bells and then she asks us what we want to sing. There is a new boy with dark black hair. He has bipolar, his anger so severe you can see it bubbling over the surface as he speaks, as he moves. The anger makes him look cool what with his slick black hair, his dirtied white T-shirts, his — I kid you not — black leather jacket. The boy's name is Jake; he asks to sing Silent Night. All the anorexic girls in their seats, including me, start to squirm. Silent Night is a hard song to sing. The most fitting song for the hospital.

We begin. *Silent night, holy night/ All is calm, all is bright/ Round yon Virgin Mother and Child/ Holy Infant so tender and mild/ Sleep in heavenly peace/ Sleep in heavenly peace.*

I have the rhythm of Silent Night down to a T. At "heavenly," the voice rises up and up and then at "peace" the voice goes down, down again. It slips off the tongue, a natural harmony, the ups and the down, down.

We sing the last words: *at thy birth,* and look around at one another. We don't want to sing another song, singing en masse like this seems childish or distorted — torturous, when the songs are sad. Quickly, Jessie starts laughing. He rocks back and forth, the laughs rolling out of him like he's heaving, having an allergic fit. Jessie raises his arms up high and says it: *Merry Fucking Christmas.* He can't stop, he says it again: *Merry Fucking Christmas! Merry Fucking Christmas!* He slaps his knees with his hands, puts his hands over his face, covers his eyes, rocks back and forth, *rock the baby to sleep, rock the baby to sleep.* Jessie can't stop, he is tortured. Merry Fucking Christmas.

Jessie's nurse asks him to stop. Sarah asks him to stop. Dr. Kay asks him to stop.

"NO!"

"Jessie, if you do not stop you will have to go to the quiet room."

"MerryFuckingChristmas, MerryFuckingChristmas!"

The words become stutter, like those childhood toys you wind up to watch them jump around — when they hit a wall they can't move. They keep jumping to the wall, jumping to the wall, jumping... "MerryFuckingChristmas!"

Jessie's nurse grabs Jessie with both of her hands — she gets him at the sides of his chest underneath his underarms and she yanks him up, roughly. Jessie starts screaming and gets out of his nurse's hold for a moment and then she grabs him again, quickly, at his two wrists. You can see that she is hurting Jessie, his skin turns pink/white next to the point where she squeezes his wrists tight. His nurse hunches down, squats her legs and starts walking backwards, pulling Jessie to the quiet room. *"Ho Ho Ho!,"* he says to all of us patient dummies watching him, horrified and not knowing what to do.

Is there any way we can raise our arms up, behind a white flag, and say: *Yes, yes I agree with him? MerryFuckingChristmas* — that's how I feel. Any way I can agree, any way I can support

Jessie, without throwing myself into the flames, too? To plead the fifth? To raise my hands up.

In the quiet room no one is ever quiet. We kick the padded walls, we scream, we curse the stupid camera with the stupid red light, watching us in the corner. We scream, *"Let me out!"* We scream, *"Leave me alone!"* We scream, *"Shut up! shut up!"* We say we feel angry, sad, not angry, fine, sick. We say we hate ourselves, and as they come inside, to console, we retract: Never mind. *No, I hate you!* That's what I meant, why can't you listen? *I hate you!*

In the quiet room Jessie screams, "Fuck! Fuck! Fuck!" He emphasizes each word, at each syllable there is pain, there is drama, there is life, and there is also this immediate, urgent demand for death. It's like a mating call, the sound so specific and routine to each animal. Jessie says "fuck" and his voice starts so low and then it rises up, and up, he ends like he's on the edge of a cliff, screaming for dear life as flames smoke up his legs.

Fuc-k-k-k!

When a man screams and you hear the strength of his voice, it can be scary. But when a boy screams, when his voice cracks, when the embarrassment of his high pitch is so clear and yet the real need, the real hurt, is so pressing that he decides to keep screaming through the cracks... it's heartbreaking.

That's it. Code Red! Mayhem! Red flag! Alert! Alert!

Dr. Kay tells Jessie that he will lose his privileges if he continues acting out. Does he even hear? Jessie takes his shirt off — we can see because he keeps on jumping up and down in front of the door's window. One of the anorexic girls — I can't remember her name, she got here yesterday and will leave tomorrow as her parents, we assume, pluck her out — starts to laugh at Jessie.

I try to do my part in protecting Jessie, I eye the girl and I tell her, with mean eyes, *shut up, shut up!* Quickly, Jessie has turned his shirt into a scarf and he wraps it around his neck. Everyone in the group must know what is happening, and they say, "Oh no." *"What?"* I ask Sarah, *"What is happening?"* Sarah tells me, "Shhh."

Dr. Kay tells Head Nurse June to call security. "Jessie, you have to stop, security is coming."

This is what is happening, I am too young, then, to fully realize the scope: Jessie has turned his T-shirt into a noose. Jessie is trying to kill himself. To be exact, Jessie is trying to kill himself with a T-shirt on Christmas morning in the quiet room of a psych ward during morning meeting. He is jumping up and down, hoping that, in the end, it will stop. He'll break.

To die.

This makes me sad, today. Ten years later tears fall from my eyes, they puddle down my cheeks, fall to my chest.

How could I not know? I was too young, then. I was too young, and much too naive, to know that on the morning that Jessie woke me up with a card, my gift, he would come so close to breaking just three hours later.

To sleep.

What was I supposed to do? Yes, there was Dr. Kay there. Head Nurse June. Sarah. Jessie's nurse. But what was I supposed to do? Jessie and I had a special contract — we never spoke it out loud and yet still it was there: I will take care of you if you take care of me.

For the first time since I came into treatment, Jessie has stopped noticing me. He used to watch me as I ate my three meals and snacks — I always finished that way — and I felt responsible to him for finishing. It worked because I trusted him. I wasn't responsible to him like I am to my family or my outside friends or the nurses and Dr. Kay. I was responsible to him as I really am. *I know this is hard but you must, food is necessary, you must eat your food.* Sometimes all it takes is for someone to recognize your pain, to see you as you really are.

Will Jessie see me anymore? He didn't at that moment just as I, really, didn't see him. I saw his pain, I saw his anger, I saw his desperation. What I didn't see was his theatricality. I didn't see that he fed off of his torture, that his life was so not important to him, that he could, in effect, turn his life into a circus. I saw his person and I saw the swamp his schizophrenia held him in, but I never saw these moments of choice — not the suicide attempt — because I do not believe that suicide is a choice so much as a quick-fix solution — but the full extent to which Jessie lived in his screams, the fact that his screams were real and pressing and free of any delusion — I saw that, but I didn't see that the screams were also fun for Jessie. I didn't see that he fed off of those screams just like I would later feed off of binging, those moments when the hunger is so strong, like bones and blood, we can't quit. So yes, he may have helped me, by virtue of being there as I tried to finish all of my calories, by being there as I cried over the Christmas cards, by being there on Christmas morning to greet me with my very own gift before anyone else could wake me, but if he leaves me now he won't be helping me at all. All of his help will wash away, much worse than had he not been here at all. I will know love, or something close to it, and then that love, that love I have come to expect, will be taken from me. The memory worse, the reminder of what I no longer have.

Does he even remember me? I can't forget him.

I no longer know where Jessie is, what he is doing, how he is. It doesn't matter — the feeling of needing to protect him hasn't left me for an instant.

Jessie keeps jumping up and down as all the patients watch. We can't take our eyes off of him. He is fear, he is torture, he is passion, acting out what he feels most necessary. Dr. Kay, Head Nurse June, and Jessie's nurse huddle by the exit door. Two big security guards come to the door, on the other side of the exit sign, outside. Dr. Kay opens the door, they come inside. Whisper.

Jessie calls out "Merry Fucking Christmas" like it's his last time. He puts his all into the scream, makes his voice louder and higher than we ever possibly thought it could go.

The security guards walk past me and I swear, from their heavy stomps, I can feel my wheelchair shake. To me the guards look as ominous as the angels of death.

I don't want Jessie to die. I don't want a stampede of security guards, dressed in black, to walk by me fast. I don't want my wheelchair to shake. I need calm.

Close my eyes. *One Mississippi, two Mississippi, three.* Breathe fast, breathe slow. Pinch your arms to feel your presence until your nurse shoos you away from yourself, no more acting out, no more real world metaphors for pain. We're stuck inside this cold, cold world and we can't reach out. What happens if you take your T-shirt off, if your shirt becomes a noose? The things you thought were safe are weapons.

Jessie is picked up like he's flying. Then he squirms so much that one big security guard holds his legs tight while the other holds his upper half. They start to walk and Jessie keeps on squirming so much, and calling out his favorite tick: MerryFucking-Christmas, MerryFuckingChristmas! Jessie gets out for a moment, falls to the floor for a moment, and starts to get away. The big guy once holding Jessie's feet grabs Jessie by the two shoulders, clamps him in like a sheet of metal, and lifts him up, the other big guy grabs Jessie's legs, tight.

They walk past me in the circle, heading towards the exit. Jessie bites the arm of his new keeper, the one clamping him in like a metal sheet.

Jessie gets taken out of the room, poof. And just like that Dr. Kay continues the morning meeting, we sing "Here Comes Santa Claus," and Dr. Kay goes over our special Christmas Day plans.

Just like that. We don't talk about him, mention him, cry for him. We just go on with our day. Merry Fucking Christmas.

We go downstairs. The old ladies who support the hospital, fund-raise and hold arts and crafts sessions, have found people to sponsor the hospital and hold a Children's Medical Center Secret Santa.

Here is what we are supposed to do:

Walk up to the rounded Santa, sitting down in his red suit, his fluffy and scratchy long white beard, hold out our hands and receive a gift from Santa, something special from a bin filled with presents by his side, all wrapped up, no one can see.

Of course we are to say *thank you.*

I wonder if the people who bought all the gifts for the sick hospital patients knew that some of those gifts would go to the psychiatric unit, to the kids sick from bipolar, schizophrenia, eating disorders, to the people who are suicidal, would they still have donated? Yes, of course, the good people of the world should donate to the little children, sick and dying from cancer. But what about me? My sickness is inside, too, but it's different. Past cells and failing kidneys, my sickness is emotional so who is to say it's really a disease? Dr. Kay, of course. But what about the people donating to the sick dying kids? The people who don't know me?

The school I go to always has fund-raisers, canned food drives, holiday present donations for those less fortunate. Every winter my mom takes my sister and me to the mall where we go to the Christmas tree in the center, and we each pick a paper star. On the star is a name of a person, less fortunate, and a gift they want. Often they want a new backpack for school, shoes, a new warm coat. My mom walks around the mall with us to find gifts for our two less fortunate kids — one for me and one for my sister — and she helps us to find two gifts for each: one what they asked for, what they need, and one for fun, a present, what they might wish for. My mom says there is a difference between what we want and what we need, in between the two there is a great sea that parts like when Moses asked it to. There is need — it is real, pressing, it is blood. There is want — it is ever changing, light as air, it is flesh.

I want warmth. I need touch, I need to feel my hand, held.

If I were someone not myself, one of my friends at school or my friends' parents or their parents' friends, I would not think that I, who I was then, in the hospital, was a fitting less fortunate person. Just last Christmas, I got a Tickle Me Elmo and a new pink puffer coat for someone less fortunate. Now, the tables have turned, I am the less fortunate, and she?

I hope, yes, that she is warm. And I hope, while my friends donate cans of food for those recovering from hurricanes, clothes for the homeless, while they ship off their favorite dress from yesterday, fill that used-to-be-special spot of their closet with their new favorite dress, their favorite dress of today, that they don't think of me. I am not a less fortunate person. *I am fortunate.* I know that is something I am supposed to say.

We walk downstairs and the room is filled with sick and dying kids. Because visiting hours are later it seems like everyone here is a kid, with only some nurses here and there in my peripheral vision. To my eye we, the mature and depressed psychiatric set, are the most adult of them all. In my memory I am also walking. I am not in my wheelchair. I know it didn't happen like this but at the time I felt so high, so superior, like my darkness could overshadow all the petty light in the room. I saw the truth, I was real world, I knew what it was all about.

When we go out of our part of the hospital, something magical happens with the nurses. Once they are away from Dr. Kay and Head Nurse June, they become our friends. We are twelve to fifteen. They are mid to late twenties. Yet our ages match up when you count the great wisdom and aging that comes with being a mental patient and combine that with the rest of the world, with the people who aren't sick and are as such much too young for their own age. We slide into place. We laugh like it's summer camp, talk about boys and girls and celebrities, things people our mutual ages like to talk about.

Sometimes one of the nurses will take me to the side and ask me, casually, about how I dieted. They want tips. Me of the lowest weight, the most successful anorexic in terms of time it took to get from healthy to hospitalized. I don't want to share — after all I know the pain hurts deep and I know I'm not evil, I know I'm not blind to where I am, to how I got here — so I dance around the subject. Give them the answers without the whole answers. It's simple really: It happened so fast

One of the old ladies asks us what unit we're from. Jake says we're from THE PSYCH WARD and we laugh like they do in A *Clockwork Orange*. We are dark, we are angry, we know where we are, how we got here, and we think it's hilarious! So funny! We'll laugh in your face! We'll throw out our fears and push them all onto you. If you hurt us, we will hurt you more; if you are scared for us, we will make you scared even more. We multiply, make it worse — why not? — after all, it's pretty much as bad as it can get. So bad that it has become, of course, hilarious. So bad that it has become the opposite of bad, that it has become familiar, and so, also, good.

I walk up to Santa and hold out my hands, say thank you.

Inside, my gift is a Barbie doll. Her long white legs, her smooth white skin, her cute button nose, her ocean blue eyes, her shiny straight blond hair, her perfect pink manicure, her feet, perfectly pointed, perfectly made to ease into her pink little heels, a perfect fit, her poking little fingers.

My nurse Sarah takes the Barbie doll from my hands as everyone laughs — not at me, with me.

"We'll find you something else, this is very inappropriate." Sarah is obviously angry. In her eyes it's so clear: *Don't they know?* In her eyes, "our society" should have skipped over a lot of bad steps by now, we should have evolved, we should have stopped buying the same gifts for kids that we did in the fifties, before girl power, before we knew that sticking two fingers down your throat is a real disease, within the body.

A new memo must be written:

Do Not Give Inappropriate Gifts to the Less Fortunate. Make it clear that this category includes all things with long legs and porcelain skin, all things that cut, all things that celebrate violence, all things that are Diet, all things that are Fitness, and, as we've now learned, T-shirts.

We go back to our side of the hospital, open the door. *Mrs. June, guess what I got for Christmas? A Barbie! Can you believe it? Can you believe it, Mrs. June?*

I don't remember anything else from the day. My memories are distinct and isolated and don't relate. With my family or without. Sad or funny. Holiday or not holiday. Merry Fucking Christmas or Confiscated Barbie. There are memories but they don't connect, and if there is no reason for me to remember them, I don't. It's like I have muscles without tissue, organs without skin, no bones to connect my dots into anything that makes any sense, stands the test of time, lasts longer than a blink, a flash, of the eye. A fleeting memory. If it weren't for the hospital I wouldn't even have a what, why, or where. The hospital, of course, is the constant. It at least tells me why: *I don't know.* Close my eyes. Throw away the key, watch it fall into blue waters, sink and thud. *I don't know because I don't want to know.* That's a good answer. It couldn't be any more concrete, the heavier to sink with.

In my memory my family never left me on Christmas, just as they never arrived. All I remember is opening up one gift. Untying the pretty ribbon, tucking my finger into the breaks of the gift wrapping paper, finding the tape, peeling it away from either side, pick a side, taking off the shirt of the gift, looking inside.

What was inside the gift doesn't matter, I don't remember. What matters is my family is here. I can feel my sister's warm smile and her big chocolate brown eyes. I can feel my mother's hand, so soft to the touch, running up my back and down. For a moment it doesn't matter how bony I am, how embarrassed I feel when my mother touches my bones. For a moment, all that matters is once I was a little girl and my mother rubbed my back and sang me songs so I could fall fast asleep at night and now she's rubbing my back again, for a moment, as I unwrap my gift.

If you close your eyes, the memory can last forever. It's just, once you wake, you won't know where you are.

Merry Fucking Christmas.

13

FAMILY MATTERS

October 21, 2011

You can say it's all your family's fault; you can say your family had nothing to do with it. The fact is your family has everything to do with it and it was no one's "fault." The fact is one's relationship with one's parents, with one's family, can be incredibly complicated, so complicated that placing blame on any one person is entirely impractical, if not pointless. The point is someone got sick and that someone had a lot of people in their lives that influenced them — and it might not defuse more than that. You can't put people down pat in linear boxes, like dolls, saying, *"You go in the culprit's spot, you go in the avoider's spot, you are certainly the victim, and you must sit here,"* because, who knows?

Who knows the influence you had on me? Who knows what the good did? What the bad did? It's hard to tell. Things get mixed with other things, and the words you didn't say can mess me up just the same.

While it's near impossible to know exactly why, it is possible to see it broken down in tiny, microscopic, portions. So maybe I can't be sure of the big picture or of the most specific cause and effects, but I can organize the influence of one's family on eating disorders into bite-sized bits, free of contamination, purely theoretical, and on a case-by-case basis that may have nothing to do with your own experience.

The first self-contained bit starts with loyalty. I am loyal to you because I am a child, or insecure, or human, and I have no one else to look up to, to aspire to, to trust. I am loyal to you because my sense of self is small compared to my sense of self ascribed to me by other people. In a group, I become what the group wants me to be. In a friendship, I become who my friend wants me to be. I start to laugh like her, dress like her, do the things she wants me to do because — as we try not to admit — I believe in her opinion more than I believe in my own. I cannot be happy on my own. I can only feel good when the people around me give me the positive feedback to make me feel safe and wanted, to make me feel like the laughter is genuine. If they think I am popular, I am popular; if they think I am nice and pretty or smart, I am nice and pretty or smart. You show me.

I pretend to put up a tough shell. When I hear a negative critique I fake diplomatic sincerity as if I'm capable of handling rejection. When I've lost all the right-sized top parts for my screwdriver I still manage to build my cheap furniture up all by myself, hang the pictures on the wall. *I did it myself.* I should be capable — I am. But I still don't truly know who I am without you. In fact, how you treat me determines how I act, who I will be for the day, how I will feel about myself after I take those consequential steps from alone at home to out and scrutinized in the big, bad world. My day-to-day life. Before my eating disorder and even much later when I was still struggling and in its grasp, you and your friends' influence over me was 100 percent. So I turned to anorexia. I knew that if I were to be the self that is informed by you, I would be, as I am now, all over the place. So I turned to anorexia — she told me who I was, how to be, how to feel, and it was easier as she was one instead of many. I could listen to her and the relevance of all the other many people and faces was quieted.

Today I hear many voices. I work hard on protecting and nurturing a solid core within myself, but I am easily swayed. If I smile at you and you don't smile back I might rethink my whole life plan.

The eating disorder was easier.

Child psychologists talk about many things that support how I feel about people's huge influence over me. Many would likely say that I have not properly grown into a fully functioning, emotionally competent adult. Perhaps my "lack of self" indicates that I am influenced more by the "group" than I am by my ego. Perhaps I am stuck forever in the "mirror stage," where people's reactions decide how I understand myself and how I behave in a given setting. Perhaps the child psychologists and their friends would say that when I am in a classroom, I play the role of the student, that when I am with my family I play the role of the daughter or the sister, that when I am with my friends I play the role of the friend — according to what they think that means and how I perceive it. Perhaps these people think that if a gang came up to me and wanted me to join, to put tattoos on my face, I would join split-second because I do what I am told in groups. The child psychologists would assume that I had a troubled upbringing, no real comfort or sense of security as a child, that my identity was spoilt before the age of seven, or at least twelve, and that I have no dependable, healthy foundation.

Yet I had a good childhood, my parents doing everything, or most everything, they could to help me grow both safely and happily. But I have to admit that my childhood wasn't perfect. *An eating disorder at thirteen.* How much more of a red flag do you need to know that something went wrong?

People suffering from anorexia feel a need to please that can feel innate, instinctual. It takes enormous effort for such a person to avoid her (or his) impulses and not do what the other person wants, not assume the role of the person that would best fit according to the other as they stand in line together, talk over dinner. We spend so much of our time pretending, playing with who we are so we can better please others. Over time, all this pretending leads to a real habit of foregoing yourself for other people's interpretation, based on other people's expectations.

It's instinctual — you are no longer sure of who you are, all you know, the only thing, is that you need to be perfect, *to please,* to be the person everyone else wants you to be. In time, wearing too many masks increases the odds of you losing yourself entirely. It becomes a habit, something hard to break, a habit of self that you can so easily learn to mistake or replace for who you really are.

You become loyal. You don't want to hurt anyone's feelings, so desperately needing to please in order to feel that boost in confidence, that so-close-to-truth-feeling sense of self that your interactions with others provide. And so you're loyal, simple as that. You do exactly what they tell you, and in doing so, you trade yourself in for the other person. Part of the trade happens because you trust the sense of self that you "receive" from the other person more than you do your own sense of self. The other part? You simply cannot be loyal to yourself and loyal to another person, let alone many other persons, at the same time. There is going to be something you have to trade, to swallow, to deny from yourself. A healthier person should be able to accommodate everyone without losing themselves in the process. But someone with an eating disorder can't do that. If they can't accommodate the other person, they cut away at themselves until they do.

Guess what this tendency means for eating disorders within the family? We lose ourselves, get rid of ourselves, replace ourselves — for you. Gone goes our impulse to reach out when we want to be comforted and need the touch of affection. Gone goes our ability to speak up when we no longer feel safe. Whatever it is that doesn't fit within the rules and ways of being standardized by our familial structure, gone. For instance, I'm not so good at doing a thousand things at once. I can juggle well when I have to but I much prefer to focus on a couple of things diligently rather than spread myself out too thin. However, my parents are entrepreneurial, hardworking, creative people. My parents think it's fun to do a lot of things all at once really well, and I agree, because I was raised to think like them, but the truth is I can't hold up. My brain gets stuffed. My heart flutters in a panic attack.[11] Yet, despite the shaking fingers and the eyes bugged out in stress, for much of my life, I felt as if I had to abide by my family's way of doing things. I felt I had to juggle all I could hold and more.

When I was ten I had to go, at 3:30 p.m., from school to extracurricular art class, singing class, girl scouts, piano, dance, swimming. I didn't tell my mother that everything was too much because I didn't know I had the option, and, it's true, I enjoyed everything I did and there's not much one can complain about when allowed to draw until the sun goes down. But the truth was it was too much for me. I often felt overwhelmed, like the world was spinning along at a rate too fast for my own, and while I wanted to dive in, because that's how my family works, once I dove it always felt like I was hitting my head against the rough surface. I was taking on too much.

Later on in high school I would do the same thing. I had swim team at 6:30 a.m. and I stayed in school for all the extracurriculars until 9 p.m. when I had to come home and study late into the night for my AP classes. I don't think I learned much in high school. I just *did* a lot.

My family is reasonable, understanding, and supportive. The one main thing I could have done to better my under-twenty life was speak up. Yet I never spoke up because that felt impossible — for people in the grip of eating disorders, speaking up feels like it's not an option at all.

---

11   My family does not agree with the above, in fact they say I have it all wrong: I'm the one who likes to juggle. Looking at my life, how I really live, that's pretty clear, yes, I like doing a lot of things at once. But looking at how I feel, well, that's a different story. I remember my first panic attack, the only real one I've ever had. My first finals freshman year, first few months in NYC, the snow piled so high on the ground that when you took your first steps your legs got iced to the knee. My heart started beating so fast I thought, surely, this is it. I called my mother, I cannot breathe. I called my doctor. She made me take my pulse over the phone, telling me where to put my hands on my wrist. It's too fast, I can't count! I had to wait 16 slowmo heartbeat hours to go to the nurse at my school. She prescribed a week's worth of Xanax. I swallowed the pills, finished my exams and have forever since been afraid of what I equate with winter — my death chill — the cold icing my knees, the inability to breathe, all the weight on my shoulders; when I feel the panic coming I tell myself, just breathe. Please stop talking. I'm going to have a heart att...

Of course I did the same thing with my friends. I was loyal to a fault. When the Hanson craze hit the states in the fourth grade, my friends fell in love and sang "MMMBop" for three consecutive years. I never liked Hanson, but my friends did, and so for three years I pretended that I liked them, *loved* them, too.

I suppose this fake band-worship seems like it's not a big deal, like it's part of adolescence. But a person with or at the risk of developing anorexia has an impossibly high sense of what is right and wrong in the world, an inescapable moral compass. When I was ten years old and pretended to like a boy band that I, in fact, couldn't stand, I felt, in the pit of my stomach, vile. I felt like I was doing something terribly, terribly wrong. Like I was deceiving people and lying to my friends, like I was selling bits and pieces of myself and, soon enough, what would I have left?

I wonder, when I was nine years old, could I have predicted what was to happen to me in just four years? I feel like I knew that something was coming. Like soon I would arrive at a fork in the road and I would have to decide between myself and other people. For most people, there is a negotiation; it is possible to maintain close friendships and relationships without sacrificing one's own desires, hopes, dreams, and identity, and yet, I felt I had to. I think I knew that my compulsion to sacrifice was distorted, but I couldn't verbalize it or understand it completely. I didn't know I would soon find relief from putting my fingers down my throat or that I would spend so many dinners turning my food into numbers and calculating my level of guilt. But I knew that something was wrong with me. There were too many gifts that I was born into and beautiful things that I had already experienced to not know, from a lack of full delight, that something was off inside.

Again, I did not develop an eating disorder and then get sick. I was sick and my eating disorder was my misguided attempt to fix myself. I think that you have to, you must, understand that in order to attempt to recover. You have to understand that you weren't fine before the eating disorder. Instead, you were probably dizzyingly trading in yourself for your selves according to the wants of others and you probably turned to the eating disorder in order to help you find balance again, to shut up all of those damn voices and listen to that little voice inside.

If I close my eyes today and listen, my little voice says it wants to be safe, to be comforted, to be held, and it says that I can find that comfort by being hyper-organized, by being in control, by looking both ways and backwards and never walking out the door. That's anorexia — and it's also my inner voice deep, deep inside. It makes it very hard, throughout one's life, to know whom to be loyal to, whom to trust, and it also makes it very easy to assume that the people to trust are the people closest to you, your family.

It's true that when I was in treatment I had no will to live for myself. It was my love and my loyalty to my family that helped me to fight. Eventually, as I fed my body and got closer to reality, I realized that I also had to fight for myself. But it was my loyalty to my family that was stronger at the time than was my loyalty to myself. I was able to funnel that to my advantage in treatment, but it's also part of the reason why I was sick in the first place. *You cannot take care of others before you take care of yourself.* We've heard that sentiment so much we think it doesn't matter, that it's irrelevantly juvenile. But as we back ourselves into a corner, we'll see it happening: conforming our personalities to meet the needs of others forces others to live in moments that are untrue and forces us to lie for simple, fictitious comfort. Personally, I wish my sister and mother nothing but the truth.

When you speak to people who have "recovered" from eating disorders, many report that their families were a big part of their illness and separating from their families helped them to get well. In some cases that might be true, but it's more like getting better happens when you learn to trust yourself, be yourself, love yourself and, moment by moment, manage to say *No* when your twisted instincts tell you to sell yourself to please. If you haven't learned to stay yourself while with others, than 800 miles separating you from those who might have helped enable your illness can't hurt, but that's like putting a nice throw over a stained couch. Eventually, the stains will reveal themselves, and it's not a lifelong solution — especially if you have that strong moral compass that makes your stomach sour when you don't act decently and truthfully.

You are loyal to your parents when you are a child. You learn to be disloyal and rebel in your teens and then, eventually they say, you accept yourself as you are; you understand yourself in relationship to others and you learn to not sacrifice yourself for the sake of others. People suffering from or at the risk of developing eating disorders have not learned to rebel in a way that doesn't injure the self, or in a way that truly expresses their hurt, and thus have not learned to forge their own individual adult identities; instead they are more like perpetual children, running scared from place to place trying to be loyal to this person, then this person, for the sake of survival. And when they "act out" with their eating disorders, it's not them acting out on their family or their friends. It is the manifestation of a lifetime of soul-selling habits accumulated into the final punch. Finally, the disloyalty they have punctured themselves with repeatedly, for the sake of being loyal to their families and those close to them, has caught up with them to the point that it is physically evident in their bodies and behavior. They are no longer just saying yes too much and smiling too much and saying, "Okay, sure" when they don't genuinely mean it. Now, they are killing themselves. In truth, that's what they have been doing all along, long before the calorie restricting, long before the over-exercising, long before the time spent over the toilet in the 24-hour fast food chain.

I understand, *you didn't mean to do it to me!* But, since your expectations of who I am supposed to be around you are so rigid that I couldn't, and you could never, see who I really am, then didn't you really intend for it to happen? Was it less literal?

The me you wish I was.

You didn't mean for it to happen, did you?

· · ·

Portrait of an Anorexic Family:

Perfect. No screw-ups or arguing, these families are high achieving, with clean homes, coiffed and combed hair, kids that take out the trash, do their chores, go to sleep on schedule, wake up on schedule, achieve, excel, accomplish, and win, *just like their parents!* To an outsider, this family is perfect-perfect. Perfect, like a fine-tuned machine that does everything you want it to do, wins all the awards, as timely and quietly as possible. Perfect, like the things you could have been, would have been, should have been, if only you were born as one of Them. If you ask one of these lucky types what it's like to be a part of their circle, they report: "We're great," "Everything is fine," "It's perfect."

I should know. Before my eating disorder and the colossal family divides and heartache that followed, I was one of them. We were perfect. My mom was high-achieving, beautiful, smart, and accomplished. She decorated our house like an in-demand interior designer; drove us around like a full-time chauffeur; fed us like an organic chef; clothed us in things with frills that scratched at the collar like a haute couture devotee; took care of our colds and flus like a registered nurse; handled our trips and falls like an emergency room doc; planned our family fun like an event planner; handled our Family Christmas Cards like a big-time PR rep; and made sure we were *here*, then *there*, perfectly and on time.

My dad fulfilled (I think) his fatherly requirements — albeit with no dependable clockwork. He told great stories, his tummy a soft pillow to read and sleep on, and on a summer beach vacation he showed me the stars and the many galaxies, mapping the solar system out with a flashlight so I could follow. He taught me how to ride a bike, how to ski, how to throw a softball (though I wouldn't pick me for your team). He taught me about cherry pie and how, at a fair, you can lose all your money, and that's okay, as long as you come home with a big, hairy toy bear just like the one he didn't get when he was your age, after running out of the little money he had with no win in sight.

And my sister and I, we also fulfilled our daughterly requirements. But here is the kicker: My parents were new-agey, smart, and conscientious. So my sister and I didn't just play with dolls, we also climbed trees, played with largely gender-neutral toys. We were raised to be polite, but we were also encouraged to voice our individual opinions. We ate dinner every night as a family where we were, again, encouraged to speak up independently. We were tucked into bed at 9, but we weren't scolded if we couldn't sleep and if we wanted to read another chapter aloud in bed we could. Even when my sister decided that the violin was not for her, she was allowed to quit and discover singing. But we did follow one family requirement: we achieved. It wasn't like our parents told us that we had to — they never would — and it wasn't even like our school or respective society ever told us, explicitly, to achieve. Rather, it was just something in the air, a given. We had to achieve, and it didn't matter that no one told us, we just knew. Our parents achieved, the people around us achieved, the people celebrated in the magazines achieved, so, of course, we had to achieve as well. Whatever our new-agey parents and our Montessori-education turned us on to — dance, swimming, summer reading lists — we understood the message behind it all: excel, compete, win. Do your "personal best," and then multiply it by three.

Some therapists will say that the problem with the perfect family is that it carries with it an undercurrent of coldness or don't-come-too-close sentiments. I don't particularly relate because, prior to developing an eating disorder, my family was warm and loving. I felt protected. I felt free to be my own individual. I didn't have to like something just because my parents did. But I heard the family lullaby. *Keep on pushing, keep on fighting, reach for more, keep going, do more, do better.*

It was the family mantra, *do better, do more.* We never spoke it aloud, and maybe that's why it grew so powerful. Like the forbidden chest you cannot open, *do better, do more*, grew more powerful each night we failed to see it.

Even "good" (as in supportive and non-destructive) families are privy to the high-expectation buzz; it's arguably unavoidable if you want to participate in our world and actually Be Somebody. But the cold families do exist, I saw them in the hospital. When such families would openly question their part in their son or daughter's illness, I wanted to scream, *"Really?!"* Really, you don't know how your absentee parenting, how your unreachable academic, athletic, and beauty ideals hurt your kid? Really, you think you are untouchable, that you did absolutely nothing wrong?

If you deny your child the appropriate support and nurturing that she or he needs, or over-control them in an effort to squash your own self-doubts, then the kid can easily grow up hungry for love, an addict to artificial comforts such as eating disorder behaviors. Desperate for the attention and recognition they never got, the kid can become disillusioned into thinking that they will find such appreciation if only they were more disciplined, more unlike the whole person that he or she should have been allowed to grow into. It doesn't take much smarts to figure it out. You just have to be open to the fact that you might not be perfect. That your family might not be perfect. That you might actually have to change some things in order to move forward.

One could say the Portrait of a Bulimic Family is the opposite, but that is an overgeneralization, especially considering how common it is for a person with an eating disorder to play musical chairs between the two.

While a person who first develops anorexia stereotypically comes from a perfect family that, either warm or cold, overly values achievement, a person who first develops bulimia stereotypically comes from a family that is disorganized and emotionally confusing; while the anorexic family often sends one distinct message (*succeed!*), the bulimic family often sends many mixed messages: be thin/eat cake, love to learn/hate to read, laugh and play/shut up this minute. Someone who develops bulimia typically grew up in an environment where they didn't know what was going to happen next and, instead of hyper-rigidity, they suffered from a lack of structure and the sense of security that a more steady sense of schedule and direction helps to create. Perhaps their parents were never home or perhaps their parents had intensely conflicting aspirations — one minute up, the next minute to the right... their actions or inactions caused a sense of being at sea, of being a paper-thin sheet away from out of control.

Often, the bulimics I knew would confide in me and say that, growing up, they felt like whatever they did was not good enough.[12] I would tell them how lucky they were, how growing up, I felt like everything I did was just a good first step, like I always had that mountain ahead of me to overcome, and like whatever I did, even if it was good enough for everyone else, even for my high-standard parents and friends, was never good enough for me. In actuality, I don't think that either way of thinking is better, or particularly distinct, and I don't think bulimics are lucky.

The one thing that, generally, the bulimic has that the anorexic does not is a multitude of ways to act out. From doing drugs, to stealing food, to plain old binging and purging, the bulimic can feel like the things she or he does are acts of revolution, methods of breaking their suffocating position and expressing their deep understanding and experience of the chaotic. What the anorexic has that the bulimic does not is societal approval. It is cool to be disciplined, cool to have such a tight control of yourself that you look pre-pubescent and at the risk of passing out. For a time the anorexic can take pride in themselves over other people, especially the bulimic, but eventually she or he must realize that all eating disorders are just a form of numbing-out, of using food or lack thereof as a narcotic, a noise-eliminator, a muzzle. And

---

12   Not being good enough is different from the anorexic's haunt. The anorexic is good enough, she just has so much more ahead of her to accomplish whereas the bulimic's not good enough = why even try?

if they stay sick long enough, there is a great chance that the anorexic will swing to the bulimic side and vice versa — it's just too hard to stay at one extreme for so long without needing to jump to the other end, to wave goodbye to the one person that you've truly understood and disobey who you thought you were.

Even today, after everything I learned and suffered through, I still take pride in the fact that I was an anorexic first and that I came from a perfect family, first. I won't admit it readily, but it's true: I am proud of the fact that I was once a practicing anorexic and embarrassed by the fact that I was once a practicing bulimic. I will much more readily tell you that I "used to be" an anorexic. But a bulimic? An over-exerciser? Maybe one day I'll quietly admit that I used to put my right index finger down my throat, that the hours blurred into years. But I would never admit that I also used to chew and spit powdered sugar donuts and take so many laxatives that I had to frequent different drugstores for fear of worrying the cashier. I told you now, I know, and I am already so embarrassed. I want to ask you to please not judge me. Instead, remember that I used to worry, before I was dirtied by bulimia, about whether or not I should include the 5 calories in a stick of gum in my daily calorie allotment (*sure you burn them while you chew but should that really count?*). Instead, remember that I used to run for so many hours on end that I still can't look at a person jogging without flashbacks of needing more, more, and memories of how I am not enough.

The fact that I value my supposedly "perfect" family (and the anorexic outcome) over the stereotypically all-over-the-place bulimic family can seem like a class issue and to some extent it is. Yet the numbers don't say that a rich family may lead to anorexia while a middle or lower class family may lead to bulimia. Instead, I think, it slides into the theoretical. A family that values excellence above all else should be, theoretically, economically privileged, while a family lacking structure and emotional consistency must be, theoretically, economically disadvantaged.[13] That's what our system tells us, and it's part of the reason why it is cooler to be an anorexic than it is to be bulimic or — to speak of the unmentionables — an EDNOS or overeater.

The truth is there is no such thing as "one" family — a family cannot be merely structured around the need for perfection, or emotional control, or emotional unrest, the need for a sense of liberation. Rather, all families vary according to whom you talk to. The mother thinks one thing, the father (or other mom/two dads/what have you) thinks another. The oldest thinks one thing, the middle another, and the youngest something else entirely. Part of the varying perspective is due to your position within the family and the different perspectives and roles available to you. Another bit is that people are simply different and the fact doesn't change once you get down to the workings of the family. For instance, when researchers question women with a history of bulimia about their upbringing, such women often report more familial coldness and overprotective mothers than do their healthier sisters. Such women also tend to be more nervous and have less confidence than their sisters, "By nature."

Sometimes who the child is, by nature, meshes with his or her larger family structure, as in a child who loves the dramatic and the over-the-top, who feels welcomed and understood by her or his like-minded family. This kid can easily join the family tribe. But what if next comes a child who is insecure and shy, one that favors calm surroundings? Now the family won't mesh as well and the child, by nature, will feel some level of unease. Perhaps the kid will try to deny her or his natural temperament

---

13   *I KNOW.* Gross sentence.

in order to fit in better with the family and perhaps this method will work, for a bit, until the teenage years hit and the temptation to live out one's own path becomes more undeniable. What then? Then the obvious temperamental breaks between the members of the family are brought to light. Then, it is time to decide: do we fix this? Will we learn to respect the separate members of our family, somehow finding a way to work together? Do we accept that our setup is not working? That, in order to go on as a family, we must actually become a family?

More importantly: how are you getting in the way? Problems follow when you don't walk your talk — that's a big one. I know plenty of screwed-up young women who say their mothers did nothing but encourage them to be everything they could be, do whatever they wanted to do, ask for what they wanted, and take it if no one acted quick enough. But almost all of these same mothers didn't follow what they preached; instead, it was more like they were saying, *"Please do this because I couldn't, my generation couldn't, I wouldn't know how."*

I have friends who were taught to love to learn and think big and who were given the greatest gifts of education but then, once they aged a bit more, were advised by those same mothers not to take a "real job" because juggling work and kids is impossible. I have friends whose mothers taught them that they were beautiful no matter the narrow societal beauty ideal, that "the inside" was more important and then, once they aged a bit more, were offered a singular love through sparkly clothes and plastic surgery graduation gifts by those same mothers. I have friends who were taught to love healthy foods and the occasional treat, to love to move and be active and to live a healthy lifestyle but then, once they aged a bit more, grew up to the fact that the instructions of moderation came from militant discipline and that going to the gym and eating like a bird were really worshipped principles that their mothers subscribed to out of fear. I have friends whose mothers taught them how to throw up after "accidentally" eating too much — a beauty trick, they said.

There is something to be said for being at the absolute pinnacle and still having shit-out-of-luck problems.

An eating disorder is a call for help and the person with an eating disorder (the victim) is the messenger to the family (and her world at large). She says, *I am sick, we are sick, we are killing me.* You have to listen if you want her to live. You have to wake up to the fact that you can't be a shitty mother (or father) without consequences and that just because your life sucks doesn't mean your daughter's has to.

It is far past time for mothers in this glitter-world to blow off their ways of always being smaller.

Time to admit that our self-obsessed memory foam bubbles aren't helping.

Every anorexic has a mother, every obsessive-dieter has a mother, every overeater has a mother — even a memory of a mother, an idea of a mother, an absence of a mother so great she exists in every particle. I had a mother. Did you?

4/11/12

Dear friends,

I overheard, actually I was told, by someone my own age, someone who used to be my friend, someone who was in school with me way back when, someone who wrote and participated in the contest during that seventh-grade school camp-out, someone who wrote in my name, today I heard them say, "that doesn't matter."

In fact, to put it in quotes, the person (a he), said: "that's absolutely childish. Boys will be boys. That is not traumatic. Btw I know I listed you as the hottest."

To him, I would like to say: fuck you.

My hurt is not yours.

Thank you, friends, for listening.

14

INTENSIVE OUTPATIENT

January 18, 2002

In the hospital they try to scare you to change by talking about death.

They say, as it's true, that eating disorders have the highest mortality rate of *any* mental illness. Can you imagine? All those crazy people — the bipolars, the schizophrenics, the sociopaths, the many-identitied — and my kind drop to the floor first. Of course I know that when they say "eating disorders," when they say *death*, that they are talking about anorexia. To me, they say that studies show that at least 5 to 10 percent of anorexics die within 10 years of "contracting" the disease, that at least 18 to 20 percent of anorexics die after 20 years and that only 30 to 40 percent ever really recover. To me, they also say that *at least* another 20 percent of people suffering from anorexia will prematurely die from complications related to their eating disorder, often heart problems, even suicide.

Am I scared?

Do you know how hard it is to look at someone so close to death, so wholly and entirely consumed by anorexia? Do you know how hard it is to look at their bones — that's all they have left — to see the sunken skin, to see them, really, disappear as they turn to the side? Do you know how hard it is to walk and talk and think when you yourself are so close to death by anorexia? How impossible, how absolutely impossible, living any longer can feel and still how soft that fire is, that small want to live, and the fear that the fire will be blown out, will disappear?

That's my answer. *I know.*

Anorexia is death, I don't need anyone to tell me. I see it in the other girls. I feel it in myself, in my disappearing will. Five days before Christmas and my parents are told that I might not survive the night, say *goodbye, Jordan*, say *goodbye.*

When you're so close to death the world slows down to milliseconds and the greatest pain, the greatest pain, is knowing, somewhere, that the strength to live a few days more is there, and still knowing even worse that you can't find it, that you can barely walk, can barely talk. To form a sentence is impossible, to ask for help — it's past that too.

I know that I am dying. What I want to know is, will it stop? Can I?

If I close my eyes maybe I can fall fast asleep. A release from hurt, a soft pillow to lie down on, covers to pull over my head, that's what I want. An extreme, an ultimate, the most thorough package. My very own death.

I am sorry that I am just thirteen and ready to go.

What I want to know is, did I do this to myself?

I know that life isn't so easy for some people. That for some people death can come most naturally. But I also know that I never asked for this. I don't want my will blown out like a birthday candle and just because I can't find the strength to find it, to protect it, to understand it, doesn't mean it's all my fault.

Because I am fragile right now, because I am, in fact, becoming death, you can't tell me what you really think. If my feelings are hurt just one bit more, I might break. Even if they aren't hurt, I am, I might. And I'm not, we're not, she's not.

My mom. My mom is not ready for me to die. That, I know. That, I can depend on. That, it keeps me from doing what I think I might want to do, it keeps me from doing what I don't quite want to do, it keeps me, here. Here for now, I can promise that when we speak in milliseconds.

One Mississippi, two Mississippi, three.

I love you and you love me, and that, I know, is how it should be.

In my Treatment Team meeting, every Friday, I sit with Dr. Kay and two other doctors. I tell them, every Friday, that I would like a sip of Diet Coke. And salt, and pepper, especially salt.[14] I tell them that I have been good, that every day, every meal and snack, I have "met all of my calories." I have. And I try to convince

---

14   Salt, pepper, and diet drinks are disallowed, forgotten privileges. Salt because of water weight, heart palpitations, and electrolyte imbalances. Pepper primarily because anorectics tend to abuse it — as a calorie-free flavoring agent. Sprinkle it on, nay, totally swamp the food with black pepper dust. Looking at the nutritional label and seeing "zero," you can't understand how awesome that is for an anorectic. You have to check the label multiple times to make sure you're not dreaming. Diet drinks, of course, are the drink of choice.

them that I should, in fact, start practicing my life in the "outside world" while I'm still inside. The Diet Coke, the salt, the pepper. At this point they remind me that they are still increasing my calories, every day they go up and up. They start the calories, low, on the first day, so that I don't have a heart attack. Then they gradually increase, by 200, 100, 300, each day a higher number until I come to "a stable weight gain" that lets me meet my "stable healthy weight." They show me on the chart where I should be, they say that it is a range, it can go up and down give or take a few pounds, maybe five, but that that's where I need to be. I am not even close.

Sometimes when the less experienced nurses walk by me as we count our calories before our meals and snacks, I like to sneak a peek at the other girl's caloric needs. I am amazed when it is so high, jealous when it is so low. *"Why are they making me gain so much weight?"*

The first week, actually, I lost weight. My metabolism got a boost from the higher calories so I lost and everyone got scared — even though this is very common, predictable even, my parents were told it would happen. At my Treatment Team meeting they blamed me — it must have been my fault. Exercising? Purging? Hiding my food? No. All the same they made me stay at Level 1, I couldn't leave during Rec Therapy when the other kids could. They got to go outside, to play at the swings, to soak up the last rays of the sun while I sat with my nurse inside the confines of the psych ward, at the wrong end of the exit signs.

Once I apologized to Andrea. I told her, "I'm sorry I'm still at Level 1 and you are stuck with me."

At the Treatment Team meetings on Friday I tell Dr. Kay that I am trying hard, working hard, not to listen to myself and to Recover. I tell her that it is hard, so impossibly hard, yet I want to get better. I do.

Dr. Kay tells me, while the other two bosses of my team nod, that I can go up to Level 2 and that even still I cannot have any Diet Coke or salt or pepper. In my mind they become huge monsters, chewing flesh and bones, burping out to me: *gain, gain, gain.* Of course that's what they want me to do, both in the real and the imaginary, inside and out.

I take out a piece of paper that I made especially for this day with Sarah. She helped me practice my speech. On the paper it has a list of pros and cons as to why I should or should not get to drink a sip of Diet Coke. Also, on the paper, it has a light bulb of an idea, Sarah's: that I should get to drink a sip of Diet Coke with my family, on New Year's, as a gift for doing well, for gaining, for "meeting all of my calories."

I read the paper:

Jordan's Diet Soda Proposal

Pros:

- *Calorie free*
- *Carbonation settles an upset (and too full!) stomach*
- *Tastes good*
- *I have and will promise to continue making my calories*
- *Water is not so easy to drink in 16 oz.*
- *Food is more enjoyable with a diet soda*
- *I'm working very hard*
- *It will help me to learn how to, in a hospital, drink "the drink" in a normal amount*

Cons:

· *I might get full from soda (if this happens I promise to still eat my calories plus the carbonation will settle my stomach)*

And they agree. They agree! Like magic, just this one time they agree with me, and yet the memory lasts forever, it does. They say that I can have a sip of Diet Coke, one ounce to be exact, on New Year's Eve with my family during visitation hours on a couple of conditions. First, replace the words "Coke" with "Sprite" — no caffeine, better for the heart. Second, we must wait on the actual day, just minutes before, to know for sure — Head Nurse June must give the go ahead based on how I've been doing, by the minute. Third, I cannot ask for any more diet drinks after that. Also, I can't have pepper, and especially I can't have salt.

I'm not used to Treatment Team meetings going well and getting what I want. Even before my first I knew the bad prospects as the other patients had told me. So this one went well, yes, and I'm grateful. But the next one doesn't, that's the truth.

Later on in my treatment, my Treatment Team will give me the privilege of having cream cheese as a condiment whenever I need an extra 30 calories to fit my meal plan and two saltine crackers (25 calories) just won't do. So what do I do? It just so happens that the cream cheese they serve in the hospital is nonfat and has seven grams of protein per serving![15] Seven grams! It also just so happens that before the hospital, when I got sick, I Abused protein. Previously a vegetarian, today a vegan, I read in the nutrition books when I was thirteen that everyone needs protein and so I listened, eating more protein, even meat. The number of what I needed in terms of grams of protein grew in my head until every day I was counting calories as well as grams

15   Yeah, that's a lot of protein per packet. Mind you, they were big packets.

of protein, both of them equally important and non-negotiable. When I got into the hospital, one of the scariest things, besides the upped calories, besides the inability to exercise, was the complete lack of sufficient amounts of protein in the hospital's food items — according to me. I talked to the nutritionists assigned to me, *"But maybe some people need more protein than others, and maybe I'm one of those people!"* They upped my calories, they didn't let me exercise, but in my head all of this could be made just a little bit better if I was allowed to get even a little more close to my preferred daily grams of protein. Before the cream cheese, that wasn't possible. I'd count the grams of protein up, secretly, in my head and it wasn't even close. Of course I had my fair share of pointless calories like white bread and crackers, and I'm sure butter was slathered all over the meats and veggies, I'm sure, and we weren't even accounting for them, but I didn't have enough protein, not my *enough*, and this was most important.

Sometimes I'd tell Sarah, "I keep counting the grams of protein I've eaten today and I can't stop." Sarah would try to help me with distractions. She would remind me that I didn't need to count protein grams like I did, that it wasn't healthy, and I would try to listen to her. But still, the need, my protein. Before the cream cheese that need wasn't met and then it was! Like that! Immediately, I started Abusing the privilege. The first day I had three cream cheese substitutions, the next day five, the next I even substituted an apple with two servings of cream cheese and one half square of graham crackers. Can you imagine? I abused the cream cheese protein for a whole weekend, Friday, Saturday, and Sunday.

Then Monday came. Bam! Boom! Trouble! The poor little patient girl cannot be trusted, cannot have privileges. The poor little patient girl must be very, very bad. They say it all the time:

She must not want to get well.

That was the end of nonfat cream cheese substations for me. In fact, that was also pretty much the last time I counted grams of protein in my head. I knew it was too heart-crushing in the hospital with my meal plans so controlled, and by the time I got out I sincerely didn't want to count protein anymore — calories, sure, but protein was (almost completely) out. And I'm happy to report that today my vegan self couldn't care less about overeating protein, and so miracles really do happen when you're not looking.

I tell Head Nurse June that I'm tired of being held like I have cancer. What does that mean? When people hug me they lightly pat me as if my shoulders are sticky, as if I could break, as if I'm infectious... I'm tired of that. Head Nurse June tells me, "Shake it off, Jordan, shake it off." She demonstrates what shaking it off looks like — like a person having a seizure while standing upright. I laugh, ask her for another. Head Nurse June hugs me tight, like she's not afraid of me, and her warmth is so great, her body so soft to the touch, I feel better. A few hours later I'll ask her for another hug, then another.

Why do I do this? Because when you're in the hospital over the holidays and there is no "school in session," all you do, you'll find, is still. You'll find that stillness is sickness — not the reason why per se but the reason *how*, the reason *for what*. You stop so that you can find stillness, so that you can become stillness. And then of course you find yourself in treatment and still is all around you, mirroring you, reflecting you, calling out to you, still.

Hugs from Head Nurse June are the only thing I've found to wake me.

In Group Therapy we meet a new patient. She conveniently had her stomach pumped at the ER and soon after, they shipped her up to us. She says her stomach was pumped because she tried to kill herself and it did not work. As she talks, I think back to something a friend had told me when I was still in school and healthy. My friend said that girls survive suicide more often than boys because girls use things like pills and cutting whereas boys get what they want, they die, because they use guns and ropes and high places. I look at this new girl and I almost want to laugh, to slap my knees, *"You messed up, you took the pills! Wrong answer!"* It might not sound funny, to you, on the outside, but to me it is hilarious, to me it is life-supporting, finding the funny and the twisted and the should-be ironic in our pathetically everyday dark-quiet. *So you tried to kill yourself? So what, join the club.*

I don't think the new girl, Margaret, likes her name. Each time it is called out by one of the nurses, she flinches. Margaret, *flinch*, Margaret, *flinch*, like clockwork. Margaret says it hurts when your stomach gets pumped, she says it feels like hell, like the worst possible thing, and she had no idea it would. The next time, when Margaret tries to kill herself again, if she does, you can see it won't be by pills.

We smile at Margaret the Suicidal and say, "It will get better." She's older than most of us, in high school already, and as we console her, I feel like she is here as some sort of warning, *"You should see what high school is like."* I feel like as we comfort her she should, really, be instead warning us.

In the hospital I've learned that I won't like high school, that it can get so much worse than what I've already experienced.

I know, I must know, that what I have experienced so far is not that bad. Padded school life, secretly off-kilter family life, high expectations for future. Nothing too tragic here. Yet as far as I can remember, I always thought that life was close to torture.

It can get worse. The hospital taught me that. That, outside of all the dumbed down preaching, the *just one day at a times*, and the *first take care of yourselfs*, that things can get worse, so much worse than what I've already experienced. I knew that before the hospital, but the hospital confirmed my doubts. These are called Unintended Psych Ward Preparations for the Outside World. When things got worse, I knew they would.

Here's what I'd like to know: If I wasn't prepared for such bad things to happen then would they still have happened?

At least in the hospital they put a mirror up to my quiet and I saw my pain, I saw my future pain, and I accepted it. *High school will be bad, got it. Check plus.*

I promise I am not obsessed with words: the stillness, the quiet, the cold, to remember, to sleep. The soft covers to pull over my head. What I am is a little girl, even when I am all grown up, that's still who I am inside, how I feel. I am scared. I am timid. I am alone. No matter what you do to make me feel more safe or secure, it will not work. I perceive you as so much bigger, always looking down on me. I'm never enough. Insufficient, immature, incapable, self-obsessed, self-focused.

I am not you. In fact, I am much less than you.

I should be in charge of my own agency, my own destiny. I should be able to choose how to take care of me. I should know what's best for me.

But little girls don't take care of themselves — though we can pretend.

I just wish you knew, when I say leave me alone, what I really mean is come closer.

Group is finished and everyone walks out of the room with our new suicidal in tow. I wait four seconds, that's all, and Sarah comes to wheel me out too. Time for our afternoon snack. I have an apple, two two-cracker packets of saltine crackers, a small carton of milk (eight ounces), two sheets of honey-flavored graham crackers, and one serving of string cheese. The graham crackers taste good, they crumble as you bite and melt in your mouth. All I want to do is open up the carton of milk so it becomes a glass of milk and dunk the graham crackers into the milk, let them get soggy like milk and cookies do, every particle of food expanded and dissolving into the liquid.

When I was little I would do that at my grandmother's house. She would bring my sister and me lemonade and graham crackers as a snack and we'd dunk the graham crackers into the lemonade and eat the sugary, lemony, crumbly goodness. It's comforting, and it tastes good. Yet I can't will myself to do it. One of the other girls — she's been in treatment twice at this hospital alone already and she's my age — does it: She opens the milk carton and dunks her bread in the transformed milk cup — *her bread!* She dunks her white bread in the milk, and I can't even do that with my graham crackers. If someone from the DSM-IV[16] was here, I'm sure they'd say milk and submerged bread is "distorted," milk and submerged graham crackers is "normal." I know this, but I can't take the leap.

It's not that people are watching, it's that it feels improper and I, if anything, am buttoned up. Polite. *Do not what you want to do.*

---

16   The Diagnostic and Statistical Manual of Mental Disorders — it's the bible of the psych religious.

It's sad, really.

When afternoon snack is finished — everyone met their calories — we go to the main hall where we have morning meeting to play a game. Games are a big deal in the hospital, and we play them all the time. They are called distractions. We take the sad and the ugly and we turn them upside down, willing ourselves to laugh or even play. When I first got here I thought that was stupid, distorted, even. I thought all of the distractions were a harmful displacement of true emotions, a stupid filter. I thought, as they say in the hospital, that you can only fill a bin with your trash — your true emotions — for so long before the trash starts to overflow. I still think that but the distractions and games are close to fun and so, eventually, I start to willingly partake. To laugh, to try to play. During our meals and snacks we also play games, almost every time, and if someone is having a particularly hard day finishing all of their calories, or if someone is new, than we play even harder.

The games we play during meals usually have to do with alphabets. The game we play the most starts with one person saying the name of a movie that begins with the letter "a" and then the next person at the table, fast, has to name an actor that played in the movie and then the next person, fast, has to name a movie that begins with the next alphabet letter from the celebrity's first name. So, for instance, Renee Zellweger is followed by *Saving Private Ryan*. However, I should warn you, I am bad with these games because I don't really know the guidelines. I didn't listen when they told me at first and then, as the week went on and I came to more, the time had passed for me to ask for help and I just had to play along as if I already knew.

Today we play charades. We've never played the game

before, but I suppose everyone is bored of the usual so we have to incorporate games more outside of the box. The nurses warn the eating disordered to not move around so much when it's our turn, *no exercising*, and we begin. Al is called up first and she acts goofy and everyone laughs. She sits down and Jessie is called up, he acts goofy and everyone laughs. He sits down. My name is called. I stand up. I walk to the spot in the center where we are supposed to, and I start playing the game — everyone is staring at me. Why? *On no! Oh my!* I stood up, me! I stood up and walked, on my own free will, completely forgetting for that brief moment that I was sick and dying and stuck to my wheelchair. Everyone looks at me, wondering, *will it happen? Will her heart give out? Now?*

Still is a synonym for quiet and calm. These words sound sedentary, tranquil. The truth is they are the opposite. Not even the quiet before the storm, the stillness, the quiet, the calm, is chaos. It is dark and forbidden. What should be up is down, what should be down zooms left and right. You close your eyes and you see your head is stuck in some dark coffin, crashing to break the surface — not for breath, not to stay alive, but to test out death as far as you can take it.

Define happy. Define torture.

· · ·

In my memory nobody is in the hospital on New Year's Eve besides me and Al and the one male nurse with the most gentle-looking wrinkles around his eyes and the cool dreadlocks that fall an inch past his shoulders. It couldn't have been this way, really. It must have been more like: Al and I are the only ones with the combined privilege and age allowed to stay up until nine while all the other kids must go to their rooms to sleep. But in my memory, it's just me, Al, and the dreadlocks. The halls quiet, all spaces deserted.

I feel sad, lost, and forgotten and I know Al feels the same. No matter how much I don't like Al, or no matter how much I'm supposed to not like Al, I do feel connected to her since we had intake at just about the same time. Even though we both feel sad, lost, and forgotten, we have to put on our respective faces, pretend, fake happiness and a general interest in the everyday in order to not ruin the other person's New Year's Eve.

You must think, for me, that the New Year is symbolic in some sort of way. I could approach it as a turning point, a fresh start, a bookend to close the darkest chapter. Refresh. Start over. Instead the heartbreak from Christmas in the hospital, the mass quiet, the sheer awareness that life is not worth it, that living is too painful, that things will always get worse, has made me completely devoid of optimism, of seeing the brighter side. It's simply another day.

We play bingo and the clock ticks on, slowly, patiently. All we have is time to fill, great gaps of time with nothing to do but think — something we don't like or want to do, something we, in fact, shouldn't do. Think about how we got here and what we will do to Change, maybe. But nobody thinks of that. Instead we think of how we can get out, of what we would do if we could, if there were no cameras watching. We think of our Disorders, how much we cherish them, how they fill the space. We think of how there used to be a great need, the elephant in the room, how the disorder came in and, for us, the needs were met, all problems solved.

Time passes on and then Al has it, she holds it in her hands. "Bingo!" The nurse smiles, he is a nice guy with looks both cool and kind. Forever smiling, he hands Al her prize, a slightly larger than travel sized bottle of purple sparkly body wash. Al says thank you and smiles. Al clicks open the top cap and smells the body wash and then lets me smell it too. It smells synthetic, with a dash of vanilla. But it makes Al happy and so it makes me happy too. Happiness, sadness, great big laughs that help you shake it off, cries of terror or rage — that's all contagious here.

In the hospital there is so little to look forward to, so little to take comfort in, so little to call your own that material treasures take on their own life. They become *mine*, mine in a sense that we never had before. Mine in a sense that, even when you have nothing, you still have the Get Well cards and the flowers, you still have the ChapSticks and the sweaters. Our old neighbor sent me a pair of pajamas with hearts on them, and I love those pajamas, every time I put them on, I smile. *Mine*. The old neighbor also sent me a card, the card said those typical trite and meaningless things: *You can do it. We love you. We're thinking of you. Pray.*

I smile at Al, she smiles at me, and the nice guy nurse hands me a slightly larger than travel sized purple sparkly synthetic body wash, too. Everyone's a winner.

So that's one memory from New Year's Eve. I also have another. I know that both memories are true, that they both happened, because they are both stuck in my brain, the stuff I can't forget. What I can't explain is how they both happened the same night. The two memories are completely distinct, existing in their own singular space and time, and they contradict, they can't exist together. But they do. I am all alone; I am with my family.

I am with my family. My mom, my dad, my younger sister with her big chocolate-brown eyes. Sitting together I am allowed to drink one ounce of Diet Sprite, just one sip. Head Nurse June gave the A-okay, I am a good patient girl. Sarah measures one ounce exactly in four different cups. When the clock strikes, I don't remember the time, I just remember that it did strike and that we were waiting for it to strike, we were expecting it, we counted down, and that when it did strike we all drank our one-ounce exactly.

I remember I close my eyes when I take the sip and, not wanting the Diet Sprite to leave my taste so quickly, I swish it around in my mouth slowly, relishing the little bubbles tickling my tongue and swooshing around. When I open my eyes everyone is staring at me. I am supposed to swallow. But what if I don't want to? That doesn't matter, it's distorted not to swallow, distorted to be so obsessed with diet drinks, to need them to the extent that I do, the best part of the day. I look at my family, the tears in my eyes. I swallow to say I'm sorry.

I'm sorry for you because I am distorted, because I am not who I am supposed to be.

I'm sorry for me because even when I know what I want to do, I can't.

My mother's birthday is coming up in just a few days and I am sad for her because I am in the hospital and so that makes me a bad daughter and her birthday a bad birthday. Head Nurse June tells me to draw what I am feeling. She knows that I like to draw; I always have my sketchpad with me, and she thinks that I must be working through my feelings when I draw because there are always tears in my eyes once I am finished. Sometimes I feel like drawing is all I do in the hospital, since school still isn't "in session." I tell Head Nurse June I'm tired of drawing; she suggests I take out my journal, the one my mom left for me my first night wherein I wrote, "I will get better." At this point I say, always, no thanks, and get out my sketchpad instead. To me, journaling is dorky and self-indulgent. And the fact of the matter is I need to get out of my head, not further in.

I start drawing a robin — it's my favorite kind of bird. I draw its beak, I outline where its two little feet will rest on the page, on a twig.

When I was little my sister and I used to stay over at our grandparents' house on Fridays and sometimes we would visit my grandmother's best friend, she lived just two doors down on the same street, on the same side. At her friend's house it seemed like there was always a rotating showcase of fine porcelain dishes, crystal cut candy jars, and Madame Alexander dolls. My favorite thing of hers was a porcelain dish with robins hand-drawn in the center. My mother, it turns out, drew it when she was sixteen.

Head Nurse June thinks I work through my feelings when I draw but I know better: I'm silencing them.

On my mom's birthday, January 5th, I don't remember anything significant. I just remember that Jessie helped me draw a big sign for my mom on green cardboard paper that read, "Happy Birthday, Mom," and that for all of the visiting hour time, Jessie referred to my mom as, simply, "mom," and I remember that that freaked my mom out.

The next day, on the 6th, my vitals improve and I'm allowed out of my wheelchair and two days later, it's my birthday. Isn't that funny how close my birthday is to my mom's?

Like I need one more reminder that I am my mother.

You would think I would remember my birthday, but I don't. You would also think I would remember getting out of my wheelchair, but I don't. Now that the wheelchair is gone I understand how much I liked being pushed here and there, taken care of, a special emergency patient. I understand how nice the two soft pillows were that I had to keep underneath me to sit on because my butt is so bony that it hurts to sit. I liked the way I kept my sketchpad and pencils underneath the wheelchair, and I liked the two little legs at the bottom where I could rest my feet. I liked everything about the wheelchair, you could say, except when we had an hour or two to spare and the nurses took us outside of the ward, on the other side of the exit signs, and we had to go in the elevators to go to a different floor, and in my wheelchair I would never fit with the other "psych patients." And we had to walk by all the other non-psych patients and I had to lower my head, apologizing, *I am not like you.* And when one of the nurses would accidentally bump my feet into the wall, bruising me, or when I'd forget to put my feet up on the foot rests before we started moving and my feet would get all dragged along the floor.

I guess you could say I didn't really like the wheelchair when I had it, but now?

I am sorry I'm not like you.

One afternoon while I'm waiting with the other eating disorders for Eating Disorder Group Therapy to start, Jessie walks over to me and hands me a present, a piece of yellow paper, the same kind that I used for my family's Christmas cards that I drew on Christmas Eve.

On the paper is a drawing of a single flower. A dandelion.

Jessie says, "For you."

I thank Jessie for my present and ask him how he is today.

Jessie looks at me, seriously, with eyes like the end of a sentence.

He says, "It is you."

Next Dr. Kay comes and Jessie is taken away from me. Hand-held, he never comes back.

15

TALKING BONES
Purge Binging

When you do it, it's never because you meant to.

Instead, you do it because it feels good. Because the world gets so loud everything starts to smell like hairspray, full of static and sticky chemicals. You do it because sometimes you just need to eat a whole family-sized bag of chips without thinking twice. Sometimes you just need to eat sour candies until your tongue hurts; until the chocolate evidence is smeared to the right of your chin; until too many cookie crumbs fall to the floor. Sometimes you just need to eat until you are so disgusted with yourself that all you care to do is fall asleep, erasing the past.

Sometimes it makes sense to use self-disgust as a gauge for when to stop. Self-disgust is past full, past satisfaction, flying to the breaking point.

Sometimes that feels good.

You eat until it hurts. You eat until you cry. You eat until it stops feeling really, really good and you have finally, for the moment, had enough. You eat until you are sick. Until the world stops moving round and round and you have found your cave. You eat to feel and to stop feeling, to listen to yourself and to hear nothing, to feed yourself the things you want and to allow yourself to enjoy and to say, *tomorrow*, tomorrow I will be good. Tomorrow I will start fresh and this will never happen again. This is a goodbye, a goodbye eat.

You don't eat out of desire. In fact, it often feels like you have nothing to do with it. Like there is a monster inhabiting your body asking for more and you are a mere vessel for appeasement. You had nothing to do with it. It was not a conscious decision. It was an inner need, an inner longing.

You can call it an addiction, but I think it's more like one's bones, talking. Your bones have had enough. They decide it's time to deconstruct. Time to take in so much and yet feel nothing.

Time to purge. Purging is the obvious step, the progression. It's like brushing your teeth: It's the final to-do, the bookend, and if you go to sleep without doing it you are going to feel really guilty. So you walk to the nearest restroom. Depending on where you are and how you purge, this restroom could be anywhere. It doesn't matter really. Just find something that you can use to hide the evidence as fast as possible, to clean yourself, to get all of the excess out of you so that you can feel pure again.

Because the binging makes you feel like you are in a tunnel, or a vacuum, and time stops and everything goes quiet and still, you also feel very slow. You walk to the restroom, you drive to the restroom, you stumble and crawl, whatever you can do, on autopilot. When you reach the toilet it can feel like a miracle. *Finally!* Finally I have found my personal solution, the tool to hide my indiscretions.

You lift the seat and you begin to question yourself. Your hands are already scabbing up from the tough friction against the back of your throat, the stomach acid making the tops of your hands even more red and inflamed. Your throat hurts just at the thought of one more time. Even though you are sick and you know you shouldn't do it, you can't help it. Your stomach is expanding like a balloon ready to burst. You are forgetful. You can't think clearly. Your throat is sore and your face is puffy. You promise yourself that this is the last time.

You lock the door and you purge. Out comes the calories, out comes the fat, out comes the grease and the butter and the things that troubled you before the binge. Out goes all the little bad things of the world and the big bad things and the medium-sized bad things. You are free. You are pure. Safe from the calories, safe from the bad thoughts.

And then, just as soon as they left, they come back. *You are scared. You are shit. You are nothing.*

You try to ignore the bad thoughts but they are impossible to ignore. You close your eyes, you go to sleep, you hide. You suppress and try to get by but eventually the bad spills out over the rim and onto your fingers. Eventually you come home and in the swift moment between turning the knob and opening the door, you know. It is time. Time to binge. Time to purge. Time to numb your thoughts through food and over-consumption, time to numb your guilt through purging, through evacuation and punishment. It's a cycle and both the binge and the purge feel like hell, like the worst thing you could possibly do with your time, and yet you keep up with the back and forth. Because as bad as the cycle feels, your everyday feels much, much worse. Your everyday is so bad that your bones take over and you binge, you purge, you cope as best as you can.

Caught dead, you're guilty. And hungry. Much too guilty and hungry.

You're tired, maybe even finished. Of course. Of course you want more.

16

SEX & THE LITTLE GIRL
To Body War

We restrict because we're ashamed. We restrict because we're scared. We restrict because we know what's going to happen to our bodies, and we want it to stop. We restrict because the world is so great, we feel so small, and we know everything is topsy-turvy and we want to feel secure. We starve because we have to. And when we still the outer world our inside world can quiet. We can find peace, find that singular thing to hold onto, nothing else matters.

We eat because we're troubled — we feel so much and are torn so far. Sometimes the pain is so great, so confusing, that we need to feel numbed. If you eat your emotions instead of thinking them through, that can feel safe. That can feel like home. Our bodies get bigger and bigger, but the addiction is great and the will to hang on is there; it tells us we are shit. It tells us to keep eating. We eat because it hurts, we eat because we want so much, we eat because we can't be satisfied, because we never even thought to ask. We eat, it seems, because we started.

We purge because of guilt. Because of the steps to forgiveness. Because it's part of the routine and when your throat hurts and the slimy yellow acid from the pit of your stomach covers your hands, you feel it. The guilt, it eats away at you.

We over-exercise because if we keep moving then we won't have to stop — that's the goal. We hide in our sheets, we don't leave the house. It's warm inside and who can say the same for the outside world?

We take laxatives because sometimes purging isn't enough, not physically but figuratively; we take diet pills because the celebrities do, and also because we wish they didn't.

We do these things and they can all seem quite different, but the truth is, really, they are the same.

We do it because we are ashamed, we feel guilt, we see the world as it really is, or as we think it really is, or as we've been told it really is, and we don't approve. We want more; we don't want anything at all. We want so much that the galaxies spin out of orbit and the whole world stops, the stars stop, the Milky Way stops, and when silenced, we can feel it. Cold. Quiet. Numb. Nothing. It's nice to see things as they really are, and it's nice to get things to shut up.

I don't want to talk about it.

Around 30 to 40 percent of eating disorder patients are survivors of sexual trauma. Trauma is the thing that pulls the trigger, enacting the blueprints within our DNA.

Can you imagine all the people trying to survive?

Take away the sexual trauma and abuse, and there is still something.

Way before our 16th birthdays, we've been catcalled, we've been under or over-valued because of how we look, we've been taken for granted physically as if our looks are all that matter. We've seen the ads and the movies and our friends have already started the game of Compete for the Man. We've been taken advantage of, without our consent.

When I see my body, I see hurt. You don't see that, I do. And even though it can't be calculated, by you, it can be, by me.

When was your first abuse? Was it when you were ten years old, afraid of growing up and with DNA like mine, so closely nudged to the eating disorder surface, or was it when your identity was already more supported? Had you already accepted the status quo, had you learned to accept the things that offend you or had you learned to fight? Were you supported by those around you? Did you feel safe? Some people can be surrounded by the most loving people in the world and be totally, completely, hand-held safe and still not feel secure, as if the questions of who they are and if they will survive the night are still up in the air. Some people can trust their family and then learn the hard fact that most sexual abuse occurs at the hands of someone they know.

It sounds so rational. You are sexually abused and you keep on eating, so that you never have to be seen as a sexual object again. You are sexually abused and so you stop eating, you stop partaking; you restrict in order to try to control the very little that you can in this world, the mere bites of food you put into your body. You restrict because the outside world is dirty and you want to be pure, clean, light years away from adolescence and widening hips and the venture into the adult world that most certainly guarantees more abuse. You binge and purge because you want two different, disagreeable sets of things, and once you start the cycle, the brain can't stop. *I am good and so I won't eat.* Yet restricting is hard and so I eat. *I am bad for eating,* so I eat more to compensate for the feelings, and then I binge to clean myself, so I am good, and then I feel guilt, so I eat more, again.

In many ways an eating disorder is about the avoidance, or response to, one's sexuality and a culture which, no matter how much we resist, requires us to sexually partake or be taken. The disorder is the mess of an attempt to hide our anger, our frustrations and fears, and in doing so provide an outlet where we can refuse to conform to the ideal and thereby feel safe, feel as if we matter, as if, even in this world that gives us nothing, we've found a sort of power.

My eating disorder was a recognition of the fact that I had little control over my life and where it was headed. The disorder was the solution. *I refuse. I am not your meat.* It works because, as a good girl, as an anorexic, I cannot show my anger and I cannot hold any feelings of resentment. With restriction I have it all and yet no one knows. I can be angry, I can protest, I can *refuse* and I can still avoid having to actually stir the pot. And I know I had shame regarding how I looked, and I had shame regarding how I was going to look, the growing female parts, and the shame was very real. And so, like magic, the eating disorder serves two purposes: first, it's the solution to vent our anger while still remaining perfect and good, and, second, it's the thing that helps us harm our bodies in retribution for the great shame we feel. It's self-punishment, that is the solution.

Sometimes when I eat, I cover my mouth with my hands as if I am talking out loud, even though I'm not.

If you do something wrong, if it is your mistake, I will still apologize. *I am sorry.*

Psychoanalyst D.W. Winnicott said that all people experience three interconnected lives that together shape their identities, almost like an extension of Freud's three states of consciousness. The first life is totally inside a person and consists of their "truest" emotions, sensations, and imaginations. The second life consists of one's relationships with family, friends, and partners. The third life consists of one's observations and experiences with society and culture garnered from avenues like the media, politics, and work environments. These three lives are supposed to, in a perfect world, develop like the interconnected circles of the Olympics' emblem so that one's inner life (the first) is perfectly centered in between, and so assisted by, one's close relationships (the second) and so, perfectly, almost magically, unencumbered, or unthreatened by, one's experience with her or his cultural environment (the third). That perfect circle gives people a strong sense of self, supported by those they love and trust, allowing them to respond to culture independently, as a sort of third-party observer who is healthily detached and whip-smart regarding cultural inequities like sexist advertising and misogynistic media roles. Winnicott's theory, in reverse, then, sums up an anorexic or eating disordered person powerfully. Instead of living connected and according to their "inner" selves, i.e., their most basic instincts, anorexics live by the moment, exposed to the tosses and turns that the everyday brings;

they are not strengthened by but vulnerable to relationships. They equate cultural requirements as a basic belief system, thereby living outside in instead of inside out.

When you live from the outside in, you have such a low sense, or trust, in yourself that you have to rely on others. Pity you're the only one, it seems, who gets totally, life-threateningly screwed up.

Separate from healthy perfect people, people with eating disorders have relationships that have less (constructive) criticism, less intimacy, less openness than most.

How is it that I can need, from you, the whole world, the moon and the stars and every last bit of love and support and, yet, at the same time, expect nothing, want nothing, ask nothing? How is that I can see what my world wants from me, and follow, almost killing myself, and yet the whole time still refuse, still say no, still go my own path and hide deeper and deeper inside? How is that I feel like I don't know who I am yet at the same time know that who I am is killing me? How is it that I find comfort in my disorder and also no comfort? How is that this disease heals me, completes me, and most literally kills me all at once?

How is it that when I feel I go numb, I still feel too much?

How is it that I ask for death, that I am obsessed with death, and yet I am still alive and fighting for life?

I know I have a problem because, when I was twelve years old I started covering my mouth when I smiled, just like I did when I was eating, sometimes.

You are not supposed to hide. You are not supposed to find fear in your life where there is supposed to be happiness. You should not have to apologize for being who you are, who you really are. You should not feel ashamed.

That's what matters here. It's not the facts, it's my story, how I feel, the sense of shame in who I was, in who I am, that I shouldn't have felt. The shame I have, even though I never asked for it. Even though I never said yes.

THIS IS THEIR STORY.[17]

1/23/02 progress record 11:20 am points 18/30 goals: meal plan take care of self ask for support, still ambivalent about eating disorder. Mother very upset that patient named her disorder. This am, Jordan announced she has "given up" her disorder, because it tried to kill her

1/23/02 progress record 10:20 chair to be pulled close to her table when she eats. Shakes her leg often and stretches her legs out. Rearranges her food during meal, which is an indication that she is struggling. Patient said in family therapy that she is frustrated with her progress. While on Level 1, patient is to interact only with level 1 peers and not level 2 peers. She can only play cards with staff, journal

1/23/02 progress record 12:00 patient said it has been too hard for her today to think about not having her illness

1/23/02 progress record patient says she knows which staff she can manipulate and does

1/23/02 progress record patient had her sister ask staff during visiting hours if they could watch a

---

17   Their story = excerpts of medical mush pulled from my patient file to document their side of the story from intake to inpatient to outpatient to discharge.

movie even though patient is on Level 1

1/23/02 progress record 1:30 still expressing much ambivalence re: growing up - verbalizing fear of letting go of anorexia nervosa. Affect anxious, mood anxious, easily overwhelmed

1/23/02 2:14 progress record had angry outburst yesterday, but was able to redirect herself and make her calories after getting support from staff. In Treatment Team requested that parents redo meal ED 1 and 2 so they can do a better job of stopping her attempts to manipulate them at meals

1/23/02 4:15 patient drew a tall tree with strong roots. She has, per her report, always felt anxious and wished for sturdy roots. Patient used dark colors for the ground because she expects life to be hard. She sees herself as a survivor but she wishes she had less anxiety

1/25/02 5:40 progress record bright, interactive, sarcastic at times. Verbalized enjoying idea of going back to school and telling peers she's been at a psychiatric hospital and treated with antipsychotics. She likes how it "scares people." Silly, giggly. Continues to complain about frequent night sweats

1/29/02 finally able to say she is "scared." Knows

eating disorder is strong and unsure if she can continue to manage it

1/29/02 12:15 patient is starting to express feelings more appropriately, but still suffers with people pleasing and her illness has been the "glue" holding family together

Disposition - benefits maxed out 2/6/02

2/02/02 11:17 during lunch is when patient needs lots of support from staff. Patient used peer interaction and support by way of staff to complete lunch

2/03/02 patient attended chapel and started to want to work on receiving communion without feeling guilty

2/3/02 2:30 patient stated that parents think of her as perfect angel and never does anything wrong. Stated parents think too highly of her

2/3/02 3:37 patient to speak with dietician about consuming too many dairy products and strawberries as well

2/08/02 weight has fluctuated and nurse thinks she has been exercising

2/08/02 5:05 patient participated in group by

discussing what depression feels like to her. Patient said she has an empty feeling when she is depressed and her friends did not help her with the feelings but now she knows how to help herself

3/14/02 3:40 patient reports feeling "upset" about almost being in her healthy weight range since then her "eating disorder will be over"

Free write therapy assignment:[18]

I really miss my family. I need them right now. I need the warm hugs and comfort. I miss them so much and so little at the same time. I have no motivation. None. I don't really want to do anything. It all takes so much energy and it all seems to have no importance. I need my family right now. Why can't they visit me now instead of at seven? I can't wait that long. That's what it feels like I'm doing. Waiting. I don't want to think of what I'm waiting for. I'm pissed off. I'm full, I have energy, I need to exercise, I miss my family. Michelle got to go home after exactly two weeks, if I'm lucky I'll get to eat with my family in two weeks. I want to SCREAM. I miss my family so much. I should have a special visiting hour for my parents because I'm only thirteen and I miss them. I don't want to be here but I don't want to be home, either. I don't know why I'm here. I just want a break. That's what I deserve, a break, a rest, but I never allow myself to and never can. I miss my family.

---

18   A free write therapy assignment written in the beginning of my treatment by me, filed by them.

17

OUTPATIENT

January 14, 2002

Sometimes flowers are named after what animals they look like. Tigerlillies are named after tigers because the colors are so similar. Cattails are named after cats because they are tall and lean but strong-looking, like a cat's tail. Gooseberries look funny and cute yet mischievous, just like geese. And dandelions are named after lion's teeth because the French thought the flower looked like a row of sharp triangle teeth so they called dandelions "dent de lion," the tooth of the lion.

Yet dandelions aren't sharp, they aren't hard, they aren't tough. Dandelions are fuzzy and the petals are easy to pick, eeny, meeny, miny, moe. Dandelions don't bite, of course. They are stirred into tea, stomped on, overlooked. And even when you see them all you notice is the color. Yellow. How happy, how sunny, how bright. In a word, yellow is joy. In a word, yellow is meaningless, pure pettiness, pure luck. Dandelions aren't tough, they have no thorns, no bristles, no long roots to grow to the bottom of the earth and anchor them to the pit. Dandelions are, in fact, nothing like lions. Lions are strong. They are serious. They crouch in lion's dens, and when they strike you hear them roar. Lions are tough — they are not flowers. They are not yellow. And when Jessie leaves, lions do not cry out for him, they do not say *I'm sorry*. They do not ask, again and again, *"Where did you take him? What did YOU DO TO HIM?"*

Jessie knows I'm not a flower, he must. I am not a flower, not a lion. So why would Jessie call me a yellow dandelion? Why would he say, *"It is you"*?

I know it's not me.

Dandelions are long and lean with a great big fuzz of hair at the top, but Jessie couldn't have called me that for *that*, Jessie knows it's not about the exterior. I know he does, Jessie saw my pain, he saw it plainly, just I saw his. Jessie was tormented, a hopeless case, he believed there were devils out to get him and only so few angels out to protect him. Like a video game. In the hospital Jessie believed that I was one of his angels, sometimes, when he was in a fit. I always thought he was mine. And then right before he leaves he hands me a drawing and on the drawing is a flower. There is no explanation, no reason why, just a simple proclamation: It is you.

He could, at least, have told me who I was before he left.

And I could, at least, have rescued him. That is after all what angels are for.

When I was little I believed in God. Well, no, that's not true. When I was little I believed in God, unquestioning, I felt him. Then when I was in the hospital, I believed in God because I had to. He had a capital, God, and He listened to my prayers, I could confide in Him. *Please God, let me die, let me contract some horrible disease, please make this stop,* I would pray. God never answered my prayers, and today I am sorry to say I don't believe in him.

I am my keeper. I am my shepherd.

When I prayed to God I talked about petty, selfish, self-centric things. I prayed by me, for me, according to me. I asked for death.

Yet when I pinch the flesh at my wrist I trust that I can feel it, that I can say it out loud, *ouch*.

My mom remembers the day I accepted Jesus into my heart.

My dad and I were going for a walk around the block, my first childhood home, and my dad was talking about the Protestant God and Jesus and The Heavens. I understood it and we prayed, "Please God, welcome into my heart." We came home, and God was inside me. Before I had my confirmation, but now God was a part of me and when the wind blew I told my mom that is God blowing kisses for you and me. Later on we switched churches, and we started another Sunday school, and I decided I'd like to be baptized. I got dunked in the water, I held my breath. God is inside of me, believe it. And as a kid I knew I had two guardian angels, I just knew it. One boy and one girl, they'd watch over me.

One night I left my two guardian angels some candies to nibble on while I slept. I woke and the candies were still there as I left them. I said, *next time.* Then my grandmother lay on her deathbed in my own mother's childhood room, and we prayed before she passed. Then I Got Sick and I prayed even more.

Please God, let me die.

When my parents divorced, or when my mom first tried to divorce my dad, the church was mean to my mom. Many of the men at the church, a good Christian church, told my mom that a wife should stay with her husband even if he beats her, either emotionally or physically, that it is God's will and God's plan. In my high school, I think everyone believed in God.

Eat my flesh, drink my blood.

The thought of a God, a higher power, has helped many people recover from addiction.

Sometimes God can be good, sometimes God can be bad, but does that mean that sometimes God can be real?

Just because I believe in my disorder and just because I believe that Jessie meant it when he called me his angel, that doesn't mean my disorder is real, that doesn't mean I'm an angel, that doesn't mean I exist as I know I do or as I want to or that I'll even be here tomorrow.

Let us stand. Let us sing. Let us cry, *"Amen!"* as we go on with our lives.

When we lose a life — *I am sorry for your loss* — I do know that it is nice to pray.

I do know: *Dear God, Please keep Jessie's devils far away.*

. . .

She walks into the room and smiles; unaccompanied, turns out she's been here twice already. Head Nurse June inspects her bags, takes out the gum, the magazines, the tennis shoe laces. She laughs with that big, heaving, ho-ha laugh of hers and I hear her and in hearing her I grow smaller. I sink down in my chair. How could she be *here, right now,* with me? Samantha.

In the summer we'd drink slush puppies out of coffee straws and dive head first into the cool blue water with the rays of light glistening over the surface. We'd dance in the water and our bodies would make little waves and the light would reflect up off the water and onto the blinded lifeguards, they couldn't see, the sunscreen and chlorine stinging in their eyes. In the summer we'd make friendship bracelets as we waited — *for what?* — on white sticky lawn chairs. Greens and purples, pinks, yellows, reds, I'd tie a knot and hold it tight in between my kneecaps as I braided the friendship bracelet longer and longer. In the summer I'd hand out friendship bracelets to all of my friends, and I'd make a special one just for myself, everyone said I made them so well.

What happened to the summers? This last summer wasn't spent at the country club pool. And the last? Where did those summers go, my summers with Samantha, my sister, the friendship bracelets, and the slush puppies sipped out of the little straws?

On the Children's Medical Center of Dallas Psychiatric Activities Therapy Assessment, they ask me questions and I answer, and someone, not myself, writes the answers down. I don't remember the questions, the answers so very far removed.

They ask me, the woman, *"Do you have a best friend?"*

I *say;* *"No."*

They ask me, "What do you like about him/her?"

I say, "Let me be me!"

But I had many best friends. I could name the whole list for you now. I was best friends with Katie, Kristina, Addison, Jamie. I was best friends with Samantha. So why would I say that? *No best friends.* Just a summer ago, not this last one but definitely, it had to be the last, I made friendship bracelets for all of my friends. I held the knotted strings tight in between my kneecaps or I'd bite into the strings with my right back teeth and I'd braid the bracelets, I'd hand them off. You are my friend, thank you for being my friend, I love you.

Where did they go? The friendship bracelets, the friends. My friends from school, my closest friends, the people I grew up with, keep sending me Get Well cards and flowers and banners. You can tell they get together to make the banners, that they sign their names and write little notes at the same time. *Get Well Soon. We Miss You.* Their cheap words of encouragement form a pattern and you can't take even one *Thinking of you!* away or you'd ruin the whole form. They are together. They are still friends. But me? I said it plainly: Let me be me. I have no friends.

Samantha says, *I thought I'd find you here.* Seriously, that's what she says.

She says she remembers one day, just a few months ago, in October, when I went to her private school and had lunch in the cafeteria. I remember it too. I was visiting her school, the same high school my own mother graduated from and the same high school my little sister, eventually, will graduate from. Her school would be the top high school pick as it is the best; however I don't really care right now, I can't. Samantha says she noticed how I had lost so much weight, so had all her friends — in private schools you somehow know everyone from all the other private schools, too — and that everyone debated whether or not I was anorexic. Just like that, an easy-breezy table topic, no big deal, no life on the line. Samantha says all her friends thought I was not anorexic because I ate all the meat from the inside of my sandwich but that she, of course, knew better. She saw it in my eyes. She also saw it, she says, because I didn't eat the other things on my plate and she says she could tell that I ate the meat because I was trying to prove something. I was.

Conveniently, school has started again at the hospital after our winter break, and as we finish lunch we have to hurry back to class. Samantha met all of her meal plan requirements and even substituted a sugary cereal in for her apple. I met mine too, hesitantly, sadly.

Here's how school works in the hospital: There is a "private" school and a "public" school. The private school means that your actual school is allowing you to keep up with their actual curriculum. You go to the classroom and the teacher gives you whatever was faxed over from your real school and you keep up. I'm not in the private school in the hospital, I'm in the public school which means that I have temporarily switched over to the Dallas Independent School District curriculum. I think that this decision was made between my parents and my actual school because: 1. they don't know if I will recover so my education isn't of upmost importance, 2. even if I do Get Well Soon they don't know how long I will be in treatment so they also don't know what grade I will be in on the other side, 3. my school is very small, 4. I have already, basically, stopped attending classes because my brain is too hungry and can't retain any of the information, and 5. I personally don't want to have to deal with the embarrassment of even the slightest communication between me and my teachers. After all, many of these teachers have seen me grow from kindergarten all the way up to seventh grade when I was still healthy, and they saw me when I was sick, at the beginning of eighth grade, and when I almost totally convinced them that I wasn't. I ate a big bowl of cheerios for breakfast right in front of them during a school campout a week after September 11th. *See?* I'm fine.

Samantha and I are friends.

For weeks I have been begging my Treatment Team to allow me to start taking my meal plan with my family, because I miss my family and I want to spend more time with them. The doctors say it will be hard for me, they say it always is, and so they don't give me the privilege until weeks pass in my treatment; not until I have gained X much pounds and stopped manipulating everyone by substituting with cream cheese, stopped squeezing my legs together to exercise, started expressing my anger. When I get the privilege to eat with my family, it isn't hard, just as I had said. Instead, it's easier. I get to be with my family for forty-five more minutes, every once in a while, whenever they come and are allowed. I love it. *I get to be with my family.* Instead of it being hard, what happens, is the meals without my family become hard. *I want all meals with them! All my meals!*

In the patient reports it says my dad expressed concern that once I started treatment I started eating sloppily, crumbs would spill to my lap and I wasn't so polite. Did I become a bad girl? Did I stop being so polite? In the beginning I noticed the crumbs, when I wasn't so tired, and I left them there because I wanted to avoid the calories. But then the active choice, or rather the passive choice, the choice after the fact, the choice made out of fear instead of resolution — and so not really a choice — eventually that choice became pure laziness. I should hate to admit it, but I got tired of being neat and clean and always nice and smiling. I got tired of making sure the beds of my nails were always dirt-free and I got tired of combing my hair, dusting the crumbs off my lap as I chewed.

One day, at 4:15 p.m., I have a moment of free time and am journaling in my single patient room, in my patient bed. Head Nurse June comes in, Andrea comes in. Sarah is my nurse for the day but I don't know where she is. Head Nurse June starts looking around my room, as if someone is in here, hiding, even though she has to know that no one is or could be. Andrea starts to close the two sets of blinds next to my patient bed. My bed is positioned right next to the two windows and the blinds are always up, my choice, so I can look out and process and so that, at night, when I can't sleep, I can look out at the emergency helicopters flying up and down and rescuing people. Head Nurse June asks me if I would like to confess anything. *No.* There's nothing you want to tell me, now, nothing that you need to let out? No, I say. I have been good, a very good patient girl.

Head Nurse June reports that Andrea was cleaning up from my lunch with my family today. We ate at the booth in the hall and it was my first time to eat with just me and my family — no nurse at the table. Andrea says that she found a napkin crumbled up with chicken inside. She asks again, *"Do you have anything you want to confess?"* Really, I don't have anything. Besides letting a few crumbs spill to the floor I have been eating all of my calories. I know I need calories, and I know I want to Get Better.

I have seen other girls hide their food and sometimes they get caught and sometimes they do not but I am never one of those girls. I don't hide my food. I don't trash my food. And I know: There are starving children who have no food.

Andrea is the first nurse I met on my first night. When I confessed — her requirement — I knew right then that she was all tough and love. Andrea is love no more. Andrea is upset with me.

I tell Andrea and Head Nurse June that I didn't hide my food. *I ate all of my calories!* But they don't believe me. I lose my privileges. No dinners with family. No outside playtime with the psychiatric set. No extended bedtime hours.

The next day I tell my family what happened over visiting hours. Turns out both my mother and my little sister hide food in their napkins because the hospital food is gross, and *they just can't eat it* — yet they feel they have to, of course, look where we are. They start to take a bite, they say, but the food is so gross that they end up spitting it into their napkins and pushing the plate of food away. They admit that every time they eat with me they always end up going to a Tex-Mex restaurant nearby because they are always hungry afterwards. It's hard enough to eat when you are heartbroken, when you are around all these sick and dying kids, and when it's their fault, when their bones stick out. But when you add the mushiest, yuckiest hospital food you could imagine to the mix, eating becomes unbearable, even for my mother and sister.

You pretend to eat but when no one is looking you spit it into your folded napkin. You push it around your plate.

That's what They Do but it's not what I Do, not once in the hospital, because I want to Get Well, because I know my body is hungry, and because I learned, just a few short months ago, how to detach the physical bit of biting down into food and digesting with the emotional taste. I don't care how it tastes, I can't even feel it.

My mother confesses to Head Nurse June, and it is written in the charts. I thought that I would hear an apology but instead the fact that my family hides their food is counted against me even worse, I think, than it would have been if it were me. I lose the privilege of eating meals with my family and they write it in the charts, *Mother is not on-board with daughter's recovery.*

I Can't Eat When I'm Hungry. Taking time away from my anger, that's revolting. I Can't Eat When I'm Sad. A recognition of the outside world and the Happy Memories and The Future Moments, I can't have that. Now that my family has been stolen away from me I am both angry and sad. These feelings aren't going away. They aren't passing thoughts. They are my founding fathers. Anger and sadness is what I am. Since my red-hot sadness is stuck, now I can't eat in a way much worse than my intake and my first few days. Now it is a struggle that, all of the sudden, I do not want to take part in. I know what they are trying to do to me now. And I know that even if I do what they want me to do, I won't get what I want. The privilege has been taken away completely. I am: Patient Not Allowed to Eat With Family.

Problem is I need to eat, for many reasons. The main one being I do not want to have to drink my calories. Even worse, I really don't want to have to receive my calories up the nose. You see, they have tied me up and I'm stuck choosing between bad options. My choice is to find a loophole, to eat my calories — *but can't you please just give me a nurse and my own table and hold my hand during these thirty minute meals of eating calories, eating calories, fucking eating calories?*

That's what I ask my Treatment Team, minus the cursing which I keep to myself.

I do this because drinking Ensure, the hospital's choice of

liquid calories, is a waste. You cannot chew liquid, and if I'm going to eat, I should at least be able to taste and chew.

Samantha and I have always been friends.

I'm sitting on the floor of the hallway with all of the patient beds, right when it breaks off from the main room and becomes the hallway, almost opposite from the quiet room but a little bit past and drawing robins with their little-bird feet, bug eyes, the swooping multi-colored feathers. A girl with blonde hair and many bracelets covering both of her wrists sits down next to me, she sits Indian style like me and is maybe three feet away. As I draw the girl starts crying. She asks, "Does it get any worse than this?" I look at her. I smile. I lie, "It gets better."

On January 22, 2002, they ask us in Group Therapy who God is. They hand out pieces of colored construction paper and crayons and markers and have us draw what we think He looks like. I draw God as I have seen him in picture books, tall and white with long, straight brown hair and brown sandals that people joke about, calling them Jesus shoes. The God I draw smiles wide, his arms outstretched to say, *"Come here all my children."*

They ask us three questions, the Father, the Son, and the Holy Trinity, and I have to answer.

The first question, who is God?

He sometimes can be scary for me. For he punished Adam and Eve and flooded the world. God is someone I can talk to, a chance for relief. Sometimes when you worry you can just pray and feel better. He loves me. In a way I hope to think God is loving and fun, but in another way he is stern and strict with me.

I always imagine him to be tangible.

The second question, what questions do you have for God?

I would ask God, truthfully, why material things? What will I look like, what do I need, what will I do, who loves me, will I, etc? I would want him to hug me and I would want to know what the point to life is, what you should do during the day and night.

The third, what do you want to tell your parents?

I want my parents to know that I love them dearly. That I am working hard and that I am a good person and daughter. That I am sorry and they mean the world to me.[19]

I misheard the last question — blame it on the malnutrition. It was supposed to be: *what do you want to tell God?* For this I get some points knocked off for the day and get embarrassed and wonder, for me, are my parents God?

. . .

The girl who I smiled and lied to is named Olivia. She has big deep blue eyes, though I wish I could lie again and say that her eyes are green like martini olives. Olivia tells me how she Got in Here. I never asked, instead it's more like this silent-code the new patients sense when they walk in. *Intake. Cry. Explain to the person next to you how you aren't like them, really; how you shouldn't be here and how this isn't really you.* Sometimes people exaggerate. But sometimes, like with Olivia, their story is enough. You hit rock bottom and you can't bear falling anymore, so you speak your

---

19   This Q&A is word for word, pulled from my file.

truth plainly, point-blank, each time as if you understand it for the first time. *This is a fact.*

Olivia says that she was put in the hospital, finally, by her mom who walked into her bedroom and opened the door to the bathroom attached to the bedroom, Olivia's bathroom, and found Olivia in running clothes passed out next to the toilet with vomit in her hair and diet pills spilled across the floor. She passed out, she says.

I have met people who are bulimic but I've never really known that I have, or that they did. I think bulimia sounds dirty, desperate, slimy. In truth I think it sounds stupid, *don't you know those calories don't go away? You swallow, they stay.*

I have also heard of people who take diet pills. I think they are the same type of people who watch infomercials late at night.

I used to be an over-exerciser, but then I told Andrea my secret and now Head Nurse June won't let me sit anywhere with my legs touching..

What am I supposed to say to Olivia? Even though she is so different, we are the same. We become friends like that, split-second. In Olivia, I think I see the truth and understand it all. She knows where I've been, even though her thoughts are opposite, even though she is on the other side.

She sits cross-legged Indian style and looks into my eyes. Olivia says she thought she had died when she woke up.

Olivia and I are friends.

I have decided to name my disorder Becky. This decision has been made by me because it is impossible to detach myself from my disorder and in order to get better, I think, I need to start thinking of her parts as separate from my parts.

Olivia is two months older than me and Samantha is three. We are all thirteen.

When my mother hears that I started referring to my disorder as Becky, she flips. She calls all the doctors, every doctor. She thinks this can't be, couldn't be, no way this could be good.

Together, *Samantha, Olivia, and I are friends.* In the hospital that means we sit next to each other, defend each other, that during Group Therapy or when one of the nurses is being mean, we are by each other's side.

The obvious question: how is it that I can stand up for other people when I can't stand up for myself?

Becky was around for a week before I realized that I couldn't call her by any other name than my own. I couldn't differentiate between who I was and who Becky was. I would refer to my eating disorder as Becky but in my head I knew she was me. Sisters, twins, best friends forever. *You can't separate me.*

My dad helped me write this letter:

January 3, 2002

To my dearest friends,

I have been struggling with anorexia since the beginning of the school year. Although I tried to handle it at home with my mom and a nutritionist, the disease finally got to a point where I was not in control of it, but it was in control of me. In addition, this fall, when I was diagnosed with hypothyroidism, I wanted to believe that this was my only problem. But it turns out I was not so lucky. So on December 20th I entered Children's Hospital. Here I am working on gaining weight and learning different approaches to treat and deal with my disease. I plan on going back to school, but it will be a gradual process.

I just thought I would get us all on the same page.

Love always,

Jordan

I didn't send the letter. Instead, we wrote it for me, "To get it off my chest."

One night, before I'm sent to the hospital, I cannot sleep. My dad comes into my room to check on me — my parents know I cannot sleep — and I tell him, I think, can't say for sure, but I might be hungry. We go downstairs and he sits with me as I fix some food to eat.

I don't like other people fixing my food, and I don't like people standing over me, watching, but this time his presence is welcome, just to be with someone. My dad says I should never go to sleep hungry, that when you are hungry, you cannot sleep. He says that when he was growing up, sometimes at night he would get hungry, before going to sleep, and his parents would tell them how they had always been hungry before they slept as kids. My grandparents would feed my dad late at night so he could sleep soundly, history no longer repeating itself.

Because of the story I try to eat more for my dad. I know that I have no excuse for not eating food when it is available to me. I know that what I am doing is bad, that I should be ashamed.

When food is not available to you, hunger is permissible. It isn't something you do to yourself; it is a bad from the world inflected on the good of you — you're the victim. When food is available to you and yet you chose not to eat, despite feeling hunger, you are: selfish, insensitive, disrespectful to the hurts of the world.

Some little girls aren't so lucky to have food on their plates like me.

Some little girls would never trash their food, waste their food, spend hours calculating calories and protein in their head, waiting as they try not to eat, as if by stretching the minutes of consumption, by moving around the mush of food on the plate, they can pretend to consume without taking part.

Some girls know what it feels like to be hungry; some girls know what it feels like to ask for hunger instead. I'm the kind of girl that tries to eat more in front of my dad before I go to sleep because my grandparents knew famine while I knew family suppers. The kind of girl whose last thought before I fall sleep is *335 extra calories have to be deducted from tomorrow, 335 extra calories have to be deducted from tomorrow.*

In the hospital they say that the Goal in Telling Someone You Are Angry is to resolve the situation and take care of the problem at hand, not to embarrass or make the other person feel guilty. It's in all of the handouts. I should put it, here, in quotes.

Question: Do you know what it's like to not be able to sleep? It's worse than anything else. To close your eyes and lie in bed and know that nothing will happen, for hours. You try each night for months and nothing works. You close your eyes and you're floating over mountains and rivers and trees, your body a roller coaster, flying. In the morning you get up and you go about your life and yet all you want is to get back into bed, to pull the covers over your head. No matter how much you want to, you know you can't.

What you can do is close your eyes for a second and rest your head. You can tell someone, as it helps to let it out: *I am so tired.*

(Pause for breath)

I'm eating dinner alone tonight, just me and Sarah, because it is hard for me to meet all of my calories and so I spoke up and this is what I asked for. I can't explain to you why it is so hard for me, now, but I can tell you that it is hard. *It is hard.* As I stare at my food and back up at Sarah, back down at my food, a girl walks in, all kicking and screaming. The girl has dirty long, long blonde hair in a ponytail with a blue scrunchy and is wearing blue pajama pants with fuzzy black slippers. The only thing the girl can say is no, but it doesn't get old because she has so many different ways of saying it.

I have never hated anyone before until now: I hate this girl. I am trying to meet my calories, and here she is kicking and screaming no, no, no.

The girl is taken away. I look at Sarah and she tells me to stay calm, to focus on what I have before me, the food that I am supposed to eat.

The nurse that dispenses our medicine before our meals comes and whispers in Sarah's ear.

I am supposed to take an antidepressant pill, an antianxiety pill, and a multivitamin.

I never take my medicine. At least not usually. Or at least I try not to, usually. Just like in the movies, what I try to do is hide the medicine under my tongue, go, *"Ahhh, see I've swallowed,"* and then hide the little white and blue pills in my pocket when no one is looking, later remembering to crush them up and toss them into a nearby toilet or faucet. Every morning, though, I will take my Synthroid for my hypothyroidism — it is a little purple pill — and I will take my multivitamin, even though it has those five calories that are not accounted for, and at night sometimes I take a pill to help me sleep, when they are offered to me, even though they don't work.

Besides my obvious need for the Synthroid and multivitamin, I decide which pills to take and which pills not to take by a simple method: *what I can get away with, because I can.* Meaning, when I am in the mood to rebel, I do and I don't take the pills. When I am in the mood to repent, or to change, I take the pills. Each swallow an admittance of personal shame, a spotlight. *I can't fix this all by myself.*

Once I am discharged from the hospital, I will sometimes sneak into my mom's room late at night to tell her that I can't sleep. My mom will take a big white oval pill from her medicine cabinet and cut it in half. I will take one half and she will take the other. By this time, my parents are separated and my mom — she tried so hard for a divorce, to save the family, and finally she got it, and we were saved.

In the hospital, when I do take my pills, I swallow them all at once, even though there are sometimes like five or six to swallow and only one or two ounces of water. I swallow them and say, "Ahhh," and I smile, inside, knowing how cool it must be to swallow so many pills at once. Sometimes, even, I don't drink the water.

Sarah looks at me with heartbreak eyes and in seconds the girl that can only say No is sitting at my table for dinner, the table that was supposed to be for just me and Sarah as I spoke up and said I was having a hard time and needed to eat alone with Sarah just this once, please. Now, Sarah must watch us both, be both of our nurses at once and in this I feel, not forgotten, but abandoned. Just because I am not new does not mean I don't deserve your help; just because I am not new does not mean I don't hurt just as bad. Sarah tries to tell me she is sorry, with her eyes, and if it weren't for No Girl's feeding tube going straight up her nose maybe I would forgive Sarah.

How am I supposed to eat my food when there is a girl with a feeding tube pushing calories up her nose sitting right in front of me? The feeding tube is gross and plastic. The liquid pushing up a pungent beige. Medical tape stuck like a cross keeps the feeding tube pushing upright. Soon enough Little Miss No Girl will have blistery red skin surrounding her nose from all the scratching, drippy-beige irritation. *No.*

In my eyes, this girl is rock bottom. Samantha and Olivia agree, she is the pits. Her first night she kicked and screamed by the exit sign for mere minutes and then she stopped, she was placed at my table. All energy gone, she's got nothing to hold onto and while all of us here, even though we are so sad, so mad, so hurt, we have something. We hold onto it, whatever it is. Even if it is just our anger, we hold on. We go into the quiet room, we hammer the walls and you know that we are real. Even if it just our hallucinations, like Jessie, at least that's something. When I cry and the tears hit my kneecaps my whole face gets warmed from the ooze of the tears. It's like a volcano erupts inside me, and I keep crying. I can't stop.

All No Girl does is sit, and when the nurses aren't looking she lies down. The nurses push her to sit upright, at least. And this plays out for the rest of her time here.

No has given up. The thing you are Never, Never, Never-Ever supposed to do.

I would like to write No this letter, but then I decide not to:

Dear No,

My advice is to Say Yes to the disorder instead of no. Say Yes to recovery. Say Yes to something, just anything, just never Say no. No is a too-short word, and when you say it, doors close.

Olivia and I walk to Eating Disorders Group Therapy together. We're late because we were helping Head Nurse June clean up the loose crayons and markers from Art Therapy. On the floor we spot a forgotten medical piece of paper, crumbled slightly and dirtied by stepping feet.

It says, in Andrea's handwriting: foster care. Grandparents negligent, taped mouths of children.

This, this has to be No's story.

Head Nurse June says I must learn to say no if I ever want to Recover.

I look at No Girl lying down in the middle of the hall, and I tell Head Nurse June, *"I could never."*

Never is very different than no.

Three times a week No Girl goes on the other side of the exit sign, for an hour, and then comes back. Samantha's nurse says it's because No Girl goes to an independent therapy. But when No comes back her face is red and she is all sweaty. One day Olivia asks No, even though No doesn't talk, "Why are you all red after independent therapy?"

Olivia says, "It looks like you were exercising." No girl smiles. We get our answer.

Before I met No I thought that even the girls that don't want to get better, do want to, sometimes.

I wrote this in the hospital:

Reasons Not to Tell My Friends About My Meal Plan:

- *They have been stressing me out, making me not want to eat, making me want to exercise, and making me scared of the social scenes.*
- *They are not GOOD friends.*
- *They might spread rumors.*
- *They would find out they were right.*
- *Then their parents would know.*
- *They will be even more watchful when I'm eating.*
- *They probably aren't mature enough to be supportive or understanding.*
- *It would make me feel like I wasn't as sick as they — doctors — are telling me I am.*
- *I SEE (the big test to get into private high schools).*
- *Graduation.*
- *I'm intimidated by them.*
- *I've been trying not to think about them for months.*
- *I fooled them and made them believe I didn't have an anorexia problem.*
- *I could get rejected.*

I wrote this at the end of the list and then I crossed it out:

- *I might have to go back to them and start all over.*

Samantha, Olivia, and I decide that we would like to go to the hospital's church service today at 11 a.m. The church is open, for all religions, every hour, and we imagine that many families come for their sick patient kid and pray, ask for help. But not today. Today there is no one in the hospital's church room except for me, Samantha, Olivia, and Olivia's nurse. Just us and the pastor.

At the end of the service we sing a song and communion is offered. Samantha, who is so sick, and who has been for so long, opens her mouth and takes the body of Christ. Olivia, who passed out with diet pills spilled on the floor and vomit in her hair, opens her mouth and takes the body of Christ. The pastor stands before me and I take two steps away, bumping back into the seat from which I rose. *I can't.*

I can't take the body of Christ.

I want to, I really do. I want to be graced by God and I want to be comforted — I want to do something that would make my mother proud, to be part of something larger, to be grateful and forgiven and blessed with angel wings.

The thing is, with communion, there are calories in the bread of Christ that are not accounted for in my meal plan. The ten, fifteen, maybe almost twenty calorie bites of Jesus would be unaccounted for, ten, fifteen, maybe almost twenty calories that I do not have to eat in the laws of my meal plan.

That would be a voluntary sacrifice.

We walk back into our ward and I confess to my nurse, *I could not eat the flesh.*

I am sorry, mom, that I could not take communion.

I am sorry dad.

I have a pamphlet from the church service that day in the hospital.

It reads:

In your anger do not sin; when you are on your beds, search your hearts and be silent.

I will lie down and sleep in peace, for you alone, O Lord, make me dwell in safety.

Samantha, Olivia, and I are friends. I know this because we laugh together, cry together, protect each other. With them, I feel safe, I feel included. I look into their eyes and I know them, they know me. I imagine that when we get out we can go back to the lives that we once had, Samantha and I, for a moment. I think that Olivia can come along too and we can all be friends. It won't work, I know. Friends are things that happen in the hospital. They cannot happen outside. And, as they say, once on the other side of the exit sign, us friends cannot communicate outside of Treatment. Bad Influences.

I wish that I could hold onto these moments forever. Not the hurt, not the pain, but the fighting, the inability to say no, the understanding. You could look into someone's eyes and you could see them. That's the stuff that can't happen in the outside world, the stuff that I want back. And it's not that I want to go back, necessarily, it's just that those were moments, real moments, and every year I grow further away.

Will I forget? I already am.

I wish, when I was in the hospital, that I walked past my room in the patient hallway, just once, and that I peeked into all of the other patient rooms. I had a single, because I was so sick, and I was thankful at the moment. Olivia and Samantha shared a room. I wish I looked into all the rooms and stockpiled all the images, Exhibit A, Exhibit B.

I wish I had a picture. I could look at it and I could say: *I was there.*

The only pictures I have from being sick eighth grade year include a picture of me with my friends Katie, Kristina, and Jamie on our first day of school. It was the first day they had seen me for two months and I had gotten so thin. Jealousy was there, hidden within the moment. There was no fear in their eyes, there was no pity — pity was a look exclusive to the adult world. For my friends, it was jealousy. After school that day we went to a fast-food restaurant and I panicked, I didn't know if I could eat. Instead I went to a bagel shop next door and brought back a whole-wheat bagel with strawberry cream cheese, an orange juice, and a fruit plate. I ate it all and that made them feel better, I could see.

I have a picture, in my head, of a month later, September 11th, 2001. That night we went to our church and we prayed outside and I thought it was the end of the world. I have pictures from my school campout a week later; I don't want to look. I have a picture from the family Christmas party we held a week before my intake, the night one of my mom's friends told her I looked like I model. I have a picture, in my head, of how my mom looked at that moment: angry at the world, forever taken aback.

I wish I had seen their patient rooms. When you get to your room, you can't walk on. That was the unwritten rule.

Had I known that Samantha was anorexic, before I was in the hospital? Yes. I suppose I'd always known, even before I knew what "anorexia" meant, I knew.

Had Samantha always known? Even before I was "anorexic," had she known?

Jessie hands me a piece of paper, the yellow dandelion drawing, and says, "It is you."

Perhaps you could say we never knew. If you did, you'd be lying.

18

DIETS, CELEBRITY, & ADDICTION

I want the span of my stomach to dictate nothing in my life. I don't want to be an exposed thigh. I don't want to be a body fat percentage. I don't even want to be a test score or a GPA. I want to be me. My body, my mind, my self, all as one. I want all of my parts to support the other. I don't want to hyper-distinguish one or diminish another. I want to love all of me, to live with all of me, to respect all of me the same.

But it doesn't work like that.

We live in a world where perfectly waxed and tanned anonymous legs sell refrigerators. Where every successful new product is marketed with the same profit-making premise: You are shit, if you buy this material thing, maybe you can be less shitty. And I am here to tell you that eating disorders do not exist because of celebrities endorsing diet pills. But to some extent, they do.

My body is less mine than it is everyone's. Everyone has a part of me, owns a part of me, knows a part of me. My body is a thing and that's simply what happens to things: they get used, get taken, are bought and sold and eaten up, chewed, diminished, praised, equated into dollar signs. My body has become a piece that you can own — it is not just for me. And it's not because I made it so. In fact, I have very little say in what happens to my body. I cannot help that it has become my billboard, my calling card, my defining feature.

I can't help that your body is your calling card, too. I can't help that, with your body, people place you in your box. That, with your body, people think that they know who you are, where you come from, whom you can and cannot sleep with. I can't help that you have assumed the right to take my inventory and stare me top to bottom before you give a fast, split-second, automatic, and largely effortless estimation. I can't help that, with my body, you decide how much I am worth.

Some say we can be both smart and beautiful. But how?

Let's talk beauty. Being a size "0," 2 or couture-4 is physically impossible for pretty much everyone — but we still try. Let's talk sameness. As in, when did beauty become synonymous with "same?"

This is what we know as beautiful:

Tall but not too tall, 5'9" is perfect, 17–25 years old — no exceptions — white features like small button noses and shiny frizz-free hair, impossibly plush lips, big eyes, big breasts, small waists, legs that look like caterpillar legs, legs that prompt everyone to say, "Put some meat on those bones!" And all this beauty, all this beauty that is all so impossible has to be yet one more thing. It has to be effortless. Effortless! *I just got out of bed! I was born like this! The clock stopped at twenty; it's pure luck! Lucky me!* So that's a problem, because that's not really what beauty is, right?

Is beauty impossible, a total airbrushed illusion? Is beauty defined by culture? Or is beauty universal?

Do our ancestors determine our beauty? Is it our genetic, caveman tendencies?

These are huge industries we're talking about here: Dieting, Makeup, Fashion.

Do you think, because I am a woman, that I have to hate my body? Because I am a woman, and I do hate my body, do you think that means it has to be this way, forever?

We already know it's bad, we have for some time, and yet we keep participating as if there is no other option, as if it's better to take part than not to take at all.

Imagine all the hours we spend obsessing over our bodies. Nothing can be that important, can it? Especially not something that is always changing. If we took all that time and put it towards building huge monuments out of limestone, that would make sense, because the monuments would last forever, much past our own lifetimes. When we obsess over our bodies we're not helping anyone — except, of course, the big beauty, lifestyle, and diet brands.

Sometimes I decide to be a pretty person. It's not a conscious choice, it's subconscious. I stop studying so hard and wear too much makeup, enjoy my clothes more. But I always refer back to brain over matter. Does that mean I'm ugly? Does that mean I'm nice? That I have to be funny to have friends?

Some say eating disorders are the more extreme versions of what all moms and daughters do on a daily basis. I don't agree. There is a sea of difference between dieting, even at the most extreme, and eating disorders, even though at times the lines can seem very narrow. Both dieting and eating disorders are tortuous, they are not fun, they are not healthy. Both have become lifestyles for many women, a being by way of routine. But an eating disorder is based on something much bigger, much darker, much more within ones foundation while dieting is rooted more in vanity.[20] Dieting is personal, superficial, one person's individual "issue" to the next. That does not mean that the personal isn't political, that these societal pressures to look like the impossible ideal shouldn't be changed, that dieting is not harmful, is not indicative of larger social constructs that harm the female, her body, and her mind. That does not mean that these societal pressures are not pressing. But it does mean that my eating disorder almost killed me, it was such a dysfunctional, devastating, *disorder*, and in order to get by every day I need to know that my disorder was separate, unrelated to dieting.

No matter how bad a diet can get, an eating disorder is not a diet. They are not the same. One deals with an attempt to become the beautiful body. One is an attempt to escape our world completely.

20   Disclaimer: Dieting, here, means dieting for appearance, not health. Of course, one's health is important, always, and so proper foods must be eaten and dieting must happen, sometimes. But let's ask ourselves: Would the sometimes legitimate need for dieting happen, would Obesity happen, in a world without the much more superior size tiny? Extremes depend on each other in order to exist, overeating processed fats and sugars so often fueled by shame.

Most doctors will tell you that while the "gateway drugs" to eating disorders are often simple, everyday sorts of diets, there is only a minimal, insignificant, impossibly small cultural influence in anorexia. They say that dieting does not cause anorexia, that dieting is, rather, only like one more flicked match in an already burning structure, that anorexia can happen, that it does happen, no matter the culture. But an eating disorder arose like a volcano so quick, maybe even within minutes, after I began a so-called everyday diet. I wanted health. I read diet books and magazines and then, with the snap of my fingers, the disorder took over.

Doctors talk about how anorexia has the highest correlation to temperament of all of the psych disorders. In other words, the fact that I was born with a temperament prone to being overly disciplined, wary, controlled, calculating, and perfectionistic with illusory but still real-to-me feelings of inadequacy puts me at greater risk. Bulimia is also considered to have a correlation but not as much as anorexia and, since I developed anorexia long before I did bulimia, I am considered a tried-and-true, bare-bones anorexic.

Doctors also say that girls in families with no history of eating disorders (no genetic markings), run a less than three percent chance of developing anorexia. Less than three percent! I hear three percent and I think: my disease is not a diet, I am separate, intense, disordered.

I hate pettiness. I hate popularity. I hate fluff, celebrity, pretense. I hate having to fit in all of the time, the dress codes and the spot-free clean.

I hate having to smile at you when I really want to walk away.

I hate that I am lying.

I love pettiness. I love popularity. I love fluff, celebrity, pretense. I love the simplicity, the sparkle, the glitz.

How can I want two things for myself, to run away and to come closer, that are so different? Just because I criticize doesn't mean I'm not subject to the same self-hate that everyone else is, too. It's one thing to notice the problems but to take meaningful steps away, to *Make a Difference?*

Just because I admit I'm an anorexic doesn't mean I can change.

Some anorexics will try to convince you that anorexia is a lifestyle, not a disease. Of course this isn't true. Lifestyles have to be sustainable. Anorexia never is.

Our dieting and pretty, popular, fluff culture isn't sustainable either, in that it is largely pro-anorexia. How?

Yes, the glitz asks for extreme thinness and offers up a singular representation of beauty. Yes, the glitz delegitimizes those that don't fit in. Yes, the glitz tricks people into thinking that they will be happy once they are thin enough, and yes the "enough" is never met.

We praise perfectionism, discipline, overtime, control, power, superiority, structure, purity. We require both virginity and the appearance of promiscuity. Youth and power. Flexibility and determination. We say that nothing good will happen without some suffering, we use hard work to justify the pain, as if hard work is a synonym for sustenance. We let our jobs define us. We value control and To Do lists over everything else.

We diet. We eat crap. We diet more. Billions of dollars are spent to make sure that we keep feeling dissatisfied with ourselves so that we keep dieting. The fashion industry recycles the same ideas, the same pretty models and celebrities, all of which serve to keep you consuming more. *Fashion is better than you.* If you buy this foundation than for two hours your face will be in camouflage, you'll look natural.

If you are pretty enough, if you play your role deftly enough, then maybe you will meet your soul mate and get your happily ever after.

In the morning, you wake before the sun to put on your spandex and run through the park — just a few decades ago, what would they think of you, running around in rubber tennis shoes? Of course, anorexia was still present way back when and gender roles were even worse. Look how far we've come.

Look how I can complain about my white picket fence dilemmas when the majority of women suffer, immediately. Take the whole world: women do 66 percent of the work yet receive just 10 percent of the income, own only 1 percent of the land.

We ask our little girls to smile, always, even when they're sad.

We ask our mothers and sisters and friends, grown women, to never consider themselves anything more than girls — they are not *women*, they are *girls*.

One out of five women are sexually assaulted in their lifetimes. On college campuses, the number could be higher, though who really knows as less than twelve percent of sexual assaults are reported in colleges.

If a woman gets raped, she gets blamed.

It was her fault. She asked for it.

Your womanhood is not a mask, it's not your clone, it doesn't make you part of some team that throws away your individuality at inception.

Your womanhood is not your girlhood. Girl Power was a marketing ploy, a rhinestone-encrusted excuse of a need to beg your parents to buy more purple tank tops with peace signs and BFF half-hearts.

I'm sorry you have to grow up in a world like this.

Plastic surgery, reality TV. School dress codes where skirts must fall past where the hand meets the thigh though popularity requires skirts much shorter. The influx of ads that tell us what we need, the video games and ridiculous songs, each summer flick more explosive than the last.

Taking away the mini-skirts and bikinis won't do anything; the sexless being and the sexualized being are part of the same game.

What's most important is to notice that there is a right and a wrong, always. There is a black and a white, always. A smart or a pretty. There is a who you are now and a who you could be tomorrow if you work hard enough. The point is to recognize that we have no middle ground to fall back on. We can zoom to the left or zoom to the right. That's our freedom. We get to choose our side. And, in choosing, we give up everything.

At this time I would like to remind you of a popular metaphor in the eating disorder world: Genes load the gun and the environment pulls the trigger.

Bang.

19

PROMISE ME PERFECT
OR: REMIND ME LATER WHEN I FORGET

I will not be perfect.

Being perfect is not healthy, it's not nice, it's not conducive to a proper, healthy life.

I will not be perfect.

Being perfect does not and cannot exist. There is no such thing as perfect. Perfect is for the wimps, the scaredy-cat kids, it's protective and it's not real.

I will not be perfect.

There is nothing one can gain from perfection. No higher understanding, no rewarding experience. Perfection is bad for you. Perfection can kill.

Type A's, sorority brats, professional Ivy Leaguers, bankers, celebrities. I am not one of them.

I will not be perfect.

I think perfection is something some people can achieve, but not me. I'm imperfect. I spill things and food falls to my feet when I chew. My silk pants have coffee stains on them; my white blouses ink. I am not perfect.

I think that if I were perfect my whole life would be better. I think if I were perfect I could finally be happy, free, and perfectly, perfectly content. Perfectly me.

I think I can be perfect, the idea itches inside me and I think maybe one day I could be. But not today. Not tomorrow. Perfection is something so great that I would have to work really hard to achieve it. I would have to sweat and bleed and go sleepless for a really long time.

I want to be perfect but I don't think I have what it takes.

I have doubts. I have insecurities. I have fleshy legs.

I want to be perfect. But I don't think I have what it takes.

Sometimes I wonder, a lot of times I wonder, what other people think of me. Do they think I am perfect? I think a lot of people who aren't me are perfect — and certainly they can't all be.

Is everyone perfect but me?

Make me perfect, higher power! Let me snap my fingers and open my eyes, let me wake up and become a top-shelf, porcelain sliver of my former self. I don't want to be me, to be here, to be here like me.

Can't I at least be the smartest person in the room if I can't also be the prettiest?

Please?

I want to be perfect, to have the perfection I see everywhere but inside me. Is that too much to ask?

Just let me be perfect. I'm desperate, I'll do anything. I will sacrifice five years of my life to lose 10 pounds. I will sell this thing we call my soul. I will lie, I can cheat, I could steal for a newer, truer, more perfect self.

For a boyfriend that looks like a Ken doll, I could push my best friend under a bus. For a bracelet that shines like the moon, I could give myself to you.

I just want to be perfect. And since I can't be perfect, since perfect does not and cannot exist, can't I at least appear perfect?

Can't I at least have the things that announce to the world that, if perfect were a real thing, I would be a real and perfect person?

I don't think perfect is too much to ask for because perfection is everywhere. It's accessible, one quick pill and a pair of sparkling jewels away!

I can be perfect. I can be it, have it, become it. Give it to me! Give it to me, please!

I want to be perfect.

At night I dream what it might feel like and sometimes it feels so close, sometimes it feels so far. And I think one day I might have it. Not today. Not tomorrow. But then?

Then I will be perfect. It's not a when or a where or a what, it is a then. Then, I will be perfect.

At night I stare at my reflection in the mirror and I see my perfection like bones underneath the surface. I just need to peel away the fleshy exteriors and I can have it.

I reach for the scissors and I think, why can't it be this easy? Why can't I just cut off my thighs, my stomach, the tip of my chin?

If I cut, do you think it will heal and I can be perfect?

This is not a rare fantasy. It is common. We dream we can cut away to perfection.

I think if I were to be perfect I should have to work for it, to struggle. I don't think I could stand a perfection that was done by the hands of someone else to me, for me.

Then that wouldn't be my perfection. That would be their perfection on top of me.

I don't want their perfection. I want mine. My then.

If you are perfect, I just want to be the same as you.

I know that if I have just one, others will follow. With the perfect looks so too will come the perfect career, perfect purse, perfect furniture, perfect husband, kids, and Windex-clean life, the serving utensils all laying flat as I chew.

It's so far yet I can smell it. I close my eyes and I can touch it.

This is what happens when you are not perfect: You Get Forgotten.

I will never be perfect.

Put it on record that I'd die for you oh dear perfect.

I would do — you've heard me say it — whatever it takes.

I tell myself that I will never be perfect but as the morning comes I've already forgotten.

Remind me later, I don't have what it takes.

20

DISCHARGE

December 20, 2011

Have you ever seen a schizophrenic up close? Have you seen the great fear in their eyes, the shaking? The way they look, really, like they are the most inside of their selves and are also so detached? Like they looked inside and all they saw was black?

Have you ever seen a bipolar in a manic rage? Have you seen them sink until they are just three years old, throwing a temper tantrum, angry over spilt milk?

Have you ever seen a suicidal depressive? Have you heard them talk about their death and seen their face light up? Have you seen them and, in looking, seen their ghost, seen them dead? Have you already said goodbye? Have you predicted just when it would happen and did it?

Have you ever been manipulated by someone who has no limits?

Have you fallen in love with a narcissist?

Have you seen a borderline personality up close? Did you pity them? Were you tossed and torn?

Have you seen a dissociative identity click and turn from one person to another? Have you wondered if they were faking it? Did you stare into the click and watch them fall, for a heartbeat, did you see their dark?

Have you seen a person imagine snakes, did you have to hold them tight, to look into their eyes, did you have to scream, *"There are no snakes!"*

Have you seen a sociopath up close? Were they beautiful? Were you scared?

Have you seen an addict dig a grave below rock bottom? Did you wish they would pass? Did you think, really, how pathetic, how low?

Have you talked to someone and have you understood that when they're lying they're really telling the most truth?

Have you been supervised while you showered? Have you had your shoelaces confiscated? Have you ever been so looked down on? Have you been hugged like you had cancer even when you didn't, even when it was your fault? Have you been told that you must say goodbye? Have you seen an anorexic up close? Have you seen her hunger?

Imagine that you are in a room with all of these people, all at once. Imagine that they are younger than you, younger than 18, and so even more timid and scared and vulnerable and even more eager to please. Now let them start talking, start *itching*. Imagine all the stupid cliches on the wall, imagine the Get Well cards, imagine the flowers sent — they had to take out the metal posts. Imagine your T-shirt — it can also be a noose. Imagine the words Illness and *Dissss-eeease* and Disorder. They have to repeat them to you so that you think it's not your fault, so that when you get out and walk to the other side of the exit sign you can tell people "Disorder," tricking them into thinking it wasn't really you.

Have you been told, by an expert, that when someone important to you hurt you, that is wasn't really their fault? That they couldn't help it, that they loved you? Was the writing all over the walls and did you know it and still wish it wasn't true? Did you let the voices kick around in your head and did you rock back and forth, holding yourself, trying to self-soothe? Did you know that the rocking was the most important part? Just because you hurt me doesn't mean I want you to. Just because I'm hurt doesn't mean I should have been. Just because I see my pain doesn't mean I can get rid of her.

Imagine all the people, even when you close your eyes you can't not know they're there.

That's where I am. Right now. I haven't left.

It's ten years later to the day. The early morning of December 20th, 2011.

Ten years ago, I would be secretly finishing up my morning exercises, my mom would be getting dressed for the day. Hours would pass. We'd go to lunch, we'd split the hamburger, well-done, and then we'd get the call. I'd leave. Things would change, today. They did forever.

In many ways, I didn't plan it to happen this way. Chapter 20, my discharge, written in the early morning of the day that I was first a patient, ten years ago exactly. It's a cycle. It doesn't stop. You blow the candles out, and you're still right there. You try to explain it to your present world, and no one can understand. How could they? You seek out the patients from before but you can never really talk. Bad Influences, Triggers, Anger Management, Denial. You're alone. You're scared. Very little has changed.

And you say we survived.

Almost, I'm proud. I hid the pain and sometimes there isn't any pain to be had. Sometimes I really am happy, sometimes I really do feel normal. When I talk to people I try to emphasize it: *I survived.* I am fortunate. I should have died. I am lucky to have such a normal life, I am lucky to be here; I worked very hard, I fought, it was one of the hardest things I ever had to do, one of the hardest things a person ever could do, and it's the thing I don't want to talk about because it hurts, that's what I say. I say, *"I just want you to know where I am coming from, that I fought and that I should be dead."* They agree with me, like that, split-second, and of course it's not enough, of course I want them to agree even more, to get it so that I can get it, too. After all, unless they understand, I can't. After all, I need them to acknowledge me, to see me here: I am a victim and I am also not.

I thought that when this day would come, something would be different, that I'd have closure. Instead, I've found there is no closure to be had. Not even a drop.

· · ·

In the hospital they ask when I remember being happy. I remember I was in seventh grade, on a school camp-out, running around with a friend joking about how much we loved hot tea, how we were going to start a company together, how we were going to sell teas and call our company "HotTea" (hottie). We thought we were hilariously inventive and I remember, really, being happy. I remember, for a moment, thinking *this is it.*

How could I be so happy in that moment when, if you remember, that same time is when Best Body happened? That same time is when my whole wide world began to break.

We do not have moments that we can look back on to sum up our whole lives. Instead, as people, we have genetics, we have Triggers upon Triggers, we have the sum of all of our parts. And when you say *this moment did this* or *that moment did that,* I know, you aren't telling the whole truth. The truth is we can't explain it.

In seventh grade I went on a school camp-out, and that was when I was most happy, the HotTea, and it was, also, when everything started to break, even though it already had before, even though it would break, a few years later, much worse.

I also know what you think Recovery means. You think that recovery means having to choose between being so thin and so unhappy or being overweight and happy. You think that recovery means choosing to be overweight and happy. I thought it too.

Towards the end of my stay in the hospital, I was fully prepared to become like Head Nurse June, big and round with soft, calloused skin and a tummy that rolled when I sat down. I was prepared to be a person who danced, every moment, whenever I could. I was prepared to sing in the shower, to raise my arms up, and I was okay with gaining and gaining as long as that most literally meant gaining weight, gaining presence, gaining the ability to walk into a room and fill up all the space, to breathe in all the air and not apologize, to laugh and smile and to let the whole world hear me.

In my mind I was prepared to stop looking in mirrors, I was prepared to cut off the size-tags on all of my future clothes. I was prepared to choose life, to fill in all the space.

But that person who sings in the shower? That is just not who I am.

It took some time for me to realize that healing is not about trading one persona in for another. Recovery does not mean eating disorder becomes girl-best-known-for-being-nice-and-fun if that's not who you are. Instead, true recovery means learning to work with what you've got, without abusing what you've got — a feat just as rewarding as it is impossible.

But don't worry, in the hospital they taught me Positive Affirmations. I have them here, right before me, each word written with a sparkly pen circa 2002, every line a different color — first line green, second line purple, third line green.

I thought these affirmations would help me when I got out:

- *I deserve rest*
- *I'm nurturing my body*
- *I love myself*
- *God made me*
- *My family, the staff, doctors, nurses, are all here for me*
- *I am creative*
- *I am confident*

- *I am beautiful*
- *I am me*[21]

At the time I didn't know that the outside world wouldn't have Art Therapy. I didn't know that when we get overwhelmed there are no signs on the wall to remind us, "Just Breathe." I wasn't aware that there would be no more doctors or nurses. I wasn't aware that there would be no more nurse Andrea, no more nurse Sarah. I wasn't aware that when I hugged Head Nurse June goodbye, that that would be the last time.

I wasn't aware how guilt, the anxious, people-pleasing anorexic's premiere use of head-space, eats you up. I didn't know that guilt keeps growing and that when we do away with restriction, we do away with our only tried and true coping mechanism. Sure the eating disorder wasn't a long-term solution, but it was all we had at our disposal. *Express your anger. Ask for help.* What good does any of that do?

The only quasi-affirmation I still believe in might sound simple but it is profound: I am me.

It took a long time for me to figure that one out, that I am my own person.

· · ·

What happened to Samantha? She stayed sick. When I was nineteen, I visited her a lot in hospitals. Stuck in a treatment facility with adults, people that were sick for so many years, people that were so far gone, people that, you'd swear, were homeless.

---

21   Pulled from my patient file word for word.

When Samantha wasn't in treatment, she was in the cardiac unit of different hospitals. She told me she had died twice already, literally, her heart had stopped. But she always came back.

Once I visited Samantha in the hospital and she was so sick, so close, you could see, to dying. The nurse, she was Jamaican, told me to *say goodbye*. Instead, I asked Samantha if she wanted a coffee. Samantha asked for a large sugar free vanilla nonfat latte, caffeinated. I went to a Starbucks and I ordered for her. I asked for a large decaf vanilla latte with real sugar syrup and whole milk, and I asked that they mark it, instead, the way Samantha had asked: sfv, nf, no d. The man behind the counter looked at me, he wanted an answer. I told him I was a model and going to a go-see, and I had to trick my competition. The man told me, "Good luck."

I took the coffee to Samantha and for that day at least, I fed her. And then I said goodbye. A week later I brought her all of my favorite hardcover books, all the best European magazines, a fuzzy soft periwinkle blue blanket. And that was that. *Goodbye Samantha.*

Many times I have dreamed that Samantha has died. I have to choose, in my dreams, whether or not I will attend her funeral and when I wake up, the choice is still there, clearer than ever: She is dead, will I attend her funeral? In truth Samantha is not dead, she is sick. I have not visited her once since I turned twenty. I have not talked to her once. I know she is still alive because if she weren't, I would get a call.

There is only so much that you can give to one person before you have to decide for yourself that you have given enough.

I don't know what happened to Olivia. Though I would like

to believe that she is still alive and happy, my last memory of her, from when we were both sixteen, tells me differently. I think that Olivia is either dead or forgotten.

If you talk to my doctors, they will tell you I am lucky. With the severity of my case, with my temperament and with my young age and family history of eating disorders, I too was likely to become either dead or forgotten, a hopeless case.

Sick at thirteen, almost one-half the weight that I am now,[22] the same height, I laid my head down to go to sleep and I didn't know if I would survive the night. I prayed to God, *"Please let me die."*

When I look back on my disorder, back at the last ten years and the many times that I was sick, I think almost fondly of my anorexia and my time in the hospital. Those were my "bread-and-butter days," as I call them. Times were simpler then. That was before real adolescence, before high school, before the all-hell-breaks-loose family collapse, before everyone I knew before left me, before I met people in high school who were a new kind of bad. Before I learned, with Samantha, to binge and purge. Before I saw someone overdose right in front of me. Before I got in cars with boys that drove so fast I said my prayer goodbye. Before I looked into a boyfriend's eyes and knew he was going to try to hit me, before I looked into my dad's eyes... Before. Before so many things that I don't want to tell you.

I am sorry. I am hurt, and it wasn't the hospital that did it. It was the outside world.

---

22   I know I will regret, one day, putting in this detail. But against my better judgement, I had to tell you. Even the people who are so far gone can pull themselves out.

At discharge I tell my nurse, *"My disorder is a friend I don't want to let go."* I was telling the truth. I wasn't ready then; I am not ready now. I want so badly to close my eyes and go back, back to the bread and butter days.

DISCHARGE SUMMARY

In-Patient Day Hospital

Date of Birth: 01/08/1988

Date of Admission: 02/11/02

Date of Discharge: 03/15/02

"The parents describe Jordan as a driven, perfectionistic, and worried person... The patient's goals on the inpatient and partial hospitalization included a meal plan, a goal to take care of self, and a goal to express her feelings through ten-minute talks... Good eye-contact. Speech is normal rate, rhythm and tone. Affect is slightly anxious, smiling. Mood is described as 'better than before'... The patient suffered from significant emotional disturbance, including symptoms of depression and some distortion with reality. The patient's disorganized thought process contributed to pervasive pessimistic thinking, resentment, mistrust, and dissatisfaction with herself. Recommendations were made to the parents during a reporting conference to increase the structure in Jordan's routine, as well as to help her test reality by encouraging her to rethink her thoughts, and by also continuing with the weekly individual psychotherapy as well as further treatment with a family therapist in order to help Jordan and the family cope with her illness."[23]

---

23   Excerpts from a five-page discharge summary.

I will tell you this now, and fast, and you must listen because it is absolutely the most important part: I got well because of a combination of lucky breaks. I got well because, at first, I didn't do it for myself, I did it for my family. That's what worked for me. I knew that my family would have been forever lost if I passed and so I did the opposite of what the hospital tells you to do: I put others before myself, I got well for my family, for my mother and my sister — especially for my sister. It was the hardest thing I had to do, really, because I wanted to die, but I couldn't leave them like that. What would my sister say to all of her future friends? *I had a sister, and now she is gone?* In my calculations the scar of my sister having to say that was worse than me having to do the one major thing I didn't want to do. And so my damaging tendency to always put others before me had a silver lining. I gained weight for my sister, for my mother, at the time, even, for my father. Once you start to gain, your brain starts to repair itself. You start thinking differently and you learn: just keep on going. At least that's what I did. I realized that when I was still, I was most likely to forget the cardinal rule — Do Not Kill Yourself — and listen to Becky, the person I really wanted to listen to at that moment instead. And so I kept on going, I couldn't stop. I realized that the hurt was so deep I couldn't look. *I kept on going. I couldn't stop.* To this day, I know, it keeps me going. To stop and look is to let it kill you.

You have to be aware of who you are and how you feel, yes, but you can't stand still so long that you allow yourself to get lost inside your own head, especially in the beginning. Because to some degree, you cannot be trusted. To some degree, you have to use yourself against yourself.

For many years I have had to tell myself it is not my fault.

I have "recovered" when other people have not.

It's not a happy feeling, feeling like a traitor. While I promised my family health, I had promised the hospital sickness. I am sorry to those ghosts waiting in the hospital. For not fulfilling my end of the bargain. And I am sorry too that we cannot be friends on the other side of the exit sign.

I do not know what happened to Jessie. I have not talked to Samantha since a week past lying to her. She asked me, "Are you sure this is sugar-free?" I said I was sure.

I wake up hot with sweat. *"It's a nightmare,"* I've learned to tell myself. The truth is it is much more — I know that. Yet when I was in high school I had not learned to connect the heat and the dream. I would go to my doctor and say, night sweats. But now I know the truth: *Should I go to her funeral?*

I am sorry I think Olivia is dead.

When Samantha almost died twice in her medical records they didn't put eating disorder, they put *heart condition.*

For my eighth-grade graduation I wore a white dress, and I got up on the stage at our small school to give my graduation speech. I started with "Wow."

21

RELAPSE

January 1, 2012

I told you: You can only be well for so long. It will catch up to you. Some doctors say that you just need seven years of real, live, true health and then you can, actually, get some sort of verified stamp of healthfulness, some sort of guarantee that you probably won't get sick again, that you probably aren't an addict, that you probably will be just fine.

They are lying.

There is no stamp. No guarantee. No on/off switch. And when you are recovering, please, tell me, how are you supposed to complete seven years without an episode? Seriously? *Seven years?* That is just not possible.

I was diagnosed with anorexia just over ten years ago, and since then I've had handfuls of healthy/happy months. Not fistfuls, not bucketfuls, just handfuls. And I'm one of the lucky ones. I've had a relatively so-called average life, did the standard things, both good and bad, that someone my age is expected to do. My body mass index is comfortably in the middle, not too far to the left, not too far to the right. I am supposedly happy, healthy, free. But I have never had seven total years of total health, and it is not on my wish list; just as I don't think there is a rainbow awaiting me on the other side, I don't think seven years is possible — because there is no other side. Once you are an addict, you can never, truly, be well. It's like being a burn victim and saying that one day you might look like a normal person. Sure you might put all your hopes and dreams into some non-invasive miracle surgery and maybe one day your skin will look normal to the non-discerning eye. But you will always know it's there. You will always know you are scarred, you were sick, you almost died. And brought back to life, you will always know that a part of you is still buried in the earth, waiting for you and calling your name.

I was sick and now I am not healed. I might look normal. I might look healthy. But I'm not. When I picture myself I see hurt; when I feel myself I feel pain. I've been burned. I've burned myself.

Here is how it happens, the falls, the breaks, the heartaches: Life comes to you. You struggle. You quiver and shake. You fall. Perhaps I'm making it sound too easy but that's really how it is. Life is tough, healing is complicated, and one day you will wake up and the days, the months, the years of therapy, drugs, introspection, and self-smarts will no longer matter, if only for the time being. You are suddenly sick. You fell. You broke. It can happen in an instant or it can happen over many months,

BEST BODY: PRETTY, MISERABLE, PERFECTNESS 273

many meals, but either way I guarantee: an eating disorder is not something you completely recover from.[24] Once you know her, she will never let you go. You can run as far away from her as you can, but one day she will pull you back in. One day you will see that you never even left. That's not to say that life is not worth living, because it is. Life is wonderful. *Living* is wonderful. But you can't treat your recovery like it's a one-way ticket — I'm finally free!

Because, sad fact: you will never be normal again. It's not possible, and who is to say you were ever normal to begin with? Your eating disorder pretty much guarantees that you weren't.

As much as my eating disorder has burned me, it has also taught me many things and helped to make me into a person that, no matter my pains and quirks, I rather like and am rather proud of. Truth be told, sometimes, late at night, I fantasize about building a time machine and living my life all over again with the knowledge I have now, changing and adjusting the good and bad paths and decisions that I have made. But I have never fantasized about going back in time and living my life without an eating disorder. I know that I have severely damaged my body. I know that I am very hurt, very sensitive, and that a good moment can switch to a bad one pretty quickly thanks to my past. I know that I hurt many people that love me. But I would never want to live a life without my eating disorder. Because my eating disorder is a part of me, a part of who I have become, my history.

Yes, these words are dangerous, but it has to be said. My eating disorder isn't the worst thing that ever happened to me. My eating disorder isn't the first thing I'd change. My eating disorder,

---

24 A simple note to take as you wish: there is no abstaining from food or lack of food when it comes to eating disorder recovery. You cannot become six years sober. Instead, recovering from an eating disorder requires a balance between not eating too much and not eating too little and a similar notice/not notice of how we look, feel, what we accomplish, and how far we can and cannot push ourselves, where. We cannot wholly stop with the rigidity or self-doubting, either. Instead, we have to walk along a lifelong balance beam. (Good luck with that.)

instead, is more like a part of my foundation that is connected to every other part of me. That is not to say I am my eating disorder. But it is to say that my eating disorder was a huge event in my life and that every single moment afterwards has been and has to be affected, somehow, by the disorder.

Sometimes I think of myself and my eating disorder in terms of the chicken versus the egg. Sometimes I'm not sure which happened first, even though I know that I am not my disorder, that I can be healthy and happy. No matter what, I know that my eating disorder is connected to all the things that I do now, the things I feel now, the things I say. It is also connected to all the things that I like and do not like and wish I could change about myself. For instance, I like my severe empathy and bravery to feel things deeply. Of course, with my eating disorder, this was less beneficial, more destructive, but I wouldn't get rid of the deep-feeling now. The thing that I dislike most about myself is my penchant for superficiality and uncomfortable self-awareness. But those are very human qualities, no?

I don't think I could really be me, myself, who I am this minute, if it weren't for my eating disorder and the good and the bad that it has either given me or that I have taken from it. But here's the key: I can't see myself without it *in my past*. Because, at the moment that I am writing this, I am doing well. I do not have too many negative thoughts, too many distortions regarding how I look, how I am, and I am not conducting an entirely unhealthy diet regimen. But tomorrow, things might switch for me. I might wake up and feel very bad about my self, my life, my world. I might revert to the coping mechanism that I know best: food. I might restrict too much, eat too much, purge, over-exercise, take laxatives or diet pills. I have done all of these things many times, so many times that they feel just, if not more, as home to me as my small apartment in Brooklyn. And I am saying that I would not be the same person that I am today and that that is a good thing because, today, things are good.

But what about tomorrow? I am very busy, very far from my family, with friends that diet too much and shop too much and I need to buy a new swimsuit soon. What will happen then? Remember the superficial doesn't cause eating disorders, not in even the longest of shots, but the constant influx of the superficial definitely makes me want to escape. Remember, I live in NYC, I am in my early 20s. And what about when something *really* happens?

I'll tell you: I will relapse. How do I know? Because I relapse every second. Every minute. Some thought comes into my head, a bad thought, and I relapse for a split second. Just as I was telling you before that life was good, I was thinking in my head very opposite things. The bad thoughts come to me in seconds, and just as soon as they come there is a conscious decision that I am forced to make: Will I submit or will I surpass? Will I allow whatever is bothering me — the look of my bloated face (my fear of taking up too much space), the girlish high pitch of my voice (my fear of my capabilities), the food I ate or didn't eat (the sum of my fears and unfulfilled needs) — to take over or will I overcome them? In no way have I mastered the mind-games or learned to not be so susceptible to bringing myself down. But I have learned to look forward. I have learned to keep on going.

And in the end I think that's what recovery really means. It means living your life, as free from the disorder as you can possibly be. It is foolish to think that you will get rid of all of the attributes and influences that your disorder has given you (the chicken or the egg?), but you can live your life, do the things that you enjoy, without physically killing yourself. Doctors believe the cure exists when patients gain all the weight back (or lose the weight) that is needed and stop practicing the dangerous physical behaviors. And I don't want to, but I agree.

You cannot take a pair of pliers and pluck out every single bit of the disorder. You *can* live your life and you *can* stop restricting, stop throwing up, stop binging, stop obsessing over the numbers.

If that's how you think about recovery, then I pretty much recovered by the time I was twenty-one with only very small relapses here and there. And I am okay with that. Because I have learned to accept where I am to the best of my capabilities, to love (or try to love) myself and my history, and to forgive.

I know that when things both bad and good happen to me, my automatic response will be to practice my eating disorder. And I know that I probably have a sea of relapses in my future.

But at the end of the day, I want to live my life. I know that means staying alive. And I know that means I cannot practice my disorder. So when people ask me if I have recovered, I tell them there is no such thing but that I am doing the next best thing. I am not acting on my disordered impulses, I am not a walking, talking, eating disorder, I am not practicing. And I tell them that not practicing is such a bigger achievement than simply recovering.

It's not normal. Far from it.

When you get out of here people will ask you about control. In the form of a question that is really an accusation, they will say — as of course they know better than you — *Aren't eating disorders about a want for control?* You can clarify and answer them as much as you please but they won't listen. Their minds have been made up already, *eating disorders are about control. You had an eating disorder. You did not have and you yearned for control.*

After a while you will stop trying to let people know the truth. That's not a problem. You have to move forward, you have to look ahead. But deep inside in that spot that used to be taken by the disorder, you need to know the truth. You need to carry the truth inside of you, even if it is only yours to have. The truth about eating disorders is that it isn't *about control* so much as it is about safety, comfort, the pursuit of feeling at ease. Eating disorders are about fear and loss, hiding and denial. Eating disorders are in fact so not about control that they are about the refusal of taking control. They are about giving in. About running away. About finding a temporary solution to make you feel temporarily better.

Control implies action. It implies holding power. Images of Type-A, utilitarian-suit-clad women with hair tightly shackled; the assured male pairing of suit and dress shirt and cufflinks. But an eating disorder is not your superior so much as it is your best friend. Your comfort in feeling less-than, that most perfect spot of denying your individual right to existing truly and free.

Eating disorders are not about gaining control — they are about avoiding control, through the vehicle of control. Small measured calculations replace the ticking whole.

People who are afraid of control, of power, of the strong baritone in their deepest voice, those are the people who get sick.

A lack of control, a lack of power, a lack of say in one's standing and circumstance both present and future — that's a good place to start the narrative for your little seed of truth. You did not get sick because of a need to find control; it was the absence of control combined with your fear of taking it.

Tell your friends. Tell Head Nurse June and Andrea and Dr. Kay. Perhaps recovery is not the thing to go after. Perhaps it doesn't exist. Perhaps we will stay sick together forever. But there is a difference between being sick and practicing your eating disorder, just as there is a difference between wanting control and taking control, the kind eating disorders do not give.

I say you go out there and you step as far away from your eating disorder as you can. I say you stop practicing. Stop giving in. You take control, instead.

In Samantha's Name

Samantha was alive — at various stages of recovery, sickness, and relapse — during the writing of this book. However, Samantha passed away the summer of 2014, a result of her eating disorder. It was a summer day much like the ones we had shared, a summer day when, had the eating disorder not come, she could have been swimming.

Samantha was sick for fourteen years before it took her. She never read this book, or even knew it was coming.

I am ashamed for not talking to Samantha since I was nineteen. I would not have been able to talk to her and stay well — I know that. But Samantha was deserted by so many childhood friends, just as I was, and from so many people that she loved.

We are all accountable for the huge loss of of life that was Samantha.

In her name I'll do my part now to spread awareness and fess up to what we'd all like (because it's easier) to sweep under the rug.

I invite you to do the same, for the Samantha you know.

DEDICATION

This book could not have been made without the help of a close group of friends. Les and Chuck, you guys are the key. *Les Kerr,* graphic designing wonder man. Thank you for the book cover, the interior layout, the website design, the constant reading of email updates and email alerts and emails, emails, the *"I swear this is the last one"* decisions. You are impossibly helpful, I can't even begin — though I do think I should begin with an apology. Sorry for being a wee bit insane. But I did write a book about eating disorders, so, you know. *Chuck Dickinson,* printing hero. Without you I'd be making copies at FedEx and pushing books like I used to sell lemonade as a kid — frantically waving hands at the passing cars on the street corner. Printing with you is a nice alternative. *Glenn Hadsall,* A+ book cover photographer. Thanks to you, all the pieces came together. *Chris Walker,* A+ web-developer. Impressive. Good talker. Without you I'd have no .COM.

My continued gratitude to the team.

Thanks to Harish and Chelsea Rao *(and Kiran! And Mita!)*

for introducing me to Emily Griffin who introduced me *to Kate Kennedy* — can't recommend enough editor — who introduced me to the wonders of pressing delete. Thanks to *Arnessa Garrett* — can't recommend enough copy editor — for checking things twice and calming my fears surrounding the correct use of commas.

Amy Sheinberg and Dr. Setliff are the two professionals with the greatest impact on my recovery. Thank you for facing the deep and pathetic and miserable on a daily basis. Thank you for acting quick during my darkest emergencies. Thank you for getting me, and plenty of others, here.

Thanks to Allison Devereux, Emily Hale, and Michelle Angelosanto and that wonderful crew — your friendship and willingness to pitch in meant the world. Thanks also to Shannon Welch for being a roommate found on New York Craigslist who wasn't crazy but a whole lotta nice and fun — going through out of this world apartment nightmares is better with you.

Without proper NYC brunches with Selim Benhabib and equal doses of home fries and ketchup, this book would be 1,000 pages and would predict doom for us all. Thanks for understanding the process and for being as dedicated to what you have to make as I am to what I have to write. Never thanks, though, for the mostly bad movies.

Thanks and caffeine to the coffee shops of Brooklyn, especially Outpost and Urban Vintage, and to my favorite bodega, RIP.

Then comes the family. Thanks to my mom, my sister — *The Knape Girls*. Without you, I wouldn't have tried to survive, and this book would tell a very different story. I love you as fresh meat loves salt. More than tea requires ice, more than hot sauce from Mico — (*Meet you there in five?*). Let's do this forever.

ARE YOU ANOREXIC?
FIND OUT NOW

I. *Anorexia Nervosa.* Here is what that simple diagnosis says about me (and you?):

A. I obsess about my food intake and weight as a means of coping with my emotional problems.

1. I equate thinness with self-worth, and because I want to be worthy, I have to be thin.

2. I also have body dysmorphic disorder, so my idea of thin is different from your idea of thin.

a. I do not understand limits.

b. My idea of thin is skeletal.

B. To diagnose someone as being an anorectic, she/he must: starve themselves until they are at least 15 percent below a normal body weight for their height, lose their periods (women, of course), and still see themselves as fat — a phenomenon called "body dysmorphic disorder." That's how the Diagnostic and Statistical Manual of Mental Disorders (DSM-IV) primarily diagnoses anorexia, a disease that first appeared in The Book in 1980. I don't particularly like these core features: lose too much weight, lose your period, still think you could lose more. To me, that's a superficial diagnosis.

> 1. Other physical, or rather, other easy-to-identify, superficial, not the real disease symptoms include: extreme weight loss, thin appearance, low body mass index, abnormal blood counts, hormonal changes like lowered estrogen (estrogen being very important for healthy hearts and bones), and lowered DHEA (healthy bones). Lowered thyroid hormones, higher stress hormones, lower growth hormones (stunting growth in children and adolescents). Low blood pressure, fatigue, insomnia, dizziness or fainting. Dehydration and starvation-induced fluid and mineral depletion — also known as an electrolyte imbalance — a life-threatening condition for constantly dehydrated anorexics and bulimics if fluids and minerals are not soon replaced. The loss of bone minerals called osteopenia (occurs in up to 90 percent of anoretics) and osteoporosis, the advanced loss of bone density (at least 40 percent). Pernicious anemia caused by severely low levels of vitamin B12. Pancytopenia, a reduction of red and white blood cells. Bloated arms and legs, brittle nails, constipation, hair that is as thin and fragile as straw and that falls out at an alarming rate. Loss of menstruation — in

fact, in severe cases of anorexia, at least 25 percent of the time menstruation never returns even if the patient recovers. Fingertips that look almost blue thanks in part to a dramatically reduced blood flow. Irregular heart rhythms including the slow heart beat known as bradycardia. Bradycardia and other heart rhythm abnormalities even show up in kids and teens with anorexia, the damage is that severe and fast. While the normal heart resting rate is 60 to 100 beats per minute, anorectics experiencing bradycardia have heart beats under 60 beats per minute. Nerve damage that affects the brain and other parts of the body can lead to disordered thinking, seizures, numbness, and that odd-feeling nerve sensation in the hands and feet known as peripheral neuropathy. And the worst: a severe intolerance to cold — both physical and emotional, nothing can fix the low temp.

 a. Soft, downy hair starts to cover my stomach like I'm a young baby fox.

 b. It starts growing because I am so cold that my body reverts to caveman and grows fur to keep me warm.

2. My eyes bulge out because my skin is sinking in.

 a. Without fat and muscle underneath it, skin sticks to skeleton like papier-mâché.

 b. My sinking skin highlights all the sharpest bits: shoulder blades, elbows, knees, collar bone, temples.

3. Also, my skin is seriously dry.

a. A few months before I was put in the hospital I took a bath as a treat to calm down. My mother ordered me up into her own deep bathtub and laid out soft, freshly folded towels. I slipped into the hot, scented water, feeling the tensions of the day evaporate as quickly as the bubbles in the bath, and as I moved my mother's fancy French lavender soap over my arms, my skin began to fall off in sheets and float along the surface of the bath.

b. It looked like I had scrubbed myself raw with the scratchiest salt of the earth, when really I had done nothing but watch my skin melt off.

c. I apologized to my mom.

4. The one physical symptom I never had was broken bones. Some people break just from sitting or lying down.

a. When I was admitted to inpatient care, the head nurse made my parents buy me a special soft mattress cover to put over my hospital bed and every time I sat down, the staff made sure there was a pillow underneath me to keep my butt from breaking.

b. Nine years later, a two-second trip leaves me with a very bad third-degree ankle sprain. I have to walk around with an ankle cast and go to physical therapy for months, every day hearing, "I don't know how you did this by tripping in your dorm."

 c. Up to two-thirds of children and adolescent girls with anorexia fail to build strong bones during their critical growing period.

C. In addition to the superficial physical symptoms, I exhibit emotional and behavioral symptoms of the disease that include: denial of hunger and refusal to eat, excessive exercise, irritability, social withdrawal, flat affect or a seeming lack of emotion, preoccupation with food, depressed mood, maybe suicidal, heightened sensitivity — because I am starving, my body has regressed to starvation mode making my senses numbed yet heightened. Heightened to sounds, smells, temperatures, and light, numbed to people and cognitive thinking.

D. I exhibit many "red flags" of disordered eating that include: skipping meals, making excuses for not eating, adopting rigid eating rituals (cutting food into tiny pieces or eating one part first, then the next, obsessively and everyday the same), eating only "safe" foods, taking an excessive amount of time to eat a simple meal or a small piece of food (I could easily spend a half hour, an hour, eating a bagel or a small container of yogurt), cooking big meals for others but refusing to eat, an aversion to eating in public.

 1. I tried to eat all of my meals in front of other people, so that they would not be suspicious. This became so true for me that it became a treat to eat alone and by myself; a treat that usually ended

with me feeling guilty.

2. I once made an elaborate pancake breakfast for my whole family and insisted that they sit and eat it as I watched and ate my own special food.

    a. I have heard that some people make incredible meals for their pets.

    b. Or have extensive, obsessive, recipe collections.

E. Many people with eating disorders use herbal products, diet pills, and laxatives as part of their purging.

1. These behaviors are more in line with the "typical" bulimic patient or could be indicative of a person suffering from both anorexia and bulimia, but not necessarily.

2. Right now, at thirteen, I have never done these things.

3. In a couple of years I will.

F. I am adding my own fact. *Many anorexics are known to frequently, habitually check their appearance in mirrors.*

1. You would think they are checking to see how they look, weight-wise, but no.

2. According to me, they are checking to make sure they are still there.

G. There are other red flags, ones that people who know too-little about eating disorders assume are obvious and of paramount importance, such as weighing oneself repeatedly or complaining about being fat.

1. When I was thirteen, I had never weighed

myself besides when my family doctor did during checkups, and I didn't think I was fat, not even close.

2. Fat was never an issue for me when I was thirteen and at my starving anorexic peak.

H. Important fact to keep in mind: "Although about half of American women *and* men are on a diet at any given time and virtually everyone is exposed to advertising, the lifetime rate of anorexia and bulimia nervosa combined is less that 7 percent of the U.S. population. This amounts to nearly twenty-one million people, without a doubt a significant problem. Yet while the rate of anorexia has remained essentially unchanged since 1991, the rate of obesity has tripled, to include more than 30 percent of all Americans."

II. In the books my symptoms seem pretty clear cut, easy to identify, simple. But like most things, the diagnosis belies a much more complicated picture.

A. Biological Factors.

1. I may have been, probably was, genetically predisposed to developing anorexia. Young women with a *biological* sister or mother with an eating disorder are at a higher risk, suggesting a genetic link. Studies of twins support this idea — that even when raised apart, you get sick.

a. Researchers have identified an area of chromosome 1 that appears to be associated with an increased susceptibility to developing anorexia.

b. I like that, a freakin' chromosome!

c. For bulimia, a "susceptibility gene" has been identified, too — on chromosome 10.

2. Some argue that anorectics may have a genetic tendency towards sensitivity, perseverance, and perfectionism — all traits highly associated with anorexia — but that there is no link between genes and eating disorders.

a. These people are no friends of mine.

3. Serotonin plays a part in anorexia. Which is obvious. I am depressed.

a. Yes, serotonin also plays a role in overeating and obesity. Different strokes for different folks.

4. Being female makes it worse. As does being young.

a. The disease has been diagnosed in patients as young as six, and teens are the most susceptible, also the disease is rare in first diagnosis in people over forty. However, the number of first diagnosis in the over forty population is, in fact, rising.

B. Psychological Factors.

1. Similar to biological, I had psychological traits, either because of or in addition to the biological, that increased my risk of developing an eating disorder. These traits include low self-worth, obsessive-compulsive personality, an extreme drive for perfection, being highly self-critical, highly

competitive, and anxious.

    a. Here is my simple way of remembering the Anorectics' Psychological Risk Factor Traits: If it is something that we consider as a society to be valuable, to be deemed socially necessary to achieve status, power, or happiness, then it is a trait that contributes to anorexia. All of the things that we are supposed to be, the anorexic is. And then they say it is bad for us.

        i. You could say I'm taking it too far, that I'm bending and contorting the truth. I don't think I am. The problem, I think, is that I am too disciplined, too capable of acting out what I feel is necessary. So, while these huge ideals of sacrifice, perfection, control, structure, and precision may be unattainable to other people, and so maybe the fullness of their bad isn't clearly understood... *to me?* I'm just acting out what I thought I was supposed to, because my society told me to. Who would have thought it would be so dangerous once we fully commit?

        ii. Remember: I do not understand compromise, only black-and-white extremes. To sacrifice or to swallow whole.

C. Sociocultural Factors.

    1. Your family is a risk factor.

    2. So are your friends.

a. I'd like to say, my automatic response: *It's not true. I am not sick because of you.* And then, I, a socially responsible being, have to admit *it's true.*

b. You are a risk factor to me.

3. Your teachers. Your school.

4. Socially, weight changes bring on "trigger" comments from others. Going up can be indicative of puberty and not feeling ready and going down can cause the "weight loss high," making you feel important.

5. Middle school, high school, college, moving, divorce, break-ups with friends and lovers. Transitions are always hard.

6. Sports, work, and social activities — things that tell you that you can improve your upward mobility if you just work harder, better.

7. The TV shows you watch before dinner. The ads you glimpse as you turn the page. The cereal boxes you yawn at in the morning. The style blog. The spoiled little thing front row center in Lit 101. The six o'clock news. The ten o'clock news. The fitness magazines by your mother's bed. Of course, the films you watch; the public figures you worship; your decision of how to participate in the fashion and cultural spheres. How plugged in you choose to be with your friends online and in text, strangers on social media. Where you find your place. When you find your place.

III. Never forget that anorexia is an extremely dangerous *disease*.

   A. Anorexia nervosa is the *number one cause of psychiatric death*. Let me repeat that: number one. It's more psychically harmful to oneself, more capable of inflicting real, tangible harm — not just a life spent wasting away somewhere in a deep, unfound, semiconscious world where words can't be caught; not just a life spent roller-coastering up and down so fast you scare those around you past the point of compassion or comprehension; not just a life spent immobilized in a stupor of empty, lonely, vacant depression... but a life that is also psychically no more. A true death of body and soul. Anorexia is more psychically harmful to oneself than schizophrenia, bipolar disorder, major depression, and so on.

   B. Studies have shown that at least 20 percent of people who develop anorexia will eventually die prematurely from the disorder.

   C. The longer you "have" the disease, the more at risk you are of death.

      1. In fact, the percentage is likely higher as the deaths attributed to anorexia come from secondary causes, in the form of cardiac arrest, organ failure, stroke, and seizure — things that less informed doctors might not connect to anorexia if the patient has not been diagnosed, received documented treatment, or recently suffered from anorexia.

         a. Bulimia is dangerous as well with links to throat cancer and esophageal tears to name a few.

b. Anorexia *and* bulimia, the anorexic bulimic, she is a death prescription. A mere doctor's time of death call out of this world.

i. Don't even think about adding bulimia to anorexia — not just throwing up but diuretics, laxatives, over-exercising, diet pills or vomit-inducing pills.

ii. Don't even think of attempting anorexia at home if you have any preexisting health conditions such as diabetes, or were previously morbidly obese, or something.

iii. I am getting tired of saying how dangerous this all is.

D. Without a doubt, anorexia takes an enormous toll on the body; it can damage, really, every bodily system. And sometimes the total harm reveals itself years later.

1. For instance: the bones.

a. Since anorexia often develops during one's adolescence, the time when bones are meant to be growing strong, not deteriorating, and since bone loss can start within the first six months of developing anorexia, even the "less severe" or "short-lived" cases can result in permanent bone damage.

b. Bone damage isn't anything to disregard — it's rather irreversible.

i. I have had my bones tested repeatedly and right now I have no major signs of osteoporosis, but in five years? In twenty?

E. The most life-threatening damage usually happens to the heart.

1. The people I've known who've died from anorexia all died from complications with the heart.

    a. Perhaps at sixteen it can sound poetic. It did to me. But I've learned that to have thirty-five-year-old nurses look at you with sadness, because they know you are going to die, soon, way before your time... to have to explain to your doctors, again and again, that you *have anorexia*, that the complications are due to *anorexia* — it becomes impossible, a too-high mountain, something that can't be beat. Especially if you are the friend who watches everyone go, who can't do much more than wait, the one who gets left behind.

2. In people with severe anorexia, heart disease is the most common cause of death.

    a. The heart starves with the body. Losing size, Your Body Eats Your Heart until there is nothing left.

    b. After heart disease comes multi-organ failure.

F. Starving bodies mean weakened immune systems mean anemia and low white blood cell counts mean infections.

G. Infertility is a quiet consequence. Just as osteoporosis with growing bones, the effects of anorexia on the reproductive system can be long lasting and irreversible. When you finally "recover," gain back the necessary weight, resume a regular menstrual cycle, and eventually decide to make a family, you can't.

1. Women who recover from anorexia tend to have pregnancy complications including: postpartum depression, miscarriages, complicated deliveries, the need for Caesarean sections, and premature births.

II. Anorexia is a one-half metaphorical and one-half literal suicide attempt. However, if the measurements do not add up fast enough, there is always that dazzling, tempting piece of fruit. Up to one-fifth of people afflicted with anorexia attempt suicide, and suicide may account for as many as one half of anorexic deaths.

1. Brain scans indicate that parts of the brain suffer structural changes and abnormal activity with anorexia.

a. There is evidence that some damage may be permanent.

IV. Back to the most pressing truth: Out of all of these things that can kill you, there is one thing, one action, that can save you from hospitalization, heart disease, infertility, broken bones, organ failure, infections, lost hair, brittle nails; one simple action that will buy you more time, more life, and that is to gain weight. That is the single most important step in physical recovery. To gain weight. It seems so simple to someone not suffering from the disease. So effortless. *Just eat.*

A. To the person living with anorexia, like me, recovery makes you feel like you have to sell your soul. You have to trade in your mind for your body. And you have to make this decision because, when it comes down to it, you just can't have them both. You can either die with anorexia, or, you can betray the disease, the thing that often feels the most like you. *You can gain weight or you can die from this.* That's the choice-point where you either get your life back or lose it all, depending on what you choose.

1. *Is an eating disorder your life?*

2. *Do you exist separately from your eating disorder?*

B. I am alive. So perhaps you know the choice I made, but not the price. I sold parts of myself in order to survive.

And you?

SELECTED BIBLIOGRAPHY

CHAPTER 3

59 *Kids as young as five:* Journal of PsychoSocial Nursing and Mental Health Services, http://www.healio.com/ Psychiatry/journals/JPN/%7B0ED3F594-09E7-445D-A03B-A997949D523B%7D/Influences-of-Disordered-Eating-in-Prepubescent-Children.

CHAPTER 4

71 *Prevent a long list of adolescent troubles including eating disorders:* Neumark-Sztainer, Dianne, PhD, MPH, RD; Marla E. Eisenberg, ScD, MPH; Jayne A. Fulkerson, PhD; Mary Story, PhD, RD; and Nicole I. Larson, MPH, RD. "Family Meals and Disordered Eating in Adolescents: Longitudinal Findings From Project EAT." JAMA Pediatrics, Jan. 2008 Vol. 162. No. 1. Web. 27 Feb. 2013. http://archpedi.jamanetwork.com/article. aspx?articleid=378850.

75 *Girls with strong, supportive relationships with their fathers:* Walker, Peter. "Hungry For Dad." *Father and Child.* N.p.,

n.d. Web. 28 Feb. 2013. http://fatherandchild.org.nz/magazine/
issue-9/hungry-for-dad.

CHAPTER 5

83 *Men develop eating disorders:* National Eating Disorders
Association, http://www.nationaleatingdisorders.org/males-and-
eating-disorders

84 *Men generally account for up to 15 percent while:* "Eating
Disorders in Straight and Gay Men." *Consults Blog.* http://
consults.blogs.nytimes.com/2009/07/17/reverse-anorexia-in-gay-
and-straight-men.

CHAPTER 9

111 *Anorexia affects less economically blessed and/or non-
white woman in equal measure:* Academy of Eating Disorders
— The Myths and Facts www.aedweb.org/AM/Template.
cfm?Section=Advocacy&Template=/CM/ContentDisplay.
cfm&ContentID=1432

111 *Countries such as India, Nigeria, South Africa, and
Mexico:* Costin, Carolyn. *The Eating Disorder Sourcebook: A
Comprehensive Guide to the Causes, Treatments, and Prevention
of Eating Disorders.* New York: McGraw-Hill, 2007. 36.

111 *Even within an all-female kibbutz in northern Israel:* Martin,
Courtney E. *Perfect Girls, Starving Daughters: The Frightening
New Normalcy of Hating Your Body.* New York: Free, 2007. 11.

112 *The way we are built to survive starving:* Bruch, Hilde.
*Eating Disorders: Obesity, Anorexia Nervosa, and the Person
within.* New York: Basic, 1973. 10.

CHAPTER 13

174 *"We're great"*: Liu, Aimee. *Gaining: The Truth about Life after Eating Disorders.* New York: Warner, 2007. 141.

178 *"Acts of revolution"*: Liu, Aimee. *Gaining: The Truth about Life after Eating Disorders.* New York: Warner, 2007. 141.

180 *"By nature"*: Winnicott, D. W. *Home Is Where We Start From: Essays by a Psychoanalyst.* New York: W. W. Norton, 1986. (20)

CHAPTER 14

184 *Highest mortality rate of any mental illness:* National Association of Anorexia Nervosa and Associated Disorders, http://www.anad.org/get-information/about-eating-disorders/eating-disorders-statistics.

184 *Studies show that at least 5 to 10 percent of anorexics die within:* South Carolina Department of Mental Health, http://www.state.sc.us/dmh/anorexia/statistics.htm.

CHAPTER 16

211 *Three interconnected lives:* Liu, Aimee. *Gaining: The Truth about Life after Eating Disorders.* New York: Warner, 2007. xxv.

CHAPTER 18

249 *Bulimia is also considered to have a correlation:* Liu, Aimee. *Gaining: The Truth about Life after Eating Disorders.* New York: Warner, 2007. 21.

249 *Less than three percent:* Liu, Aimee. *Gaining: The Truth*

about Life after Eating Disorders. New York: Warner, 2007. 21.

251 *Women do 66 percent of the work yet:* "Empowered Lives. Resilient Nations." United Nations Development Programme. N.p., n.d. Web. 16 Aug. 2013.

251 *One out of five women:* The New York Times, http://www.nytimes.com/2011/12/15/health/nearly-1-in-5-women-in-us-survey-report-sexual-assault.html?_r=0.

251 *Twelve percent of sexual assaults:* White House Report, http://www.whitehouse.gov/sites/default/files/docs/sexual_assault_report_1-21-14.pdf

POP QUIZ

The Pop Quiz is a compilation of many facts from many sources. Most can be found via these four outstanding resources:

1) The University of Maryland Medical Center's webpage for Eating Disorders – Complications of Anorexia, 2) the National Association of Anorexia Nervosa and Associated Disorders (ANAD) website, 3) the National Eating Disorders Association (NEDA) website, and 4) the American Psychiatric Association's *Diagnostic and Statistical Manual of Mental Disorders* (DSM-IV).

ABOUT THE AUTHOR

Jordan Lee Knape is a Brooklyn-based writer testing the waters on the West Coast. She studied Critical and Visual Theory at Pratt Institute and works as a freelance copywriter. She has no cats, no dogs, just an Instagram account (@leeknape) and a website, bestbodymemoir.com. This is her first book.